MERCY IN HER EYES

MERCY IN HER EYES
THE FILMS OF MIRA NAIR

JOHN KENNETH MUIR

APPLAUSE THEATRE & CINEMA BOOKS

Mercy in Her Eyes: The Films of Mira Nair
by John Kenneth Muir
Copyright © 2006 John Kenneth Muir

Cover and book interior design by Pearl Chang

LIBRARY OF CONGRESS CATALOGING-IN-PUBLICATION DATA:

Muir, John Kenneth, 1969–
    Mercy in her eyes : the films of Mira Nair / by John Kenneth Muir.
       p.   cm.
    Includes bibliographical references.
    ISBN-13: 978-1-55783-649-6
    ISBN-10: 1-55783-649-3
    1. Nair, Mira—Criticism and interpretation. I. Title.
PN1998.3.N325M85   2006
791.4302'33092—dc22

APPLAUSE THEATRE & CINEMA BOOKS

19 West 21st Street, Suite 201
New York, NY 10010
Phone: (212) 575-9265
Fax: (212) 575-9270
Email: info@applausepub.com
Internet: www.applausepub.com

Applause books are available through your local bookstore, or you may order at www.applausepub.com or call Music Dispatch at 800-637-2852

SALES & DISTRIBUTION

NORTH AMERICA:
    Hal Leonard Corp.
    7777 West Bluemound Road
    P. O. Box 13819
    Milwaukee, WI 53213
    Phone: (414) 774-3630
    Fax: (414) 774-3259
    Email: halinfo@halleonard.com
    Internet: www.halleonard.com

EUROPE:
    Roundhouse Publishing Ltd.
    Millstone, Limers Lane
    Northam, North Devon EX 39 2RG
    Phone: (0) 1237-474-474
    Fax: (0) 1237-474-774
    Email:
    roundhouse.group@ukgateway.net

DEDICATION

This work is dedicated to Dr. Bert Cardullo, a mentor and friend from my days at the University of Richmond. Thank you, Dr. Cardullo for teaching me to always ask, "Why?"

And to Lila and Ezri

CONTENTS

ACKNOWLEDGMENTS

Fashioning a text like this one is hard work, and I'd like to thank all the good people who made it that much less so, starting with my incomparable agent, June Clark, and my dedicated and patient wife, Kathryn, who also happens to be a great proofreader...and tough task master. Michael Messina at Applause was a tremendous help too—and a man with connections to boot!

I'd also like to offer my appreciation to Brad Gross, Barbara Halperin, Lou Pitt, Paul Hook, J. Tomlinson, Carol Marshall, Alanna Kordell, Patty Detroit, Robert Messinger, and Aude Powell for working with me in a timely fashion to facilitate a series of interviews.

It is always fascinating to conduct interviews with the artists behind the memorable films that have meant so much to so many. To hear from their own lips how filmmakers perceive their art is one of the many wonderful gifts of my profession, and one that makes my task not just easier...but much more fun. Thus, I can't imagine writing this book without the input of such talents, and so my most sincere appreciation goes to those nineteen who undertook this study with me (in alphabetical order): Naveen Andrews, Phillip Barker, Laura Cahill, Stephanie Carroll, Ranjit Chowdhry, Mychael Danna, Sabrina Dhawan, Maria Djurkovic, Julian Fellowes, Barry John, Allyson C. Johnson, Helena Kriel, Jim Leonard, Gena Rowlands, Roshan Seth, Sandi Sissel, Sooni Taraporevala, Dr. Abraham Verghese, and Raghubir Yadav. Thanks to each and every one of you for offering your insights and memories.

Special thanks to Ami Boghani at Mirabai Films. Lastly, my deepest appreciation goes to the subject of this study, Professor Mira Nair. Thank you, Professor, for seeing the world with so much color.

"Where we love is home -
home that our feet may leave, but not our hearts."

- OLIVER WENDELL HOLMES

"I have become a queer mixture of the East and West,
out of place everywhere, at home nowhere."

- JAWAHARIAL NEHRU

A LOCAL STORYTELLER AT THE GLOBAL CINEMA

An Introduction to *Mercy in Her Eyes:*

The Films of Mira Nair

When historians of a future age debate the final years of the twentieth century and the first span of the new millennium, one trend will likely dominate discussion: globalization. Abetted by the advent of the Internet, the proliferation of satellite television, and the cheap, mass-production of DVDs, globalization is already bringing all corners of this world closer than once imagined possible.

This cross-pollination of civilizations, of East and West, heralds many wonders and tremendous potential. The better neighbors that geographically separated countries can become—through the auspices of free trade, media and e-mail—the better, perhaps, people can understand and communicate with one another and avert future conflict.

Yet globalization is not without drawbacks. How will the vast downloading of culture from one continent to another impact far away lands and cherished, long-held traditions? And what of those emigrés who attempt to assimilate the traditions of a different land, and then return home, irrevocably changed by that experience?

Shall age-old traditions be abandoned? Fiercely defended? Is the appropriate response to globalization a steadfast, conservative resistance, or a progressive, open embrace? Or oddly, is it some fusion of approaches that will serve individual nations and citizens best?

It is appropriate that some of the finest meditations on the consequences of globalization—both positive and negative—have arisen from the contemporary, technological art form of film, along with television the most influential of all ambassadors from culture to culture.

In particular, the cinema of the Indian-born director Mira Nair has focused dramatically on the subjects of national and personal identity, and more importantly, the quandary of characters who have departed their home only to find that in their new lives (often in America), they are traversing uncharted waters, forced by circumstances such as exile to synthesize old tradition and shiny modernity in ways that their parochial forefathers could not have imagined, much less advocated.

"I think the Indian establishment view—which means the Indian government—and the view amongst a lot of thinking people, is to resist globalization, because globalization, in their terms, means American domination," suggests Roshan Seth, the distinguished Indian actor who has appeared in films as diverse as *Gandhi* (1982) and *Indiana Jones and the*

Temple of Doom (1984), as well as two of Mira Nair's most popular films, *Mississippi Masala* (1991) and *Monsoon Wedding* (2001).

"But someone like Mira is a global human being, like I am," Seth continues. "We like to think that we are international citizens who belong to the world, and that's why she is important. She has a foot in America and they like her there. She certainly likes to be there, and therefore she's very well-placed. [However], she's working out of America on stories that she is culturally and aesthetically tied to in her own country."

In other words, global citizen that she may be, Nair's films are nonetheless tied specifically to her own private India. It is much more than her country of origin, it is the inspiration and bubbling wellspring for her art. Because artists' works are always tied irrevocably to their context, Nair's films reflect and represent her own personal experiences, political and social views, and even general perceptions of life itself.

An irony of this happenstance is that Nair's very personal, very local films could not exist without the very process of globalization she has often obsessed on in her art. After all, how else would a low-budget, independently produced, guerrilla-style feature like her freshman masterpiece, *Salaam Bombay!* (1988) arrive on American shores to achieve such success and notoriety? Or more recently, and to a greater degree, *Monsoon Wedding*?

And yet, Nair's films so often represent love letters to the India she knows and adores, an India that globalization could imperil, or at the very least, substantially alter. This is why she is truly a local filmmaker, but one whose audience is global.

In addition to being a filmmaker, Nair is on occasion a directing professor at Columbia University in New York. "Now more than ever," Nair has suggested to aspiring moviemakers, "we need cinema to reveal our tiny local worlds in all their glorious peculiarity."[1] Why? Because such local worlds are slowly but surely vanishing in the homogenizing process of globalization. And it's a trend that isn't stopping. In some senses and by a certain frame of mind, globalization is really just the new colonization.

"It's a constant struggle, whether it is to be resisted or embraced," muses Sabrina Dhawan, the screenwriter of *Monsoon Wedding*. "One aspect of globalization is great, because there's no denying that modern life has brought us many things. Human rights, female rights...all those kinds of things, which are a byproduct of modernization. But it's also taken away the sense of community and family and tradition and rooted-ness which people automatically had, pre-globalization.

"The reason I think that *Monsoon Wedding* celebrates this sense of family and community is because both Mira and I live overseas," Dhawan opines, "and when you're Indian and you live overseas, you tend to look back at the homeland with much more nostalgia, and globalization angers you much more than if you were living back home.

"I go back to India and I'm sad to see McDonald's and not the local chai store around the corner, but for people living in India, it's a wonderful thing," Dhawan explains. "The point of view is changed when you live overseas, because you want things to be the way they were when you left. But objectively, it's sort of better. Not all of it. It's a hard argument, and it would be great if you could find a way to settle it."

That New York embraces Mira Nair's work as easily as New Delhi (and sometimes more so...) is delightful, but one senses that this filmmaker develops her films not for the approbation of a world audience, but rather to reflect some personal need and desire to share something of her ethos. Indeed, Nair has described the process of filmmaking in the most intimate of terms, as an act of love in which flowers are "coaxed to bloom."[2]

And *identity*, no doubt, is the concept that blossoms so fully under her careful stewardship. It is something that Professor Nair, a world traveler in the age of globalization, with homes in Uganda, the United States and India, is very conscious about. *What makes me who I am? What makes me unique?* These are questions that thoughtful people may ponder, but they are part and parcel of Mira Nair's experience, and she uses her experience to create artistic meditations.

"When I left India at nineteen," she told Samuel G. Freedman in the *New York Times*, "I was rooted in a very certain reality. And since then, life has been very fluid. Back and forth, back and forth. And I realize in hindsight that I use that fluidity as part of my work."[3]

Identity is a word with a tremendous philosophical and psychological heft. It comes in all varieties, whether national, personal, ethnic, or even religious, and Nair's films dynamically focus on these concepts, usually via characters who experience, literally, an identity crisis.

The question of identity is evident in Nair's earliest documentaries in the late 1970s, as well as her first film, *Salaam Bombay!*, in which abandoned street children see their individual identities (and status as children and innocents) replaced by their function in an exploitative urban hierarchy. A little boy named Krishna becomes Chaipau—or Tea-Bread—the tea-boy. A lovely young girl named Solasaal is doomed to servitude in a brothel and becomes "Sweet Sixteen," shorthand for her value as a desirable virgin. As for the tragic Chillum, the audience never learns his real name, only that he is a drug pusher, his chosen name meaning "Hash Pipe." When he dies, another like-named Chillum promptly takes his place with no comment, fulfilling society's immediate need for a replacement drug dealer.

Worst of all, perhaps, is the plight of the smallest child on the mean streets of Mumbai. As yet, he can serve no purpose in the adult milieu and is therefore known simply and pitiably as Keera, or insect.

Nair's other films also revolve explicitly around the concept of identity. *Mississippi Masala* focuses on a protagonist named Mina (Sarita Choudhury), a young woman who is only now, at age twenty-four, beginning to forge her individual identity. She was born in Uganda to Indian parents, but when Idi Amin seized power and exiled all non-black Asians in 1972, her family emigrated to the American South and she has lived in Mississippi since. So, is Mina an Indian, an African, or an American? What traditions from each culture should she accept or reject? How is she to make that choice?

In the course of *Mississippi Masala*, Mina carefully—and after some trial and error—crafts her own answers to these questions, and defines herself in a manner that may differ wildly from the preferences of others, including her family.

In her third feature, *The Perez Family* (1995), Nair recounts the story of Cuban exiles who arrive in America in 1980, courtesy of Castro's boat lift. These immigrants rapidly come to define identity through the concept of family. Importantly, it is an ad hoc family of exiles who share only the last name Perez, not blood ties, who comprise this amalgamation.

Likewise, in her adaptation of the non-fiction bestseller, *My Own Country*, Ethiopian-born Indian Dr. Abraham Verghese, a specialist in infectious diseases, finds himself defined as an "AIDS doctor" in a small, conservative Tennessee town, and virtually ostracized by his professional peers, his concerned wife, and even the Indian emigré community there. Surprisingly, he finds that his status as a "foreigner" in America also grants him the trust of one group: his gay patients, who, like him, consider themselves aliens in this particular region of the country.

Even Nair's *Hysterical Blindness* (2002), based on the play by Laura Cahill, poses pertinent questions about how another group defines itself. In particular, two New Jersey girls in Bayonne (during the late 1980s) can't see themselves as worthwhile so long as there are no men in their lives. Their vision is so limited that they can't even *recognize* the world outside Bayonne, despite the ubiquitous presence of bridges that lead to Manhattan, the world beyond, and ostensibly more promising horizons. In fact, one character, Deb, played with heartbreaking desperation by Uma Thurman, actually experiences blindness, a telling reflection of her delusions, of her inability to see and understand what she really needs to make herself happy and fulfilled.

Most interesting of all, perhaps, is Nair's box office sensation, *Monsoon Wedding*, which really revolves around the identity of India's people as a whole. In the film, audiences see globalization, represented by the up-and-coming businessman Dubey, literally and metaphorically marry tradition, symbolized by a demure maid named Alice. Out of their joining arises a brand new and explicitly Indian identity.

From project to project, Mira Nair's film work has evidenced this remarkable thematic consistency as she gazes at exiles, outsiders, social climbers and "nowhere" people,[4] and their efforts to carve out an identity or niche in a modern world where they aren't fully accepted, and which they don't fully understand.

But if this description reads as pretentious or implies that Nair's body of work is a dry and remote exercise in identity politics in the global age, the wrong impression has been transmitted. Nair creates films not to educate, not for some overweening didactic or academic purpose. Indeed, she has pointedly refused to be "an ambassador like that,"[5] instead taking interest only in what she finds true and valuable, and hoping that because she sees the world in this fashion—and casts her films with this in mind—audiences will follow her for the ride.

"I'm wicked and irreverent and playful, not virtuous," she has assured interviewers, "I just feel a genuine joy in what I'm doing."[6]

And *joy* is truly the feeling expressed so powerfully in Mira Nair's oeuvre. "I want to make serious, passionate cinema that will get an ordinary audience, not an arty intelligentsia crowd,"7 she has noted, and it is this author's belief that she has accomplished this feat not merely with touching, human stories filled with interesting and identifiable characters, but by remembering that film is first and foremost a visual art form.

Accordingly, virtually every frame in a Mira Nair film pulses with life, color, symbolism, and meaning, and this approach attracts international audiences who might otherwise be turned off by the notion of seeing a film wherein the characters speak mostly in Hindi, for example. Or one where protagonists live in poverty on the streets.

Intoxicated with a love of life, or what she calls *masti*, Mira Nair's films are renowned for their "sensuous wit" and "sparkling personality" as well as their "cross-cultural social acumen,"8 yet they remain unique, colorful, and worthy of appreciation because Nair's dynamic compositions and choice of shots achieve a special resonance.

They are no mere pretty pictures, these trademark Nair frames, but rather compositions that draw the audience into the mood of a moment, or more specifically *extends* a special moment until the audience detects the beauty and meaning behind it, the underlying emotional truth. This technique of extending the moment is the reason why so many of Nair's films are frequently accompanied by critical descriptors like "luxurious," sumptuous," "ravishing," and the like.

Nair utilizes in-camera slow-motion photography for instance, in *Monsoon Wedding*, to lengthen a particularly relevant early moment. Within the frame, family patriarch Lalit Verma (Naseeruddin Shah) is doused in a deluge of marigolds, the traditional Indian wedding flower, as he stands underneath his daughter's wedding gate.

By capturing and extending this moment, Nair fosters the impression of this man experiencing deep emotions at the time of his daughter's nuptials. He is lost in the snowstorm of petals, much as his heart bursts with mixed emotions. He is happy for his child, sad to be losing her (as is Indian tradition), but simultaneously worried about finances, and this shot seems a perfect metaphor for his state of mind, almost as though a wedding picture has been plucked from an album and we are allowed to share the feelings it evokes for a protracted instant. Life feels fragile and ephemeral, like the flower petals in free fall.

A climactic first kiss between bride and groom in *Monsoon Wedding* is similarly lingered over, so that audiences can savor the emotional resonance and impact of the joining, this time lengthened via the cutting together of the kiss from a variety of angles, including an immediacy-provoking hand-held circling shot, and a more traditional, tripod-planted close-up.

"It's been funny," Allyson C. Johnson, Nair's editor on *Monsoon Wedding* and *Vanity Fair* (2004) acknowledges. "Mira really encourages lengthening the moment. She's so sensuous herself, and part of sensuality is that tease. So I think that when we cut something like that [kiss], it's really teasing the audience. Trying to hold back a bit.

"The way we did it, I feel like you're telling the audience, 'Okay they're going to kiss…oh, not quite yet!' 'Oh, we're finally going to get release!' Then we're moving somewhere else. It's this giving and taking away type of thing…"

In *My Own Country*, a film created for Showtime Television, the same approach is broached. Without any immediate explanation, Nair cuts periodically to a slightly out-of-focus tracking shot gazing upwards. The camera registers tree branches and rich, green leaves rolling by overhead. Rendered in quasi-slow motion, this image recurs several times throughout the film, and only in the last sequence is its significance revealed: the final vision of a deathly-ill AIDS patient returning home to the lush Tennessee valley.

This unexplained, seemingly out-of-place shot has been his view on that meaningful and tragic journey. What should be a beautiful returning is one ultimately marred by his illness—and hence the slight blurring, wobbly nature of the image. Again, we feel as though we are accessing something deeply personal and immediate in this image, a feeling of connection heightened by the grainy look of a shot, as though it were a home movie.

Nair's pictures, her very choices in framing, capture not merely a place and a time, but a texture and feeling, and that remains her greatest gift as a filmmaker. It would be tempting to indicate that these stylish shots arise from her clearly well-developed sense of womanhood, since many believe that women are keyed in more fully to nuances and feelings than are men, but that assessment only perpetuates a stereotype. These shots arise from the fullness of Nair's entire person, her rich vision of life, from a context that is much more than just a feminine one.

The aforementioned sequences in *Monsoon Wedding* and *My Own Country* represent only a few samples of Nair's visual flair, but all her films come replete with just such creative and unforgettable imagery, whether it be a masterful long shot in *Salaam Bombay!* of a child devouring a pack of crackers in the foreground, while life obliviously continues in the background, or two friends gently touching hands underwater, a cocoon far away from the social restrictions of their time, in *Kama Sutra: A Tale of Love* (1997).

These dynamic screen tableaus emerge from Nair's perspective of life as vivid and colorful, even when difficult, and she shares this view with moviegoers in a manner most singular. She has sometimes described this imagery as carnival-esque, and James Purefoy, the actor who plays Rawdon Crawley in *Vanity Fair* (2004), has related that other than Nair, he has not worked with another director who is so "precise about what she wants to see in the frame," also noting that she is an "intensely visual director."[9]

And for that reason, it is not difficult to view Mira Nair under the rubric of that admittedly overused term: *auteur*. Fitting in with this French theory of film study, Mira Nair is an artist who, if we gaze across her body of work, adheres to a consistent theme, maintains a daring and individual visual style (heavily influenced by her love of photography), and also covets a high degree of control over her art, both in her choices of co-workers and oversight of every aspect from financing a project to its final edit and distribution.

This is an increasingly uncommon achievement in America's corporate film industry. Everybody has heard the Hollywood horror stories wherein studio executive impose unwanted creative "advice" upon directors, or are unduly guided by fickle preview screeners and the vicissitudes of the market. Alternate endings are filmed, scenes are deleted to pare down running time, and all such commercial decisions, in the end, serve only to diminish a director's overall vision and control of a piece.

But not often Mira Nair's vision.

"She has an enormous, creative energy that keeps everything going very well," states legendary actress Gena Rowlands, who co-starred in the HBO movie *Hysterical Blindness* in 2002. "She doesn't get tired and let things slip, like some people do. I think she's a marvelous director, and she's very well organized. What more do you want out of life?"

"She always seems to know exactly what she wants and will not tolerate anything less," agrees Barry John, her early teaching instructor and friend in New Delhi. "She has an eye for detail as well as for an overall aesthetic."

"Mira has a wonderful grasp of detail," reiterates Julian Fellowes, author of Nair's adaptation of *Vanity Fair*, "but she is also able to embrace the whole sweep of a society, and you often get directors who can do marvelous scenes but the actual detail of the narrative gets lost. Mira can do both.

"The great luxury of her, as far as being a screenwriter is concerned, is that she doesn't want to be a screenwriter. Most directors have a sort of slight irritation that they need to have a screenwriter at all. *If only they had a little more time, they could certainly write a script as good as yours,*" he laments. "She doesn't have that, so when she gives you notes, they are that. They are notes, whereby you will then rewrite it to make it more like the scenes she wants. Which is an absolutely clear relationship and division of skill that I found very easy and pleasant to work within.

"Mira is absolutely clear about what she wants," Fellowes continues. "She is absolutely clear about what works and what doesn't. But she lets you write it, and I found her very, very rewarding to work with. I would absolutely love to do another film with her."

It is this ability to mold and control her art, to function as, in her words, "the master" of her own work,[10] that first led Nair to make the jump from *cinema verité* style documentaries into fictional narratives in the mid-1980s, a creative arena where she can control light, color and movement without the need to wait for "life to happen." And now, doing so, she wields final authority.

"When I produce and direct and conceive my own films, it's from scratch to the end," she reported to journalist Christopher Kelly. "I'm selling satellite rights at midnight, and going on television in the morning to promote it. And this goes on for months."[11]

Even more to the point, her films are a matter of *passion*, a need to voice particular stories. For Nair, filmmaking is not a task that can be undertaken with less than full commitment. She must be "totally obsessed"[12] with it.

Often working quickly and with very little money, Nair has also adopted another quality of the auteur by often working with the same cast and crew. Behind the scenes, she has collaborated with writer Sooni Taraporevala four times (*Salaam Bombay!*, *Mississippi Masala*, *My Own Country*, *The Namesake*), and accomplished director of photography Declan Quinn on *Kama Sutra*, *Monsoon Wedding*, *Hysterical Blindness* and *Vanity Fair*. Mychael Danna has scored three Mira Nair films, and on the list goes. In front of the cameras, Ranjit Chowdhry has appeared in four of her efforts, and Naveen Andrews and Sarita Choudhury, two apiece.

This likely isn't a case of a director playing favorites, but rather a plain necessity if the work is to progress smoothly. It's a special symbiosis. "It's important that I work in harmony," Nair has declared, "not just to feel good all the time, but to take each other further."13

"It really becomes like a theatre company," considers composer Mychael Danna. "It really is wonderful. She has done that over the years, and a lot of the directors I admire do that."

Being the proverbial auteur requires another sort of discipline too—and one not often seen in the milieu unfortunately now termed an "industry." True auteurs must stick to their guns about the material they vet. Sometimes this means turning down an opportunity for a bigger audience, higher visibility, and even a gigantic payday. And indeed, this is exactly the choice Mira Nair has often made. Her toughness of spirit extends to her career trajectory and her selection of film projects.

Case in point: in late 2004 Mira Nair turned down an offer to direct the fifth *Harry Potter* film. *Harry Potter* is not only a big franchise in Hollywood today, but—following the culmination of *Star Wars* and *The Lord of the Rings*—perhaps the biggest. Though she was honored to be asked, Nair demurred.

"When I consider offers by others to make films, my criteria (for accepting) is: can anybody else make this film?" the director explains. "If yes, I would prefer someone else make it. I am better suited to emotions, human beings, and less interested in special effects."14

A bold decision like that doesn't just take masti, the spice of life, but *moxie* too. And it speaks volumes about Nair's belief that artistic freedom is something to cherish more than cash, or an opening weekend in two thousand theatres.

Roshan Seth, for one, isn't surprised by her choice. "I think Mira has realized that it's not enough for her to be a mainstream American director, just some freelance director who's hired to do anything. I think she realizes her strength lies in *her* thing. She's very intelligent, very clever."

It is for these reasons that in October 2004, Mira Nair was honored as a recipient of a Maverick Award at the Woodstock Festival, following in the footsteps of her former mentor in the world of *cinema verité*, D. A. Pennebaker. In the words of festival director Meira Blaustein, Nair "fearlessly combines independence and risk-taking with social consciousness and continues the tradition of those who make feelings visible," and "who make sense out of sensations, who shine light on darkness."[15]

With her typical candor, Nair accepted the award by noting that she had to look up the term "maverick" in the dictionary, but when she did, she ultimately liked what she saw.[16]

"She's not conservative and she doesn't play by the rules," agrees Helena Kriel, Nair's co-writer on *Kama Sutra: A Tale of Love*, a period piece about the art of sex and love released in the mid-1990s, "and I don't think doing anything like that would even interest her."

As Alparna Sharma wrote in *Body Matters: The Politics of Provocation in Mira Nair's Films*, Professor Nair also remains a talent who approaches film with "a high level of tolerance for complexity, irony, contradiction, and ambiguity."[17] Still, another quality should be added to that impressive laundry list: mercy.

Professor Nair's films don't shy away from revealing some pretty unpleasant things about humans or humanity, whether it be racist Americans (*Mississippi Masala, My Own Country*), social engineers (*Vanity Fair*), or abusers of the innocent (*Salaam Bombay!, Monsoon Wedding*). Yet Nair doesn't make movies explicitly about anger, even when that anger is richly deserved. Instead, her films are filled with characters who persevere, who go on, take chances, and find their own path.

Even their enemies are not painted in terms of black and white. The pimp Baba in *Salaam Bombay!* is a thug, but audiences also understand his deep insecurity. Maya and Tara commit outrageous, thoughtless acts upon each other in *Kama Sutra*, but are never cruelly drawn. Instead, viewers recognize these metaphorical sisters as a piece of themselves, as part of our human condition.

Although Nair's films are surely designed to resist "the cultural impe-rialism of Hollywood"[18] by putting people like herself on screen, her films have also become celebrated in this era of globalization because they don't highlight our differences so much as remind us that with a few different traditions here and there, we're all the same under the skin, and across borders and oceans.

"I have a feeling that Mira is ultimately trying to do pretty much what I've been trying to do," says Seth. "We come from the same sort of social class in India. We are English-speaking Indians who have traveled abroad, who have had an education in the English language, but English as a medium of instruction, not necessarily as a language. There's a critical difference there. I have a feeling that she and I have been trying to do much the same sort of thing...and that is to put across to the English-speaking world, or English-speaking audience, what the truth is about our own soci-ety and our own culture. To tell our story in a language that is necessarily alien to us. Now, that isn't easy..."

With the assistance of some of those who have worked with Mira Nair during her nearly twenty years crafting fictional narratives, including Naveen Andrews, Phillip Barker, Laura Cahill, Ranjit Chowdhry, Sabrina Dhawan, Maria Djurkovic, Julian Fellowes, Barry John, Allyson C. Johnson, Helena Kriel, Jim Leonard, Gena Rowlands, Roshan Seth, Sandi Sissel, Sooni Taraporevala, Dr. Abraham Verghese, and Raghubir Yadav, *Mercy in Her Eyes* seeks to shine light on the career of this distinctive artist, a woman who has succeeded in the global market by being unrepentantly local, and by remaining committed to her art even in the face of tempta-tions that other directors might find irresistible.

Mira Nair has "gracefully traversed the foreign realm of Hollywood," and yet "proved adept at going home again, sending back tales that resonated as powerfully as any megaplex fare,"[19] according to *Entertainment Weekly* writer Rebecca Ascher-Walsh. More to the point, she has done so in her own fashion with increasingly little compromise.

And now quite frankly, others are following the trail she blazed. Bollywood has come to Hollywood "big time," as Dick Cheney might quip. *Time* magazine critic and film scholar Richard Corliss writes that, a "cultural stew is simmering and ready to boil over,"[20] in terms of the East's impact on Western art. In fact, "India is suddenly on Western radar screens"[21] in many arenas, from economics to art, so this is an especially serendipitous time—the age of *Bombay Dreams* and *Bride and Prejudice* (2005)—to survey the career of this increasingly influential talent.

If, as Professor Tyler Cowen of George Mason University suggests, globalization is not really a matter of either/or, but rather a trend that "fills the cultural landscape with greater choice and richness,"[22] then Mira Nair's films have been a prime reason why America grows ever more receptive to Indian masala.

"I seek the truth,"[23] Nair has declared simply and boldly of her motivation in creating her particular brand of spicy art, and that utterance is perhaps her creed.

"Mira the Amazon!" exclaims Barry John. "The new Indian woman, well-read, opinionated, a fully empowered and driven force to be reckoned with. Her ability to pull together people, resources and finance is remarkable."

Mychael Danna agrees. "[She] has a kind of incredibly kinetic, enthusiastic and life-loving energy, and she can just sweep everyone along in her vision and we all just work like crazy and feverishly to make her vision real. That's her great gift as a director."

So in that Amazonian spirit of truth-seeking and drive, let's see if we can pull together the Mira Nair filmography, and further extend the finest moments of her colorful and passionate films.

1

Mahurat: The Auspicious Beginning
of Mira Nair's Career in Film

RAY OF LIGHT

Only months after Mira Nair's birth on October 15, 1957, India officially surpassed the United States' output in annual feature film production (by a tally of 295 to 288), thus emerging as one of the world's most prolific moviemaking nations. Thanks primarily to the efforts of a talented director, and Nair's fellow countryman, Satyajit Ray (1921–1992), the world at large—and especially the West—began to recognize Indian film as a unique, powerful and separate voice in world cinema.

An emotionally devastating neo-realist film in the style of Vittorio De Sica's haunting *The Bicycle Thief* (1948), Satayjit Ray's landmark work is *Pather Panchali* (1955) a film based on the novel by Bibhutibhushan Bandyopadhyay. Unlike most Indian films produced in the epoch between the 1930s and the 1950s, it is not a carefree musical, but rather the harrowing, deeply-moving story of a Brahmin family undone by poverty, despair and delusion.

In *Pather Panchali*—a title meaning *Song of the Little Road*—a poor family's only means of support, a small orchard in rural Bengal, has been taken away as payment to debtors. Also, the family patriarch, Harihar, played by Kannu Banerjee, considers himself a poet, but is unable to acquire meaningful and regular work in that capacity. And devastatingly, the ancestral family house is on the verge of collapse due to calamities of nature and years of neglect and disrepair.

While his wife, Sarbojaya (Karuna Banerjee) does everything within her power to stretch the family's meager resources, a daughter named Durga (Uma Das Gupta) and the couple's young son, Apu (Subir Banerjee), confront the perils of this seemingly cruel life, where neighbors and local officials can't be moved to render help until it is far too late. Making matters more difficult, decrepit old Auntie (Chunibala Devi) is using up precious resources, and the family wishes she would just leave…or die.

But even in this stressful life of difficulties and shortages, there are amazing sights and sounds to behold. Apu and Durga, for instance, play one day in a vast field and happen upon a powerful locomotive steaming across the horizon. The almost alien sight of the modern train on this isolated, rural landscape serves as an explicit reminder of a different world—one of wonders and technological modernity—existing outside of the family's very personal sphere of trials and traumas.

Fours years in the making, *Pather Panchali* is shot in a spare (and bleak) black-and-white style by Subrata Mitra, and accompanied by an understated and beautiful original score from Ravi Shankar that is "at once plaintive and exhilarating."[1] In short, Ray's timeless masterpiece feels raw, tragic, and most of all, *unsentimental*, in part because Ray is a former apprentice of the realist director Jean Renoir, renowned for his subtlety in storytelling and even shooting style.

But there is also something else granting the film a special status. In spite of everything, there exists the specter of *hope* in *Pather Panchali*. According to the late, great film critic Pauline Kael, it is there because its creator, Ray, "sees that life is good, no matter how bad it is."[2]

Although *Pather Panchali* reeks of enveloping desperation, it also consistently paints its characters as identifiable human beings with complex natures, not mere good or bad guys whom the audience can root for or easily despise.

Young Durga, for instance, lies to her mother about the theft of a neighbor's beads, but the reasons for the theft are more than understandable, given the wealth and selfishness of her neighbors and the paucity of toys and treats in her own world. Some time later, Apu accidentally happens upon the truth of Durga's act, but blame or second-guessing is irrelevant by then. The family is finally moving away, cut off from their home, Durga has died, and the girl's petty theft no longer matters. Like the tradition of being bound to one's home, the stolen beads are a relic of a time past.

Similarly, Apu's father is delusional about his chances for a successful writing career, and his departure from the family for six long months—a time of strife and disaster at home—is nearly unforgivable. Yet he is never truly a hated or despicable figure. He did what he believed was correct, and his family has suffered the consequences for his actions, but like us, he's recognizably human. Fallible and fragile. Like his wife, he mourns Durga's death, and audiences cry with both of them.

Essentially, all Ray's *dramatis personae* in *Pather Panchali* are treated with compassion, with that ineffable quality of *mercy*, even when bad decisions are broached, or thoughtless actions cause terrible results. The neo-realist approach to filmmaking—natural lighting, non-professional actors and the like—only cements the perception of the film as a slice of true (if unhappy) life, not some sugary concoction of maudlin melodrama.

If it is possible for a film to concern a feeling more than a linear narrative, a mood—*a sense of time and place and its personal import*—more than a plot then this is truly the essence of *Pather Panchali*. Or, as Darius Cooper, author of *The Cinema of Satyajit Ray: Between Tradition and Modernity* has written so insightfully, Ray is a director "less interested in expressing ideas than in communicating emotional experience."[3]

In a country of strict censorship, where a Central Board of Film Censors wields the scissors on taboos like indecorous dancing, scenes featuring alcohol, and passionate love scenes (but not necessarily violence like rape...), *Pather Panchali* remains a revelation, a bastion of individuality and free artistic expression. Not because it features any such provocative images, but merely because it looks and feels so very real, and therefore totally unlike many "approved" films from India.

"Reasonable restrictions" on freedom of speech and expression has often caused Indian cinema to depict only a world of singing and dancing illusions, but not, in the final analysis, much verisimilitude.

Pather Panchali proved itself as the runaway favorite of the 1956 Cannes Film Festival, where it won a special jury prize, yet the film was merely one component of a long film career so illustrious that Ray has since become renowned as one of the greatest film directors in history. The artist won a Lifetime Achievement Oscar in 1992, shortly before his death, for his myriad contributions to this modern art form, including his follow ups to *Pather Panchali*, *Aparajito* (1956) and *The World of Apu* (1959), both of which focused on the life of Durga's brother, Apu.

In the full flower of her adulthood, and many years after the tremendous success of *Pather Panchali*, Mira Nair would acknowledge that it is this beloved film artist, and in particular, his stark *Pather Panchali*, that truly inspired her to become a filmmaker.[4]

Yet as a very young child, Mira Nair seemed removed from the universe of moviemaking. By her own words, she wasn't "one of those people who grew up knowing" she was going to be a filmmaker, making movies in her "backyard."[5] As an artist, she first had a long period of evolution to endure.

For Nair, the first family backyard was in Bhubaneshwar, the capital of Orissa, which by her own assessment, was a small town "even by Indian standards."[6] A Hindu state located on the eastern coast, Bhubeneshwar is also one of the least densely populated regions in all of India. Over a hundred miles from the metropolis of Calcutta, Nair has described Orissa, her birthplace, as a place where nothing eventful ever really occurs.

"There wasn't much to do there," she reported, and so Mira and her siblings—two older brothers, Vikram and Gautam—were often left to their own devices and the auspices of their "imagination."[7] For Nair, perhaps, this was a fine accommodation, and even at a young age, she is reported to have directed the trio's play. In this case, following the leader simply meant following Mira.

Often times, the Nair children would play among the ancient temples so prominent in that region of Orissa, temples where Nair would one day return to shoot her sensual feature film, *Kama Sutra*.

Nair has stated that in India, people "eat and breathe" cinema, but Bhubeneshwar's local movie house plainly didn't provide much diversity in its Western entertainment menu, restricting Hollywood fare to a heavily-censored version of David Lean's popular Russian epic, *Dr. Zhivago* (1965).[8]

"All you could see were Hindi movies, which were the national films of India,"[9] Nair describes.

Nor was Nair's home life one where film was frequently the topic of dinner conversation. "I come from very unpretentious stock,"[10] she told interviewer Scott Tobias. In fact, Nair is a Punjab, from one of the most prosperous regions in India, and was born into the upper-middle-class family of a civil servant, an Indian administrative officer, Amrit Nair. Described as a "remote" and "regimented fellow,"[11] who nonetheless enjoyed reading and writing poetry, Amrit was transferred to Orissa after India's independence and unification in 1947.

Nair's mother is the lovely Praveen Nair, a woman of deeply-held social convictions who has lived a life of good work, including helping the healthy offspring of the region's lepers. In 1947, Praveen began working with illiterate children of the family's domestic workers,[12] and by the 1950s, served on Orissa's Social Welfare Board. Praveen also toiled with the Red Cross on issues of child welfare, and in the 1960s was involved with famine relief efforts. If one can trace Mira Nair's interest in art to her father's love of poetry, then her social conscience seems to have been transmitted from the sterling example set by Praveen.

An interesting side note about Mira Nair's birth was reported by John Lahr in the *New Yorker* in 2002. In his detailed account, entitled "Whirlwind" (Nair's chirldhood nickname) Lahr describes how Amrit Nair had apparently pushed Praveen to get an abortion during her pregnancy with their third child, Mira. This was because a wide-ranging birth control program had been initiated in India in the mid-1950s, one advising would-be fathers and mothers to cease procreation at two or three children.

As a representative of the administration proposing such restrictions, Amrit actually advocated stopping at two offspring, and reportedly felt embarrassed by the fact that his wife became expectant with a third. He sent her to a clinic, but Praveen did not go through with the procedure.[13] As the Lahr article points out, this was, perhaps, an early indicator that Mira Nair was a spirit determined to have her way, and she has been equally determined in other pursuits throughout her whole life. Her first such dedication in childhood, was, no doubt, her quest to receive the best education possible.

When Mira was eleven years old, the Nair family transferred to Delhi for Amrit's new posting, and moved into an old mansion there. They remained for two years, and as a teenager, Nair would "swoon" over Bollywood's exotic love songs[14] but, like many of her contemporaries, also gazed often at the West for artistic inspiration. Music—both homegrown and international (like The Beatles) became an important love.

"Mira was brought up in an Indian household, but one which still very much remembers the British Empire," suggests her frequent collaborator, composer Mychael Danna. "Growing up in Canada—or an Indian household—in the same time we would have read the same books and listened to the same music and had much the same worldview in a lot of ways."

By thirteen, Nair attended an Irish-Catholic missionary school, Tara Hall in Simla, a city in the northern Punjabi state of Himchal Pradesh. It was here that she reported becoming "steeped in English literature,"[15] and her reading list including William Makepeace Thackeray's *Vanity Fair*, a novel she would one day adapt to the silver screen, as well as titles by two other significant Williams: Shakespeare and Blake. From this indoctrination in the so-called canon of the West, it was off to Miranda House at Delhi University to major in sociology.

During her young adulthood, Nair also became deeply involved in acting, and in particular political street theatre, also known as protest theatre, and in doing so, performed the works of playwright Badal Sarkar, a leading Bengali performer and activist who gained tremendous notoriety during the 1970s. Reflecting her developing social conscience, Sarkar's plays are angst-ridden, anti-establishment, anti-war and frequently absurd. A deeply charismatic man, he is the author of such plays as *Pagla Ghoda*, *Evam Indrajit*, and *Tringsha Shatabdi*, the latter an indictment of twentieth century man set a thousand years in the future.

"The first time I saw Mira was when she was on the stage of St. Stephen's College Delhi University, in the role of Cleopatra in Shakespeare's *Antony and Cleopatra*," remembers Barry John, an instructor who has had nearly forty years of experience teaching and directing children, having trained at Bretton Hall College of Education in the U.K. under John Hodgson. Today he teaches child actors at his own school in New Delhi, called Imago, and John has maintained a friendship with Nair for several decades. Among other accomplishments, he was responsible for the workshop that helped transform the street children of Bombay into actors for *Salaam Bombay!* in the mid-1980s.

"I did not know her then," Barry tells us, "but knew of her through some student friends. She was considered a pretty hot item. St. Stephens was an all-boys college that imported its female requirements from Miranda House College, an all-girls institution which, conveniently was just down the road, and had this heavy-duty actress on its roles.

"The play was dull and stilted, but that was not Mira's fault. She acted with aplomb, as the critics are wont to put it, with intelligence and excellent diction. I imagine that the role was important to her and her learning curve…," John continues. "The largely male student audience was disappointed because it was the men in the play who wore the short skirts!"

John was to encounter Nair once more when he served as the Artistic Director of TAG (Theatre Action Group), Delhi's busiest and most illustrious theatrical company, founded in 1973.

"Working in English, with a repertoire of English and American plays it [TAG] can be viewed as a post-colonial hangover in retrospect," considers

John, "but at the time it served an important function." To wit, TAG attracted the best young acting talent in the region, and also attracted large, steady audiences to its presentations.

Between 1973 and 1978, which John consider's TAG's golden era, the company mounted productions of *Jesus Christ Superstar*, *King Lear*, *Waiting for Godot*, and *Marat/Sade* among others. Nair went along to audition at TAG with a friend of John's, Khalid Tyabji (who later appeared in *Kama Sutra: A Tale of Love*).

Tyabji was Nair's first boyfriend, and the audition served as her official introduction to John.

"I remember Mira in two productions from this period," reports John. "The first was Peter Shaffer's *Equus*, in which she played the role of Ms. Strang, the mother of the boy who has blinded six horses for no apparent reason. Of course, it turns out that it is the mother who is largely responsible, having indoctrinated her son with a warped religious fundamentalism and oppressive middle-class values. Mira, of course, was actually not old enough for the role, but she was able to perform the hysteria too, when required.

"The second production was of a very different genre," John relates. "It was Alan Bennett's comedy *Habeas Corpus*, in which Mira again played the role of wife and mother, Mrs. Wicksteed. The play is a very clever and elegant sex comedy bordering on farce. It was very sporting and courageous of Mira to play the part, requiring as it did that she flaunt an enormous, cantilevered bosom, and let loose an enormous sexual appetite. She strode the stage like an Amazon, absolutely fearless, relishing every innuendo.

"Khalid Tyabji was also in those productions," John adds, "and Lillete Dubey, who would later be in *Monsoon Wedding* was in the latter. Mira's involvement in the company was limited, but sufficient to establish herself for the U.S., [and her involvement] was with the intention of further developing her acting skills [amongst other hidden agenda], and when she returned [to India], she was a film director married to an American photographer.

"I do think that her experiences of being an actress are part of the foundation of her later accomplishments," John establishes. "She is certainly inspiring for actors to work with, perhaps because she feels for them."

But before getting to that point, Nair had to acquire the best education available. Seeking to gain an outstanding education in a country where female education was not always a societal priority, Nair began applying to schools in the Western world.

She turned down a full scholarship to Cambridge University, reportedly over a chip on her shoulder about the Brits, but was ultimately accepted on a full scholarship to Harvard University in Cambridge, Massachusetts. Nair left her beloved India to attend, and at the age of nineteen was one of just three Indian students in the undergraduate class.[16]

It was during her tenure at Harvard that Nair encountered another aspiring Indian artist, Sooni Taraporevala, who was studying for a Bachelor of Arts in English literature. Born in Bombay only ten months before Nair, Taraporevala had a number of interests in common with the future director, and the duo would eventually serve as collaborators on a number of important projects, including *Salaam Bombay!*, *Mississippi Masala*, *My Own Country*, and 2006's *The Namesake*.

Sooni Taraporevala reached Harvard in interesting fashion as well. She had a friend who attended Princeton as an undergraduate and who came home to India on one vacation and asked why Sooni wasn't also applying to American schools.

"At that time, it was very rare for undergraduates to get scholarships and I was severely discouraged, but I thought that there was no harm in trying," Taraporevala reports. "So I did try, and I sort of did it on my own, and applied to colleges. Anyway, I got lucky and got a scholarship to Harvard, and that's how I got there."

Taraporevala came in as a freshman student, at age eighteen. She had never been to America previously, never been to the West, even. She calls the experience "confusing and bewildering," and notes "I don't think that I was an exception. I think it was the same for everyone else who came in as a freshman. You suddenly go from being the star of your school to being one of thousands of scholarships. It's a humbling experience."

Still, Taraporevala counts her Harvard experience as an "opening of horizons" that she didn't know existed at the time. One of those horizons involved film studies, a curriculum that in India she did not even know existed. The future writer enrolled in several film courses per semester.

Meanwhile, enterprising Mira Nair became involved in the theatre program at Harvard, and won a Boylston Prize for her performance of Jocasta's speech from Seneca's *Oedipus*.[17] Despite this success, Nair grew increasingly disillusioned with the program's focus on the American musical format, including the likes of the Rodgers and Hammerstein show, *Oklahoma!* She derided the program as being too conservative for her taste, and somewhat tired too. And so Nair transitioned to another discipline: *photography*.[18]

By 1977, Nair had enrolled in photography courses at Harvard, and her instructor in an introductory class would become an important individual in the development of her art, a twenty-five year old named Mitch Epstein. The duo soon developed a deep bond of friendship, and Epstein and Nair encouraged each other's aspirations. An accomplished photographer, Epstein later served as the director of photography on the documentary *India Cabaret* and production designer on Nair's earliest feature films, including *Salaam Bombay!* and *Mississippi Masala*. Eventually, Epstein also became Nair's first husband. Today, he is a much respected and successful photographer.

Although Nair has often stated that she simply fell into the world of filmmaking, it is not difficult to discern how her early experiences in sociology, theatre and photography shaped the artist. Her interest in sociology would inform the stories she would choose to vet—on the consequences of identity and globalization. Her experience as an actor would help Nair direct others when it came time to shoot her own films.

Importantly, as a photography aficionado who came to appreciate the artistry of Josef Koudelka, William Eggleston—the so-called father of color photography—and Nan Goldin, Nair would learn to appreciate the primacy of the image, and how to tell a story visually, within the confines of a frame.

Next, Mira Nair would have to learn the ropes of filmmaking, a *technical* and collaborative art form.

VIEWPOINT: REALITY

During the next phase of her education, Mira Nair migrated fully from the discipline of still photography into motion pictures, and at first, the world of documentaries. In particular, the artist had grown fascinated with the then-in-vogue style known as *cinema verité*, or rather *direct cinema*.

This approach, championed by adherents such as D. A. Pennebaker's *Don't Look Back* (1967) and Richard Leacock's *A Stravinsky Portrait* (1966) and *Tread* (1972), stressed a few important principles. These included: the use of a bare minimum of equipment, the recording of live sound, and the deployment of a hand-held camera to record action. The goal inherent in the *cinema verité* mode is always to record life unfolding *as it happens*, with as little trickery and movie magic as possible.

Nair's idols in this field were practitioners such as Pennebaker, Leacock and Alfred Guzzetti in their film *Family Portrait Sitting* (1975), who revealed to her a method by which to film truth as "unmanipulated as possible."[19] In her own words, documentaries symbolized the perfect marriage of Nair's interests "in the visual arts, theatre, [and] life as it is lived."[20]

At first, Nair's relatives were baffled by her career selection. She reported that her family couldn't spell the word *documentary*, much less grasp what the form was, and what it might accomplish.[21]

In spite of her family's initial lack of enthusiasm, Nair plowed forward and created several documentaries that she felt would fully examine "the culture and traditions of India and their impact on the lives of ordinary people."[22] In other words, for Nair the camera become a method by which to conduct a sociology experiment.

The first of these efforts was Nair's thesis film at Harvard, made to satisfy her M.A. requirements. The production was entitled *Jama Masjid Street Journal*, and was an eighteen minute, black-and-white film shot and edited in 1978 and 1979. Taking her cue from the hustle and bustle of the Indian street, *Jama Masjid Street Journal* represents an early form of the now-popular "video diary" that has, in much more sensationalistic fashion, become *de rigueur* on the reality television circuit.

Armed with a hand-cranked Bolex camera and shooting in 16 mm, Mira Nair prowled the streets of Old Delhi and recorded the random sights and sounds of life around the Great Mosque in the city. Much of the film involved her own presence there and the conflict it emphasized, a Westernized, English-speaking Indian female among a traditional Muslim community. Nair even described the camera as her "veil," separating her from others and creating a psychological distance between photographer and subject.

After shooting *Jama Masjid Street Journal*, Nair returned to New York, and at the prodding of others, added her own voice-over narration to complete what she had always intended to be a silent project. Adding voice-over was a decision she reportedly regretted, and a mistake that would not be made again, bending her will to those around her on the subject of her own art.

Following graduation from Harvard, Nair continued down the road of becoming a successful documentarian, but it wasn't easy. She filled her time working as a waitress, at an art gallery, and as an editor on medical films. But during this span she also actively sought out, or by her terminology, *stalked*, the guru of the field, Pennebaker. He became her mentor, and helped secure a twenty thousand dollar grant (from the New York Council for the Humanities) for her next project, entitled *So Far from India*.[23]

Not surprisingly, this second documentary was another story focusing on two divergent worlds, but one that related more directly to Nair's personal experience, living far from her homeland, a stranger in a strange land. *So Far from India*, a fifty-two minute film, recorded the life of an Indian man who was a newspaper dealer in the New York City subway, while his pregnant wife, a so-called peasant in India anxiously awaited his return home. There were major stresses in this transcontinental marriage, not the least of which was the husband's inability to treat his wife with respect and decency now that he was a "successful" American. Nair spent two full months in both New York and India to get the footage she required, often acting as mediator between uncommunicative spouses.

So Far from India is widely considered Mira Nair's first "professional film" and upon completion it played at film festivals throughout the early 1980s. Jane Balfour, who until 2000 headed her own distribution company representing shorts, documentaries and art house-style features, sold the film internationally.

INDIA CABARET

Ultimately, it was Mira Nair's third documentary that proved the artist's most controversial and high-profile early effort, 1984's *India Cabaret*. Nair raised the money for the production herself, an impressive one hundred thirty thousand dollars, and what she crafted was a powerful portrait of the female strippers populating a Bombay nightclub called the Meghraj Cabaret. The film was shot in the autumn of 1984, over a span of two months, with Mitch Epstein serving as director of photography. The temperature often peaked at a sweltering one hundred degrees inside the cabaret, and working conditions were stifling. For instance, the strippers' dressing room, was just five by seven feet in diameter.[24]

But these were only the *physical* challenges the team endured. From the very beginning, Nair also met with resistance from her father, Amrit, on the film's controversial subject matter. He clashed with his daughter over the fact that his daughter was essentially choosing to live with "scum"[25] for sixty days. Also, the male patrons of the club gazed upon the attractive Nair and considered her "as a potential girl,"[26] and that meant unwanted amorous attention.

Running fifty-nine minutes, *India Cabaret* obsessed on the ideal of the "virtuous virgin," and how that societal stereotype and ideal differed from these "queens of the night" who worked at the Meghraj.[27] It also dealt explicitly with the hypocrisy of the male customers, who would demean these women for being un-virtuous on one hand, but then spend their hard-earned money gawking at them in the cabaret on the other. A stripper or "bad" woman might very well pay for her sister's dowry, but she was still considered an outcast by her family, especially her father. She was unable even to enter the family home on the occasion of a wedding for fear of "soiling" it.

India Cabaret revealed "the marginalized lives of the strippers," who were treated as prostitutes (even though they didn't sell their bodies...) and "the double standards and patriarchal values whereby women in general are never moved to question or challenge their lot as oppressed citizens."[28]

Shot in 16 mm, *India Cabaret* became a *cause celebre* when it played the festival circuits in the mid-1980s. During this span, Nair developed associations with other participants in the burgeoning documentary film industry in New York, and began constructing a useful web of connections with like-minded filmmakers.

"Over the years, being a documentarian in New York and Mira being a documentarian in New York, our worlds converged," reports Sandi Sissel, the acclaimed cinematographer who eventually shot *Salaam Bombay!* and whose impressive career has included films as diverse as the John Kerry documentary *Going Upriver: The Long War of John Kerry* (2004) and the satirical class-warfare Wes Craven horror film, *The People Under the Stairs* (1991).

"We weren't close friends, but we knew of each other, and partially we knew each other because Nick Broomfield and I had directed a film called *Chicken Ranch* (1984), which was about women in a legal brothel in Las Vegas," Sissel states.

"So Nick and I had our film shown all over the place. I think it was 1984 that our film was released theatrically, and it did very well, and Mira had done a documentary called *India Cabaret* [and] it came out around the same time as *Chicken Ranch*, and they were on the film festival circuit together, so it was around that time that I really got to know Mira.

"Mira knew Nick, my partner on *Chicken Ranch* because Nick is British and is very close friends with Don Pennebaker," Sissel says, "and I think Mira at one point after graduating from Harvard had met with Pennebaker and they became friends."

Ironically, these documentary filmmakers, Sissel and Nair, were contemplating the same career move at the same moment, namely moving out of long-form documentary for fictional, theatrical narratives. In fact, the ever-determined Nair had set a goal—and deadline—for herself: directing a feature film by the age of thirty.[29]

After *India Cabaret*, Nair shot just one more documentary, this time for Canadian television: *Children of a Desired Sex* (1987). It concerned amniocentesis, and the manner in which the procedure was being improperly utilized in India. Apparently, in some situations, expectant parents were performing the test to determine the sex of a fetus, and upon learning it was a female, they would induce an abortion.

For the time being, *Children of a Desired Sex* represented Mira Nair's swan song in the documentary field, in part because she had already formulated the notion that it was not the raw, in-the-moment style truths of *cinema verité* that would ultimately affect and change the world for the better, but something else all together.

Perhaps, Nair pondered, it was actually "art" that "could change the world."[30]

Their final shape constructed in the editing room from dozens of hours of raw footage, Nair's documentaries had granted only the opportunity to mold that which life had presented her, not the chance to weave an artistic fabric from whole cloth. And Nair desperately sought that ability. Waiting for something to happen, as was the tradition of *cinema verité*, was often "boring as sin"[31] for this impatient, active new voice, and she wanted more excitement, more passion.

"I wanted to control light and gesture and drama," she told *New York Times'* Caryn James following the release of *Salaam Bombay!* "But I never wanted to give up the documentary…the contradictions and the way people are in life. I still wanted that kind of edge."[32]

Fostering this ideal, Nair turned her eye to this new challenge, leaping full-speed into fictional narratives. But like everything else she had accomplished so far, Nair's first theatrical feature was not going to be forged in a conservative or even particularly sensible fashion, or concern conventional or traditional subject matters.

No. It was going to be a very different proposition all together. It was going to be something unique to Nair's character and experience.

2

Salaam Bombay! (1988)

SALAAM BOMBAY! (1988)

Cinecom presents a Mirabai Films Production with Film Four International NFDC-Doordarshan, Cadrage S.A., La S.E.P.T., a Mira Nair Film, *Salaam Bombay!*

Crew:

Music	L. Subramaniam
Production Design	Mitch Epstein
Film Editor	Barry Alexander Brown
Director of Photography	Sandi Sissel
Story	Mira Nair, Sooni Taraparevola
Screenplay	Sooni Taraparevola
Director of Workshop	Barry John
Associate Producer	Jane Balfour
Co-Producer	Mitch Epstein
Producer and director	Mira Nair

Cast:

Krishna/Chaipau	Shafiq Syed
Manju	Hansa Vithal
Solasaal/"Sweet Sixteen"	Chandra Sharma
Chillum	Raghubir Yadav
Rekha	Aneeta Kanwar
Baba	Nana Petakar
Keera	Raju Barnad
Kid at Circus	Anjaan
Melaboss	Amrit Patel
Ticket Seller	Murari Sharma
Madman	Ram Moorti
Koyla	Sarfuddin Qurrassi
Salim	Mohanraj Babu
Chungal	Chandrashekhar Naidu
Madame	Shaukat Kaifi Azmi

GUTS AND GLORY: IMAGINING *SALAAM BOMBAY!*

Conceived with the title *Chull Bombai Chull!*, *Salaam Bombay!* was a narrative nurtured by co-writers Mira Nair and Sooni Taraporevala for five years before the film was produced. In fact, the project's origins went back to 1983–1984, and the shooting of *India Cabaret*. While working on that documentary, Nair lived with two dancers in their small apartment, and it was in that environment that she encountered a small tea boy, and always remembered him.[1] This real-life character—and his seeming joy in life amidst what was clearly a difficult lot—inspired her to learn more about these children and their perilous lives on the streets.

On the DVD director's audio commentary of *Salaam Bombay!*, Nair also cites another direct inspiration for her first feature film, a handicapped young man she witnessed navigating heavy Bombay traffic one day during the mid-1980s. Little more than a torso and head atop a cart, this handicapped boy used momentum—and a passing taxi—to transport himself across a busy intersection. At the completion of the daring maneuver, he exulted with a little salute of victory, and Nair witnessed the moment. Despite every hardship he faced, Mira Nair saw this soul as triumphant. Harkening back to *Pather Panchali* and Satyajit Ray, there was this notion of life being good, even when it was bad, in that unusual experience.

After the great success of *India Cabaret*, Nair wasn't entirely certain what project she should follow up with. She had pondered working on a film about her childhood and maturity in India, but Sooni Taraporevala, who had found employment as a photojournalist in India after graduate work in film at Columbia and New York University, encouraged her to look for material in a different direction.

"My reason for that was that I thought that an autobiographical film, no matter how charming, etc., would have very little relevance to most people in India. At that time, I was obsessed with trying to be relevant in whatever I did. I wanted to, perhaps, reach a larger audience," Taraporevala suggests. "Film is such an expensive medium. You spend so much money making a film that, to me, I've never reconciled myself actually to writing a pure entertainment or something like that. Everything I've written always has something a little more to it than just entertainment.

"After a screening of *India Cabaret* [in Hyderabad], the audience reaction was so involved and so visceral that I thought back to something Mira had told me years ago, that she had seen a play—a musical—called *Runaways*, by Elizabeth Swados in New York City years ago," Taraporevala remembers. "And something she said stuck in mind, when she said she'd love to do that one day with Indian kids, and have a workshop like Elizabeth Swados...did. And so I said, 'What about reviving that idea?'"

Taraporevala suggested that she and Nair should develop the idea, though at first Nair was daunted by the size and scope of such an effort. But Sooni soon provided her with a ready-made mantra: *no guts, no glory*.

Apparently, that was all that needed to be said to the determined Ms. Nair.

"When she said 'It's too big,' maybe I said that ['no guts, no glory'] because Mira loves challenges," Ms. Taraporevala considers. "And she can rise to any challenge. So that's how it happened."

But despite Sooni's encouragement, it was abundantly clear that shooting a film guerilla-style on the streets of Bombay was going to represent a tremendous challenge. Not only would the film require talented and believable child actors for the central roles, but the street itself would not be particularly cooperative in the difficult process of moviemaking.

Bombay, or rather Mumbai as it is now known, is the largest metropolis in India, boasting a population of nearly twelve million Muslims, Hindus and Marashtrians. It is a bustling, living urban center, filled with enough color and chaos to eat a film crew whole, destroy carefully arranged schedules, and transform routine logistical challenges into a full-fledged nightmare.

After walking the byways of Bombay together and meeting and interviewing two hundred street children,[2] visiting jails and so-called chiller rooms, where many of the delinquent youths ended up as wards of the state, Taraporevala and Nair were still not daunted. They developed a one hundred ten page first draft manuscript over a period of months, from summer to autumn of 1986.

"I kind of wrote it instinctively," Taraporevala states. "I had taken one course with Frank Daniels on screenwriting, which was really elementary—at Columbia—that I found quite easy, and so I really didn't know what I subsequently learned later about things like the three-act structure and character. I knew none of that. All I knew is that I watched a lot of very good films as an undergraduate, and had written extensively about them: analyzing them, comparing them to literature, comparing them for literary techniques, point of view, different things like that.

"So I think all of that helped me when I wrote *Salaam*," Taraporevala considers. "I can't remember whether I actually knew I got it right, or I didn't know. I know that certain things I didn't know [then]—which I learned while I wrote it—which was to cut to the chase. As a beginning writer, you feel that you have to set up things a lot more than you really have to. That's one thing I learned. The second thing I learned is how what you write translates into money. Which is not something you learn right off the bat…it's easy to write stuff; harder to film."

"So all these things I think I learned as I grew as a screenwriter," says Taraporevala. "As I said, I worked instinctively, and always had Mira to react and edit, and so we worked together on that and [we] made it very tight. Our final shooting script, I think, was only ninety pages."

According to Nair and Taraporevala's book about the film, *Salaam Bombay!*, the script's goal was to tell a story that was "not sentimental, but about the survival of the fittest, about children who have never known a childhood."3

"I like to be more understated and keep things unsaid," reflects Taraporevala of the script's tone. "Cinema's really all about that. It's about things not said. It's about subtext. It's not a play where you speak everything."

In crafting this screenplay, the duo also pulled together many other real-life observations, not merely the memory of Nair's tea-boy, but stories about brothels, drug dealers and other seamy and ever-present aspects of Bombay life.

"[It was] taking bits and pieces from different things, different situations, from different characters and mixing that with imagination, and the result of that is this kind of hybrid," suggests Taraporevala. "When I wrote the script, what I was drawing on was the emotional truth of what we had observed and what we had experienced. I loved the emotional truth of the situation we were researching."

Nair's intent was to augment those feelings of emotional truth by casting real street children, but then also to cast experienced, big-name adult actors around them.

In particular, Nair desired to cast Naseeruddin Shah (*Monsoon Wedding*), an actor renowned for his "use of hesitant speech and casual gesture to signify psychological complexity"[4] for the critical role of Baba, a pimp and predator. He met with Nair about the role, but ultimately found the character too despicable to take on.

The beautiful Bollywood icon, Rekha (*Kama Sutra*) was also on Nair's radar to essay the part of her namesake in the film, a prostitute and the mother to young Manju. Ultimately, neither actor was retained, meaning that the film's inexperienced young performers would have to carry that much more weight. Barry John was recruited to develop a workshop that would hone those abilities.

One highly qualified actor cast in *Salaam Bombay!* was youthful Raghubir Yadav, who had met Nair at the 11th Annual International Film Festival in India. There, his film, *Massey Sahib* (1985), directed by Pradip Krisha, was screened, and Yadav was honored with the prestigious Silver Peacock Award for "best actor" for his role in the film.

Nair consequently handed the young actor the script for *Salaam Bombay!* with the comment that she was considering him for the role of Chillum, the drug dealer. The opportunity to work with Barry John was part of Yadav's decision in accepting the part.

"I had three interesting reasons which attracted me towards the film," Yadav elaborates, "firstly the script, secondly the character was very challenging, and thirdly the Workshop with Barry John on street lives."

Yadav still remembers his feelings on the tragic character, the script, and how he would develop the challenging part. "Chillum was a brown sugar addict, so the first thoughts about him were his mental condition...with and without drugs. His normal, actually *extra* normal was on a high," Yadav explains. "And when he had no brown sugar, his life was death: agonizing, desperate, frustrating, willing to go to any level, even murder, to get drugged.

"The script had a difficult theme, dealing with the lives of street children in Bombay," the actor continues, giving his opinion of the screenplay. "It was original, and had a realistic approach, no acting but ruthless truth. An insight into the lives of the characters—no, not characters—real people."

With the professionals in the cast cemented, Nair continued to correspond with Barry John near the end of 1986, about his upcoming workshop.

"This would have been towards the end of 1986 or early 1987," John recalls. "She also breezed into my one-room 'barsati' at some point laden with laptop on one shoulder and bag-with-kitchen-sink on the other for further discussions [and] updates."

It was not long after this visit that John learned more details about the film, including its general storyline.

As devised by Taraporevala and Nair, *Salaam Bombay!* is the harrowing tale of a diminutive but spirited boy named Krishna, also called Chaipau (Shafiq Syed), a child who has left his home in hopes of earning five hundred rupees to pay for his brother's bike, which he torched. After he is abandoned by his most recent employer, the owner of a traveling circus, Krishna hops a train to bustling Bombay and becomes enmeshed in a chaotic life there. He befriends an older boy named Chillum (Yadav), a sensitive soul strung out on drugs thanks to a cruel-hearted local pimp and dealer, Baba (Nana Patekar).

While attempting to earn his rupees for the return home, Krishna works as a tea-boy and falls for the lovely Solasaal—Sweet Sixteen (Chandra Sharma), a virgin brought against her will to the local brothel as a special attraction. He also befriends a kindly prostitute—Babu's wife, Rekha (Aneeta Kanweer), and her sad, attention-starved daughter Manju (Hansa Vithal).

Over a stretch of weeks, Chaipau attempts to court Sweet Sixteen, earn his money, deal with the death of Chillum, evade the oppressive chiller rooms, and free lovely Rekha from bondage, but ultimately finds himself repeatedly thwarted in all his efforts.

Preparing to film this tale of survival on the streets was really a multi-front battle. Sooni and Mira worked on developing the script; Barry John came to Bombay to prepare the workshop for the street children to be featured in the film; and Nair herself commenced the unenviable task of raising money for the production. Sometimes this fundraising effort involved a sales presentation for financiers, including photographs by Epstein (from *India Cabaret*) and a ten minute video clip from that effort.

"Every time Mira went to have a meeting, Mitch went with her," cinematographer Sandi Sissel recollects. "Back then a woman simply didn't take a meeting alone. Now, I'm not dismissing Mitch's contribution to the film, because it was enormous, but it's one thing for a married woman to go to a meeting with her husband, it's another for a woman to go to a meeting alone. So there were many things that we did in getting the film done that were old traditional Indian ways of doing things."

Unfortunately, financing *Salaam Bombay!* was an effort that was never really settled. Backers would come in and drop out with alarming regularity, resulting in Nair often shooting the film by light of day, and attempting desperately to raise money by dark of night. In the end, forty-nine percent of the budget came from a company called Film Four on a guarantee that Nair would raise the remaining fifty-one percent herself...which she didn't. Another fourth of the money came from government funding in India, the National Film Development Corporation, a resource which instantaneously granted Nair access to such government installations as train stations and the chiller rooms. These turned out to be essential locations.

And there were other major concerns besides money. One was finding the right talent to shoot the film. Chris Menges, the cinematographer on Roland Jaffe's *The Killing Fields* (1984) was considered for a time, but by a happy coincidence, Nair connected with a game collaborator in Sandi Sissel. The two female documentarians ended up as guests at the same wedding in New York on one weekend in 1987. After the ceremony, Nair seized an opportunity.

"So at the party that night, she approached me and said 'I'm doing this feature in India and it's very low budget, but it's got a certain reality to it,'" Sissel relates.

Nair further explained that it wasn't a documentary *per se*, and asked if Sissel would be interested in reading the script. Sissel answered in the affirmative, and the next day received the script, which she read on her plane trip home to Los Angeles, where she had just recently moved. She quickly realized *Salaam Bombay!* was exactly the opportunity she had been seeking.

"At that time, it was an extremely low budget film," Sissel describes, "and for myself, even operating great big features and making lots of money, I had been asked to do a number of low budget features. But what often happens when you're making the leap from operator to DP (Director of Photography) [is] you know you're going to take a tremendous cut in salary, so I had always been a little leery about doing something that wasn't that interesting—two people in a room talking, for example. So I had been waiting for something that really interested me."

When Sissel and Nair spoke again next by telephone, Sissel told Nair she was committed to shooting the film. Nair was grateful, and Sandi Sissel proved an excellent selection, not only because she had great chops and almost unparalleled experience as a cinematographer (she was one of the first three women admitted into the New York IA 600 cinematographer's union in the mid-1970s) but because she also had direct experience shooting in India. That was a tremendous asset.

"I had been working on a documentary, and there were two directors of photography who worked with Mira at one point or another, Ed Lachman [*Mississippi Masala*] and me," Sissel explains. "On again and off again for four years, we'd alternate shooting this documentary on Mother Teresa. It required enormous amounts of travel.

"We all got very involved in it, but because of the fact that sometimes we'd get a call at the last minute, either I would not be available or Ed would not be available, so very often he would do one sequence, then they called me and I would do a sequence.

"It was toward the end of the shoot—the end of four years—and we were going to India to shoot Mother with the lepers, Mother with her sisters, everything in Calcutta that we were leading up to. So the director decided it would be good to take both crews," Sissel remembers.

"We were there three weeks in India, maybe a month, and for all of us it was our first experience in India, which of course is quite amazing. It's a completely different world from the States. I luckily had done a lot of traveling. The documentaries that I did up until that point, much more than the features I've done since, took me quite a lot to Asia and Europe and all over the place. So it was not a new experience to be in a place like Calcutta. But there was some level of being with Mother with the lepers, and Mother in a home for the dying, and all those aspects of the poorest of the poor that we had done around that country that in some way was a little bit of research for going to do *Salaam Bombay!* on the streets of Bombay."

Interestingly, Sissel's initial discussions with Nair did not concern documentary or *cinema verité*. In fact, that was something they agreed was to be avoided. "They [Nair and Taraporevala] always talked about it as a film that audiences would *enjoy*, that audiences would like, and it would be very theatrical," Sissel explains.

Nair suggested Sissel review Argentine-born director Hector Babenco's 1981 film, *Pixote*, which also dealt with the subject of street children, only in Sao Paulo, Brazil. Shot by Roldofo Sanchez, the film focused on a ten-year old runaway boy named Pixote (played by the late Fernando Ramos Da Silva), and also featured non-professionals in key roles.

The *New York Times* described that film in terms that Nair and Sissel could appreciate: "A lot of the details are tough to take, but it is neither exploitative nor pretentious," concluded critic Vincent Canby. "Mr. Babenco shows us rock bottom, and because he is an artist, he makes us believe it, as well as all of the possibilities that have been lost."[5]

Sissel was intrigued and impressed by Babenco's *Pixote*, and saw *Salaam Bombay!* as an opportunity to improve even upon the fine look of that disturbing and accomplished movie. It was a challenge she relished.

"Originally, what Mira said to me was 'We're shooting in 35 mm; We're going to be shooting in the streets of India; We're going to be doing it a certain way;' and that was what interested me in doing it," she reports. "At that time, given the enormous number of documentaries that I shot and the fact that I was moving to L.A. and working in the theatrical community, the idea that it was 35 mm, the idea that we had sixty days of shooting—[that] was all part of my desire to go do it. Had it been presented to me as a documentary, I probably would have not been interested."

Sissel's first step in prepping the film was to visit India and scout locations. "Around the time that I agreed to do it, I remember I was shooting a big AT&T commercial, and Mira and Mitch were going over to India to scout, and I was going to scout. I believe that I was to scout for a couple of weeks, then come home for a couple of weeks, and then go back to shoot."

On her sojourn, Sissel brought along a black-and-white Polaroid camera, which was often used by filmmakers in the 1980s on just such scouting expeditions, and she and Epstein traveled to various locations in and around Sooni Taraporevala's Grant Road home, a section of Bombay with an abundance of interesting places to shoot, including a market and the rail station. They snapped dozens of photographs to achieve a true sense of how the locations appeared on film. Then they collated their work and produced an extensive location book.

"There was a film that Louis Malle (1932–1995) had done about India, a sort of a documentary [*L'Inde Phantom* in 1968], and it was...very depressing, so that all you felt was poverty," Sissel remembers. "You could almost *smell* poverty. We had a discussion, and I don't remember if I initiated it, or Mitch did, or Mira did, but the discussion was that in some cases we needed to clean up the locations a little bit, so that people could actually see the humanity of the characters and not be overwhelmed by the poverty."

This discussion was part of their debate about creating a theatrical film that people would enjoy. In particular, color was discussed, and how some locations would be painted, and what sorts of streets would work better than others.

But it was at this point that further money woes arose. "I think as I was leaving India, a lot of the money fell out," Sissel confides. "There was quite a delay in production, and there was even a discussion about having to shoot the movie in 16 mm."

BACKBONE: THE BOMBAY CHILDREN

On another pre-production track altogether, Barry John and Mira Nair began to organize their workshop, the foundation from which they would ultimately select the film's cast. John had the opportunity to read the script for the first time in June of 1987, upon his arrival in Bombay. He remembers then having only a few short weeks prior to the workshop's beginning in which to decide on a training curriculum. Also, it was something of a new experience for the veteran director.

"The workshop was a rather daunting prospect for all of us," John begins. "My work in theatre-in-education and drama therapy had led to my interacting with diverse categories of children and youth, but always in some institutional context or under the aegis of some developmental agency. This was the first time that I would be working with urchins picked up off the streets, and with the objectives of fostering amongst them the skills and disciplines required in the making of a realistic feature film."

The workshop was to be a six- to-seven-week crash course in acting, and Dinaz Stafford, a child psychologist, was also involved to help the children during the long, eight-hour-a-day and six-days-a-week program.

But all that came later. First things first: the cast had to be painstakingly selected.

One of the first crises involved the age of prospective participants, as Sandi Sissel recalls. "I know that initially, Mira wanted to cast much older actors. Somebody like Shafiq was supposed to be the youngest kid. The letter writer in the film [actor Irfan Khan] was supposed to be the oldest."

But, it soon became plain that tricks like that weren't going to work. "You can get with that on stage," Sissel suggests, "but you can't begin to get away with it on film. There was that whole concept that we were going to have to look at much younger kids.

"The first few days were bedlam with over a hundred kids of various ages to reckon with, to get acquainted with, and to assess," John relates. "New aspirants kept arriving every day as word spread that training was on offer, free of charge. The responsibility for weeding out kids was undertaken by Mira...much to my relief because it was an unpleasant task, but one that, at the time, was compulsory.

"Eventually, with manageable numbers, order won over chaos," describes John, "and a regimen began to impose itself; from 9:00 A.M. to 6:00 P.M., Monday to Sunday. The first part of the day was usually devoted to physical exercises, movement and free dance, mime, voice exercises, singing, theatre games and team games. The kids themselves had a lot to contribute in those areas; regional variations of children's games and sports activities (they had migrated from different parts of the country), beach gymnastics, beach plays, jokes, songs and mass dancing."

The goal early on was not to teach the specific roles in the *Salaam Bombay!* script but rather to foster a bedrock foundation of responsibility and trust that would prove vital once the hectic pace of shooting began.

"Beyond the obvious development of fitness, flexibility, control and coordination, along with vocal and emotional expressiveness, play promotes mutual respect and dependence, a respect for rules and team ethics, trust, instinctive and intuitive responses, concentration and absorption in the 'game,'" John enumerates. "All these benefits spill alchemically into the playing that we call acting. And, above all, the kids enjoy it. You're speaking their language and they thrive on it."

"There were always four or five other adults assisting the facilitating of the workshop and participating," John explains further. "Raghubir

Yadav, an actor from Delhi who I had taught and directed, and who was cast as Chillum in the film, was inspirational and an approachable role model for the kids."

"That's a great compliment coming from Barry," Yadav says, while noting that he took his responsibility to the children (as a kind of mentor) with great seriousness and joy. "[It was not] a burden, because I enjoy delving deep into my roles, maybe due to my deep association with music, and am not afraid of hard work. I love competition and want everyone to be excellent so that I can work even harder. I love perfection in entirety.

"The process for me was addictive," Yadav explains. "I want such preparation for every character, but unfortunately, that's not exactly what happens in films in India…"

John also praises Irfan Khan, "another young actor from Delhi, whose career graph has shot up astronomically over the last few years," for his sterling participation in the workshop. Khan would return to the Mira Nair canon in 2006's *The Namesake*.

"Other cast members came in, but more intermittently," John explains. "Some sessions saw the kids segregated age wise. Other sessions, later on, were for girls only—including young prostitutes from the local red-light area, Kamathipura."

"There are so many memories," notes Yadav, remembering the workshop. "I learned patience, and how to work on any character in a very gradual way without force."

Early in the process, the acting exercises centered around each child's own personal, real-life tale. "Whether in the form of still images, solo mime, improvisations with dialogue, or pencil and drawings, they illustrated answers to such questions as: Who am I? Where am I from? What is/was my relationship with my family?," John catalogs, "What have I been through on my journey? What are my dreams/fantasies/nightmares? What is friendship? How do others see me? What is my relationship with authority figures like the police, work bosses and gang leaders? What do work and money mean to me? What is my view of rich people? [and] Where am I going?"

After watching these performances, it was time to analyze them, and a discussion time was forged wherein full-fledged debates between the children and filmmakers would often erupt. Barry describes the workshop as a non-formal education site, and he moved the improvisation period into situations "aligned more directly with the trajectory of the film's story."

These included: "Scenes from family life; running away; first reactions to the Big City; street-gang initiations; survival of the fittest; territory and possessions; violence and crime; addictions; Bollywood movies; thoughts of home; Remand Homes/chiller rooms/jails; [and] escape and freedom."

Twenty-four children were ultimately cast in the film, selected from a pool of over one hundred thirty. This group was soon introduced to yoga and Western films, including François Truffaut's *The 400 Blows* (1959), which Mira Nair felt would show them realistic rather than artificial acting, as they were accustomed to in Bollywood productions. And then it came time to focus on *Salaam Bombay!* itself.

"Ultimately we were working from the script," John notes, "choreographing action and feeding/fixing dialogue. A video camera and monitor had moved in by then, to allow the kids to analyze what they were doing, to see what was convincing and what wasn't, to know the difference between long shot and close-up, between natural and exaggerated, between being honest and being fake. In the process, of course, the camera was demystified, which took them from the position of being aware of it and self-conscious, to not caring a damn whether it was around or not."

When questioned about how one teaches children to act, John provides a thoughtful and detailed answer. "Perhaps to impress upon them the fact that it is already something they know how to do. Acting is a reflection of what people do in life. After just a few years of life, most of us know what it means to love and to hate, to be angry or frustrated or bored or whatever.

"The problem is to deconstruct and unlearn wrong or warped notions about acting that they may have imbibed from misguided parents and teachers and from mediocre television and film fare. Crucial is the relationship you build with them, based on mutual respect, trust and absolute honesty."

The workshop period on *Salaam Bombay!* is one many participants remember with clarity and emotion, and John is no different. "This particular group of kids, the core group that we were left with after weeding out, seemed to be of a special caliber at the time. Perhaps because it was my first experience of working with runaway street kids, and the intensity of it was so overwhelming. But it was a first for them too, and they responded brilliantly. They were never absent or late at the workshop; most of them would land up well before the appointed time and launch themselves into some warm-up activity.

"They began to insist that we work on Sunday as well!" John recalls. "And they dealt with everything we threw at them with great energy and enthusiasm. They thrilled at the opportunity to learn, to explore, to create and express. Having missed out on the support structures of family, and the conditions of an oppressive school system they were uniquely independent, open-minded and dedicated.

"Illiterate does not mean unintelligent," he stresses. "They make good actors because of having been exposed to life in all its rawness. They have what I call 'backbone,' a strength of character that makes them stand tall. They are fearless and shameless, devoid of masks, and ruthlessly honest—they have nothing to hide. They exude the power, the transparency and crystal clarity that are the marks of all great actors."

What Sooni Taraporevala remembers most about the street children of Bombay is "their resilience. Their good spirits in the face of all odds..."

GANPATI FESTIVAL: THE FIRST DAY...

Originally, it had been the intent of Mira Nair and her crew to complete their *Salaam Bombay!* shooting period in September of 1987, during the annual (and colossal) Ganpati Festival, a surging street parade and tribute to the elephantine God of Wisdom called Ganesh. The strategy was to take cameras into the Bombay streets, where they would film the movie's tense climax, specifically young Chaipau's escape into the overcrowded avenue following his knife murder of Baba. There, he would be separated from his last friend, Rekha. The thousands of real-life revelers and parade-goers were to serve as the impressive backdrop, free extras, as it were.

However, because of production delays—virtually all involving cash flow—there was an unfortunate reversal of fortune. Now, the Ganpati Festival would occur not on the final day of shooting *Salaam Bombay!*, but rather ominously, the *first*.

In preparation to shoot the expansive parade, some cameras were placed to catch the action from above, on rooftops, but others were directed to street level, with Sandi Sissel and her assistant, Tony McNamara, positioned directly amongst the surging throngs.

"I don't know that we really knew what to expect," Sissel considers. "Obviously, this was not a Hollywood union film, or even a New York independent film. Our Indian crew? *They* knew what was going to happen, and were all shocked, because even locations movies in Bombay were not so prevalent at that point in time. People still generally shot on studio locations, and the idea of shooting in the middle of the streets was a very unusual concept."

Sissel remembers the day vividly. "It was probably good it happened to me when I was younger, rather than today," she quips.

As the festival-goers neared in a moving parade of undulating human flesh, shooting commenced. Almost immediately, the festival-goers began throwing red powder at each other, and both Sissel and McNamara got hit right in the eyes. Meanwhile, Nair attempted to direct her actors—little Shafiq Syed and Aneeta Kanwar (as Rekha)—amidst the pandemonium, while McNamara and Sissel jockeyed for position, Sissel filming with a hand-held camera. Then the people in the crowd began to push and shove one another. Things started to get rough…

"Our producers are even in the film," Sissel points out. "You can see them almost protecting the actors and pretending to be part of the crowd."

There were also moments when Sissel raised herself up on Tony's shoulders to film the parade, because she literally could not see over the swirling, massive crowd. Sissel recalls the scene as simply "shooting from the hip, quite literally."

But filming took a more disturbing turn as the crew sought to acquire footage for the film's conceived final shot. The *Salaam Bombay!* team had a large crane, and began tracking the colossal crowd as it headed for the shore and started setting down in the sea hundreds of Ganesh icons, tiny statues of the elephant-like God that would float away to sea.

As McNamara and Sissel ascended the crane to get this shot, the crowd grew agitated by their presence. The parade-goers registered their displeasure by throwing flip-flops at the camera crew. Ultimately, and without warning, the crowds graduated to rocks.

"The reason [they threw rocks] was that they felt to photograph Ganpati was to defame the gods," Sissel explains. "If we saw these Ganeshs upside down in the water, then it would defame the God Ganesh. So they did not want us to shoot. Tony and I stayed up there quite a while in the midst of this near-riot."

When rocks repeatedly struck uncomfortably close to valuable equipment, particularly the camera, the duo on the crane reminded Nair that it was worth "about a million dollars," and if they didn't get down, they would be able unable to shoot the rest of the movie.

It was a difficult decision, however, to stop filming without achieving the required shot.

"We just had to make the decision that we weren't going to get that shot, and that if we did, it would be so upsetting to an Indian audience that it was better to come up with a different ending for the film," Sissel explains.

"Obviously this being Day One of production, this was all pretty shocking. Sooni had written this shot, and we were not going to see Ganpati again for a year. So the idea of not getting this shot made us rewrite the script right off the bat."

It's important here to state again that Sandi Sissel has worked many times outside America and knows the ropes. She has filmed in Vietnam during the Vietnam War, in Haiti, during a conflict in Lebanon, and reports that when you've done such work, "it's sort of like you sense when [a riot's for] real and when it's not.

"Believe me," she emphasizes, "this was real.

"From this point of view," Sissel continues, "Mira had probably done a good thing by hiring me to do the film, because if I had only Hollywood experience, something like this would have been overwhelming. You could have taken it as an omen and said, 'That's it, I'm leaving.'"

KUSKOO DIDI: THE TOUGH BIG SISTER

After Ganpati's baptism by fire, *Salaam Bombay!*'s fifty-five day shoot on over ninety locations proceeded at breakneck speed. Sometimes, the crew would do eighteen set-ups a day. Sometimes one set-up (like the dance sequence in Rekha's room) would require a full day—seventeen hours and beyond.

Nair celebrated her thirtieth birthday making the film and reported feeling an "exquisite terror" each morning of production, "worrying where" to place her camera as nearly one hundred crew members awaited instructions.[6]

She not only had to consider that problem, but also deal with other difficulties. For one thing, the cast often had to act in one hundred twenty degree heat. For another, the camera crew had to shoot in challenging locations (like the interior of a bus), and be prepared at a moment's notice to alter the shot (or sequence of shots) if, by chance, it should rain.

Actors also performed their own stunts, and camera people weren't afforded the luxury of reviewing dailies and thereby determining the basics; like the fact that their work was correctly in focus. In fact, Sissel and others only saw the work print once. On top of all this, *Salaam Bombay!* was also the first film featuring synchronized sound to be recorded on location in Bombay, another challenge.

Outside of these considerations, Indian mafia/brothel owners and madames wanted to make sure they were well-compensated for the use of their locations in the film.[7] After a long day of traversing such negotiations, Nair would return home to her apartment, thoroughly exhausted, only to make phone calls to potential investors. It was a delicate balancing act, and Nair reported to the press that her black hair turned gray during this span.

Not that these multiple problems affected the Whirlwind's bravado. She later reported to David Sterritt that she "trusted" her intuition "all the time"[8] while making *Salaam Bombay!* The child actors apparently picked up on this sense of confidence, and quickly dubbed Nair with a few choice nicknames, including "Danger Director" and "Kuskoo Didi—The Tough Big Sister."

As for Sooni, she wasn't aware of the pressures her friend faced. "You see, the thing is, on *Salaam Bombay!* everyone had their own crosses to bear. So I didn't know exactly what she was going through in terms of day-to-day raising of the money at night, because she and Mitch lived together then, so I was not privy to that," Taraporevala says. "I actually found out later much of what she was going through…"

Nair accomplished the near-impossible task of creating *Salaam Bombay!* in under two months through team work and careful planning and organization. Her stalwart crew, from Dinaz Stafford and Sandi Sissel to Sooni Taraporevala and Mitch Epstein, always came through in a pinch, even though for all these players, *Salaam Bombay!* was their first real feature film experience.

"To a certain degree, when people said to us, 'You can't do it,' we didn't have enough experience to know that we weren't *supposed* to be able to do it," Sissel considers. "There was a certain push forward, and you cannot on any level diminish Mitch's input. He wasn't merely Mira's husband, but he helped her produce the film. I think that our inexperience almost caused us to never give up, and we just kept going."

On top of that, they were prepared for the worst.

"For a long time when initially I went to India, I was living with Mira and Mitch," Sissel describes. "They had an apartment, and I was living in one bedroom, and Mira and Mitch were in the other. It was also our production center, so early in the production one of the things I wanted to do was storyboard the film. There was a reason—because I spoke English and some of the crew did not. My assistant spoke English. The boom operator spoke English, and my gaffer did, though he was Indian, but for the rest of the crew it was very important to me that I basically storyboard the film.

"I'm not an artist at all, but I drew little frames and stick figures in an effort to figure out what we were going to do in the locations in an effort for Mira and I to discuss how we were going to get from one scene to the next," Sissel continues. "They were very helpful, because they really made us break the script down from location to location. In many, many scenes, we followed those very carefully. It also helped the gaffer, I think, to know where we needed lights, because we didn't have great big lights. We had a number of lights, but sometimes we would use four or five lights pushed into the same place to create one big light."

Yet carefully story boarded moments could also give way to wonderful, unplanned ones, and for Sissel, that was one of the enduring joys of working on *Salaam Bombay!* Everybody, including Mira Nair, learned to be flexible, to let the children lead, if the situation merited it.

One such scene involves the character of Manju, played by young Vithal. In the film, Chaipau has presented her with a pack of crackers that she is to give to Sweet Sixteen as a token of his affection, but in a pique of jealousy, Manju goes into the brothel and munches the entire packet of crackers herself, just outside Sweet Sixteen's sight. This moment is dramatized in exquisite deep focus, with Manju in the foreground—leaning against a wall—as life goes on obliviously in the background.

"I love that shot, myself," Sissel acknowledges. "I think it was a culmination of things. One of the really brilliant things about Mira and our access to these locations was that sometimes the children just did what they did, and we were able to be loose and really figure out how to do the shot."

In this case, Nair had directed the young actress to eat *one* cracker, but the child misunderstood and gulped every last wafer, one after the other, in a single, unbroken take. There was a desperateness, innocence, humor, and ultimately a touching reality in that gesture.

"I very carefully remember that as soon as that shot was over, we all burst out laughing," Sissel says. "It was one of those things where frankly we got the shot because nobody laughed out loud. But, you know, the children did [things like] that a lot. In a sense they were playing themselves, and sometimes they just did things.

"That was one of the really good things about shooting. There was general dialogue, but if one of the children came up with something better, it was incorporated. Mira directed the children, but if they did something unusual, she incorporated it, and in many cases it was just up to us to be loose and get the shot."

A sense of spontaneity also informed director Nair's sense of casting real life extras in the film, as Sooni Taraporevala recalls. "Mira has a great feeling for faces. I remember one time, we were shooting at a barber shop around the corner from where my parents then lived, and there was this old man having his hair cut, and she grabbed hold of him and said 'Would you like to be in a film?' And he said 'But I have to go home for lunch!,' so I walked with him to his house around the corner and he told his sister that he was going to be in a film, and we took him back to the set and he was in the barber's chair for I don't know how many hours while we filmed that scene."

Raghubir Yadav remembers his preparation for one of the sweetest scenes in *Salaam Bombay!*, a night in which Chaipau and Chillum spend time together relaxing at a cemetery, bonding and laughing.

"I personally feel that relaxing in a graveyard is very horrifying, but it had to be done for the character," he describes. "To prepare myself, I roamed the crowded streets of Bombay without having a bath for two days, gathering Chillum's soul to enjoy the cemetery. So by the time I reached the location, my soul was exhausted and Chillum's soul alive, and I couldn't care less whether they let me lie in a grave or a graveyard…[I] just needed to relax.

"The workshop with Barry was what gave Syed and me the comfort level required for the natural bonding," Yadav explains. "I also had to bring myself to the age, environment, and level of Syed, and the rest of the cast and characters. Trust played a very important role during the scenes."

The *Salaam Bombay!* filmmakers clearly shared trust and an *esprit de corps*, and, as Yadav describes, this feeling extended to the young stars. In fact, the children's willingness to take risks also contributed greatly to the film's success, resulting in some of the most memorable shots. One of these was Chaipau's long run (eventually cut-up by multiple edits) through busy traffic after a daring escape from the high walls of the chiller room.

"A lot of *Salaam Bombay!* could not have been done in this country, first of all because of child labor laws," Sissel establishes. "Also, because we all know too much here [in the States]. So the idea of sitting in the back of an Impala trunk would probably not have seemed like a very good idea. A child running barefoot on hot concrete next to the exhaust of a car?"

But it happened, because the children were willing, and because trust had been established.

"While we were there, we became the family for these kids. They lived with us. They slept with us. In some cases, Mira had to be very careful to limit their diet because especially Krishna was gaining weight over the course of shooting," Sissel relates. "So she had to get him dirty again and get him to be thin again, to keep the continuity going.

"I don't remember whose car it was, but it actually worked out fine. Tony, Sooni and I were sitting in the trunk of the car, and I don't remember how long it took…this is something we just did in the middle of the street," she says.

"At this point in my career, I miss that kind of spontaneity," she notes. "Because in production meetings going into a big film, if you think you want to do something spontaneous like that, you have sixty other people say 'No, we're not going to do it this way.' 'We're going to have lights.' 'We're going to have police escorts.' 'We're going to block off the street.' We didn't do it that way, we just did it."

The spontaneity and authenticity of the film was especially heightened by the actions of the children during the daring chiller room sequence. "This child [Syed], when he jumped from one rooftop to a fence?! You wouldn't do that in this country," Sissel repeats. "In this country, you would have a little person stunt double doing that jump. You would never let a child do that! These children would do anything, and they loved doing it. I think they so identified with their character, that they really knew where they were, all the time."

Sometimes, Nair's focus on authenticity and reality took its toll on the cast during shooting, as Yadav recollects. "The most difficult and challenging day [for me] was my funeral scene. It was shot like a real funeral, where my corpse—played by myself—was tied on the bier for the whole day carried by small street kids, starting at the red light area [and going] from one bustling street to another," the actor describes.

"Whenever the shot got over, they would throw down my body—tied to the bier—unattended, creating a spectacle. I could not even think of running away. Every now and then, somebody would do a salutation to my dead body, as nobody knew about the shooting. There were hidden cameras, and I had to play dead with the poor children cursing me all the time due to my weight."

Another one of Yadav's scenes also involved serious stunt work. While being interviewed by a Western reporter, Babe begins to whip Chillum repeatedly.

"The scene in which Chillum is whipped by Baba was the least rehearsed scene," Yadav said. "Mira, Nana and I decided to shoot it spontaneously with one mechanical rehearsal for the camera. For my part, I knew that I would actually get whipped and hurt, because one can't cheat whipping a belt. So one whipping was better than many!"

Despite such difficulties, Yadav found the shoot a rewarding experience, and also a total immersion into character. "The most rewarding day was when the street kids began calling me *Gardula*, which means brown sugar addict in Hindustani," he reveals. In other words, his performance had become so convincing that to his co-stars, he *was* Chillum.

Yadav's favorite scene, and the one which he thinks best represents his work in the film, involves Chillum's suicide attempt at the train station. At the last minute, Chaipau pulls him to safety, but Chillum isn't particularly certain it's a good thing.

"It was a difficult scene because the crescendo of self-immolation and desperation had to be timed with a running train on a crowded plat-form...and then the agony of being saved by Chaipau. [I was] deep and lost into the mind of Chillum, and yet so many things had to be timed as an actor, with no chance to retake, [yet] the scene was accomplished intu-itively. The moment came due to concentration, and I think it was success-ful because I forgot that I was Raghubir.

"The most helpful direction was the faith Mira had in me as an actor," Yadav pauses to reflect on *Salaam Bombay!*'s director. "She allowed my character to grow naturally, and gave a lot of leeway for spontaneity."

In addition to orchestrating complicated scenes such as funerals and suicide attempts at a busy rail station, a new ending to *Salaam Bombay!* had to be devised during shooting, as Sooni Taraporevala remembers.

"The ending as it was originally in the script was: it's a night shoot. He's [Chaipau] separated from her [Rekha]. He's walking down the streets of Bombay, and revelers are going home. Under a bridge there's a long line of homeless people sleeping, and he goes down and lies next to them. There's a close-up of him, and a hand covers him with a tattered blanket, and then the camera moves up to show him surrounded by the other sleep-ers, and then they are enveloped by the city of Bombay.

"This was very easy to write and nice to imagine," Taraporevala explains, "but it turned out to be far too expensive to shoot because it was a night shoot, and the shot as it was imagined of the camera rising called for an elaborate crane, etc. So because of budgetary constraints, we had to come up with something else."

The new ending featured a solitary Chaipau pausing on a lonely street after Ganpati, his only remaining belonging the very toy top he brought with him to Bombay in the film's early scenes. Isolated and alone, Chaipau—as the camera draws closer—begins to cry.

"Mira came up with this ending," Taraporevala states, "on, actually if I remember right, the day we were to shoot it. It's very simple and it works very well, and it's a complete credit to her, this ending with the top."

BLUE LAYER

Once shooting on *Salaam Bombay!* was completed (during which time Sandi Sissel reportedly shed thirty-two pounds), it was time to see what the production company had wrought. But first, all the footage had to be developed.

And that's where another unexpected crisis emerged. All the footage was sent to a laboratory in Madras, and *Salaam Bombay!* had been shot with two different types of film: Kodak 93 by day; Fuji 400 by night. This was because during the late 1980s, Fuji was the only company with a fast stock that was suitable for night shooting and interiors. Kodak film was utilized for most of the exteriors.

Unfortunately, the laboratory had no previous experience processing Kodak film, and the procedure utterly destroyed the film's blue layer. It was something Sissel discovered when she set out to color time the movie. Color timing is the process of enhancing, altering, and tinting colors in post-production.

"We processed in India, work-printed in New York, and color-timed in France," she reports. "Once we got to France, and I began color timing the film, and we began to realize that the blue layer of the Kodak had been virtually eliminated, then it became necessary for us to build blue back into the film. So, it took a number of answer prints to actually get to the point where it looked natural again.

"I think that initially our goal had been to make it look like India, anyway," Sissel says, noting that the damage actually afforded the filmmakers a unique opportunity. "It was certainly not a goal to make it warm or cold, but as natural as possible. But suddenly the concept of rebuilding the blue layer almost allowed us to look at it in various ways and say 'No, I almost liked it better before, when it left more blue out.' Would it have looked entirely different had it been processed properly? I don't know…In the end, I don't think it hurt us."

Still, when *Salaam Bombay!* was released, critics heaped accolades on the film's visual conception, a fact that amuses Sissel. "That's something that I'll never fully understand, how it [the damage] added to the look of the film, other than to know that I myself got a lot of praise for this 'saffron look' to it."

Taraporevala remembers her first time watching the rushes as her personal "best day" on *Salaam Bombay!* because that's when she "knew for sure that it was really going to be a good film."

In March of 1987, foleying and editing was being forged on the film, under the auspices of a British talent named Barry Alexander Brown, the talent who has cut such films as *Madonna: Truth or Dare* (1991), and most of Spike Lee's joints, including *Do the Right Thing* (1989), *Malcolm X* (1992), and most recently, *25th Hour* (2002). In fact, Mira Nair and Spike Lee actually sat side by side in the editing room on simultaneous projects, *She's Gotta Have It* (1987) and *Salaam Bombay!* (1988), thus beginning a friendship that lasts to this day. What emerged initially from Brown and Nair's efforts was a two hour fifteen minute cut of Nair's debut film.

Nair and Taraporevala reveal in their book, *Salaam Bombay!*, that Sissel's reaction to this first cut was both bold and informative. She said she found *Salaam Bombay!* claustrophobic, exhausting and intense.

"Barry Brown, who was the editor of the film, is a very dear friend of mine," Sissel explains. "Barry and I had co-directed a film together ourselves. When I came back to New York and I saw the first cut of the film, I don't think my response was different from many feature films. When people are used to cutting on a Steinbeck, as they were in those days, and you're looking at a small monitor, people do tend to use more close-ups.

"And once you project the film, very often people discover that you need more master shots and wide shots so that it becomes more cinematographic. I don't remember exactly what I said, but I said it.

"I do remember the feeling that it seemed we had a lot close-ups and it was very claustrophobic, and at times we needed that wider feeling to it," she recalls. "Did my comments change Mira and Barry's feelings about it? I have no idea. But I do remember that actually happening, and I do know that—naturally—because that was one of the first times it was actually projected, they would have come up with that conclusion themselves."

The film's final touches included the contributions of an Indian musician and violinist, L. Subramaniam. A Grammy nominee (in 1981) and multiple, international award winner, this artist composed a sensitive but remarkably jaunty score for *Salaam Bombay!* Like Sooni and the others, he would later collaborate with Mira Nair on other films, including *Mississippi Masala* and *Kama Sutra: A Tale of Love.*

CANNES AND THE CAMERA D'OR

Salaam Bombay! was still being put through a rigorous final edit a scant thirty-six hours before it made its debut at the Cannes Film Festival in 1988. But what happened at that premiere put to bed any doubts about the film's ability to affect. After the screening ended, Mira Nair's first feature received a twenty minute standing ovation from the audience. And that was just the beginning. By the following dawn, distributors had lined up to buy the international rights, and Nair was virtually mobbed by agents. Then *Salaam Bombay!* won the coveted Camera D'Or for "Best First Feature" at the festival. It was also the winner of the Prix du Publique, awarded at Cannes for the most popular film shown there.

Within two weeks of Cannes, Mira Nair also had an American distribution deal in place for the United States. She had just officially entered the ranks of "hot" young directors.

Long after Cannes ended, *Salaam Bombay!* went on to tally up an impressive number of international awards and nominations. It was nominated as "Best Foreign Film" at the French Cesars, won the Jury Prize as "Most Popular" film at the Montreal World Film Festival, and it took home the prize for the Lillian Gish Award for Excellence in Feature Films at the Los Angeles Women in Film Festival.

Perhaps most dramatically the film was nominated for an Academy Award in the category for "Best Foreign Film." *Salaam Bombay!* was only the second nomination for an Indian-made film in Oscar history.

Salaam Bombay! proved a home run in every aspect, grossing more than two million dollars in the United States when it played in over forty cities. Critic Roger Ebert selected the film as one of the year's ten best films, ranking it at slot number five, and in all, the reception at Cannes was just the beginning compared to the critical reaction to come.

Jami Bernard of the *New York Post* called it "…a stunning achievement,"[9] and writing for the *Los Angeles Times*, Sheila Benson noted that "Nair has a wonderful eye and a truly cinematic sense of story. She doesn't tell in words what the eye of her camera can say with more authenticity."[10]

People's Peter Travers enthused that what had set "Nair's film apart is the resilience she finds in these doomed children. Poetic, powerful and disturbing *Salaam Bombay!* transcends language and cultural barriers."[11] *Film Comment* made note of the "rare authenticity" in the film, arising it believed, from Nair's "adaptation of documentary technique."[12]

Barry John still remembers his perceptions of the film when he first saw it, and how it fell in line with other critical perceptions. "I returned to Delhi after the workshop, so I saw nothing of the shoot," he begins. "Already knowing so much about the film, it still had the power to move me deeply when I first saw it. It was some kind of *deja vu*, which is always disturbing, but set in locations I had only imagined. I thought that Mira, cast and crew pulled off a miracle. During the workshop, I was aware that the project was unprecedented on various contexts, in the Indian context at least, but I was not at all prepared for the professionalism of the finished product, nor for the fact that a Hindi film was so well-received all over the world."

"I loved the film when I saw it," says Raghubir Yadav. "It is considered a classic today because everything worked for the film in totality. The theme about the lives of street children, the authentic locales, the real characters each with their own stories to tell, the realistic treatment and performances with the heart rending music of L. Subramaniam…"

"It was very successful, it was very watchable—which is really what always goes toward making a film successful—it was very believable," considers Roshan Seth, who still remembers his response to *Salaam Bombay!*

Writer Helena Kriel saw *Salaam Bombay!* in South Africa and recalls being "completely struck by it."

"I remember just standing in the lobby of the movie house and staring at the poster and staring at her name," Kriel says "and being very struck by the whole experience of watching the film."

Mira Nair, Sooni Taraporevala, Sandi Sissel, Mitch Epstein, and others forged a film of sensitivity and great brilliance in *Salaam Bombay!*, but more importantly, because of its success, Nair was able, perhaps, to achieve her goal of "changing the world through art."

Never forgetting her experience with the stout-hearted children of Bombay's streets, Nair spearheaded and assembled what is now known as the Salaam Balak Trust. A charity organized and administrated by her mother, Praveen, it consists of learning centers for children all over India, from Bombay and Orissa to Delhi. It is a sanctuary for these displaced children, one where they can imagine a better life and take steps to achieve it.

In 2005, there were seventeen such Salaam Balak Trust centers around India. More than five thousand children have walked through their doors and by doing so, taken the first step to a brighter future.

As for the specific children who starred in *Salaam Bombay!*, their lives were also changed by their participation in the project. Their salaries were paid in three parts: the first upon shooting, the second deposited in an "interest bearing account," and the final third held in a trust until the child's twenty-first birthday.[13]

LIFE IN CONSTANT MOTION

Across the span of cinema's hundred-year plus history, a number of great films have concerned the plight of children. It isn't difficult to see why this subject matter holds such resonance for so many artists. Children always symbolize *tomorrow*, the future that human beings hope to construct. Mistreat the children and what kind of future is there? Those who let childhood die are foolishly short-sighted, because, in fact, they are only murdering hope.

Like Babenco's *Pixote* before it, *Salaam Bombay!* focuses on the existence of street children, orphans without home or hearth, eking out an existence amidst the blind eye of shop owners, commuters, and even tourists. Theirs is an unseen world of danger that, paradoxically, is visible for all to see, if only people would stop to look. The smallest luxuries, ones we take for granted, are denied these children: a roof over their heads; a meal before bed; a mother or father's shoulder to cry on. Worse, they are often coerced to become involved in drugs and prostitution just to survive.

Mira Nair guides audiences into this heartless world in *Salaam Bombay!*, not an easy journey to undertake, in part because the film features so many "arresting documentary details,"[14] including authentic locations and personalities, and more importantly, stories that reflect reality. It is thus a film that seems to tear down the artificial wall distancing film from audience. For instance, it is known that the story of Sweet Sixteen is real, only adapted. That the origin of Chaipau is, likewise, true to life. That real madames are featured in the film, and that Sandi Sissel's camera grabs longshot views of reality in the film's Grant Road locations, from the train station to the market and detention homes, and far beyond, to the Ganpati Festival.

Sissel believes it is the film's realistic overtones, including real street children in real locations, which grant *Salaam Bombay!* an unusual visual veracity and potency. "You couldn't simply depend on the words. You actually had to look at it as a visual experience," she recommends. "Even though for many scenes, you have to read the subtitles to know exactly what's going on, for a lot of the scenes, the children played it in their faces.

"They didn't read," she explains. "They couldn't read their scripts and memorize them. The scripts were read to them, and they then memorized them according to what was being read, so the whole thing led to a certain visual experience. When you have this amazing acting with children, it sticks with you. It's a very real experience."

So often, Mira Nair's films thrive because the images she forges resonate in some symbolic fashion. Whether it be marigolds—the wedding flower—in *Monsoon Wedding*, or bubbles blowing by the camera, down a suburban street in a nostalgic flashback in *My Own Country*, her choice of compositions engender strong emotions.

So naturally *Salaam Bombay!* is powerful for the images it fosters, but these images work in a somewhat different way than her later efforts. Perhaps it is all part of her transition from the documentary form, but here there is no call for elaborate flights of fancy, and indeed they would be wildly inappropriate. Instead, reality is indeed the guide, and though the intent was always to create a film that would be theatrical, not *cinema verité*, the film might accurately be described as *cinema verité* taken one step further. The core of this film is in its reality, in authentic street children, in true locations, and accurate situations, and the immediacy of that effort makes the film tremendously effective.

There's a good reason so much of the film consists of long shots and includes deep focus. A bustling frame—one filled with motion and depth—suggests that life goes on *outside* the composition, and that the picture we see is literally grabbed from life unfolding. And that's always what Nair sought for her first feature, a hybrid film that would utilize her documentary experience and its strength as a form, even while telling a fictional tale. But reality and believability had to be a prelude to everything else that would come.

Yet the realistic underpinnings and supports of *Salaam Bombay!* are just that, underpinnings, and the test of any great art is the manner in which it not just records reality, but actually shapes it to address some salient point. Otherwise, audiences are literally just viewing a documentary. So Mira Nair's freshman film does shape reality, and its form *does* reflect its content. And it does so by finding and exploiting the perfect metaphor for a child's life on the streets.

To wit, the life of these Bombay kids is primarily one of *transience*. There is no constancy, not in shelter, sanctuary, work or anything else, and to propel this notion of a life with no permanence, no certainty, Nair—through her selection of shots and editing—focuses on the idea of motion, movement and indeed, stated simply, *running*.

Salaam Bombay! is a film all about motion and change. The notion dominates the picture. Upon arriving in Bombay, the first thing Krishna must do is escape from a crazed adult who chases him across the street with murder in his eyes.

Later in the movie, as Sweet Sixteen arrives at the brothel, Krishna is depicted running again, and we see him from the vantage point of the car's interior as he attempts to keep up with her. Not only is he running again, but we are separated from him by the car windows, revealing how Krishna is always separated from his goal, unable to reach it. That's an idea that is repeated throughout *Salaam Bombay!*

Krishna's employment also makes him a force of constant motion, going from one locale (like the brothel) to another and another and another, delivering his boss's tea. Indeed, the fast succession of jobs for the children—cleaning chicken cages and playing waiter at a local wedding—also indicates the inconstancy of their lives on the streets.

There is so much motion and change in *Salaam Bombay!* that by the climax of the film, Krishna actually seems old. He has lived long enough to see one Chillum (hash pipe smoker) come and go, only to be replaced. At his tender age, he wears experience on his face like an anchor, weighing down his youthful features.

As *Salaam Bombay!* races towards its climax, the pace accelerates. Motion and change persist. Krishna escapes from the chiller room in a daring vault from a high roof, and is then depicted as free, running through the busy streets of Bombay. Shot from the back of an Impala, with Syed occupying the center of the frame, the audience is treated to a frontal shot of Krishna, in mid-avenue, running towards the camera and the screen, thereby *running towards us*, the viewers of this drama.

Noticeably, he does not immediately draw nearer to the ever-moving camera. Since the car maintains its distance ahead of the boy, the composition indicates stasis of a kind. His running is endless, and the goal keeps moving. But there is something even more fascinating and symbolic in the fashioning of this moment.

Krishna's long run down the avenue is arranged, or rather *segmented and abbreviated*, in jump cuts. The audience sees the same shot staged again and again (Krishna running towards us; down the street), some four times, and only the background details change.

First we see him run on one street, then another. The use of jump cuts, which are meant to disconnect time, indicate again that this boy is— *and will be forever*—running. His life will know no constancy and continuity so long as he lives on the street. The jump cuts are symbolic indicators of this trap, that no matter how fast and how far Krishna runs, he actually goes nowhere. Time itself seems to be against him.

The motion is augmented by the fine use of L. Subramaniam's music in these scenes as well. As the escape from the chiller room commences, there is a slow drumbeat-like pulse that quickens. Upon Krishna's dash down the avenue, it bursts into full-blown, fast-paced chase music, and a feeling of tension is created.

Intense motion further informs the finale of *Salaam Bombay!* leading up to the coda. Krishna has discovered his savings missing and bumps into—in almost *Twilight Zone*-like fashion—the new Chillum. Again, Krishna has been confronted with change, and in a desperate attempt to escape a life which he now understands is hopeless, seeks out the only parental figure he can find, Manju's mother.

Krishna then kills the threatening Baba and flees with Rekha, and the frenetic motion of *Salaam Bombay!* reaches its fever pitch as their escape attempt coincides with an oncoming tide of human flesh, the Ganpati Festival and street parade. Inexorably moving forward with the weight of thousands of people behind it, this parade spirals out of control, and the hand-held, shaky camera work focuses squarely on Krishna and Rekha as they are jostled by the undulating life and physical momentum all around them. Figures rush by, speed across the frame, bump into Krishna, fight, and never recognize his presence, again pointing to his invisibility in the larger society.

But most importantly, the momentum of the parade rips Rekha and Krishna apart, and again, the movement is accompanied by a metronome-like beat, intensifying the perception of motion and speed.

And it is here in the film's final moment, that *Salaam Bombay!* makes an abrupt about-face. Krishna the runner, the boy who is always on the move but going nowhere, is seen to leave the parade, slow down (as the drum-beat-like music fades away), and sit down. Defeated. He stops cold, and after the build-up of the Chiller Room escape and the Ganpati Film Festival, the stillness is a stark contrast.

For once, the camera does not dart about, and neither does Krishna. Instead, there is a slow, deliberate, and intimate move closer by the camera, nearer his face as, alone and abandoned, he finally weeps. The contrast between the previous motion and this still, deliberate coda is one of the elements that renders this scene so powerful. A film of near-constant motion has suddenly stopped and we see Krishna alone in the frame for one of the few times in the film. His suffering goes unseen by others, but now this choice of staging and composition makes us see it without the filter of constant motion. The boy's pain is inescapable, and it is on that note that the film ends. It is a powerful and well-constructed image that can almost stop the heartbeat of a viewer because it is so powerful, so intimate.

That the boy is ultimately left with only his top—a toy—is a tie-in to the film's opening sequences, but the top is also something that, like Krishna himself, spins and spins but never goes anywhere. Although imagined by Mira Nair on the spot, on the very day of shooting, the inclusion of the toy at this climactic moment in *Salaam Bombay!* again draws attention to the idea of motion. Motion that finally leads nowhere.

Again, *Salaam Bombay!* is foremost a film of motion, of bustling avenues and life coursing through every street, and this finale counters that action and more. In a sense, it reverses the ethos of the whole picture. A very realistic film suddenly transforms. It becomes very formalistic, very theatrical. The camera is no longer merely recording life with a sense of reality, but is vividly expressing the pain of its protagonist.

Sandi Sissel remembers the staging of these memorable final frames. "We did it more than once, [And] first of all, I think there are two people who were really brilliant in getting that done. One was Shafiq, the actor, who was an extraordinary gifted, natural actor. The idea that Mira was able to get that kind of performance out of him was extraordinary. And then, I think it is not a small thing that Tony [McNamara] was dead on with the focus.

"We really shot blind," she explains. "We did not have a video monitor, so Mira was never looking at a monitor. We never got dailies back to check our exposure, or to be able to check focus. It was just a lot of things coming together."

The result of their efforts was a closing shot that has, in a way, become the film's unofficial trademark, a perfect encapsulation of the life of these street children.

"When you look at shots like that, if you get the performance, or if you get the reality of the moment, that's what makes the shot famous," Sissel says. "It's not anything technical that we do. If anything, it's that everything came together at once."

It's interesting to remember that the metaphor of a child on the run and then coming suddenly to an abrupt stop is one that has appeared in other well-regarded films over the years, notably in François Truffaut's *The 400 Blows* (1959). There, it was young Antoine Doinel as the child protagonist, and at film's end, he flees a home for juvenile delinquents outside Paris, not unlike the Bombay chiller rooms, and runs for freedom.

Unlike *Salaam Bombay!*, however, Truffaut does not fracture time with jump cuts, but instead simply stages a lengthy tracking shot of Doinel while he runs and runs. The punctuation—*the stopping*—in this case is also broached somewhat differently. Instead of a slow, deliberate move in on

Doinel's face as he reaches the end of the dividing line of water and land on a beach, Truffaut goes immediately to a freeze frame as the final image of the film. Still, the effect is analogous. We end on the notion of a boy who, for one reason or another, will always be running and is frozen in our memory in that mode.

Both *Salaam Bombay!* and *The 400 Blows* also reveal a great insight into the life (and minds) of children. These films understand and transmit the concept that children have very few "escape" options when their lives have turned out badly. One of those options is plainly and simply to run. Because of their youth, children are not permitted to drive cars, and tend not to have money for transportation, yet their legs can carry them away from danger. It is that childlike solution, just to run and run and run, that both films detect as somehow core to the condition of childhood. Ironically, both filmmakers also understand what their protagonists may not, even at the conclusion of their individual stories…that running ultimately leads nowhere.

Truffaut, Professor Nair has said, "uses children as human beings, always with such quality and such respect,"[15] and that is a characteristic she likewise shares. Mira Nair is too in love with life, and too in love with these children, perhaps, to simply present an image of street children that is wholly negative or destructive (like *Pixote*, for example). *Salaam Bombay!* is not designed to be a liberal balm, and for that reason, the children in the film are respected, and treated with a complexity—and mercy.

While it is clear that the children are lonely and exploited, they are more than figures for Westerners to feel pity for. Their very names represent what duties they are expected to fulfill in Bombay (Chaipau, Chillum, Sweet Sixteen), yet *Salaam Bombay!* sees two sides of every issue. Although there is squabbling among the children, there is also "a camaraderie that gives it the feeling of a coming-of-age movie," suggests *Washington Post* critic Rita Kempley. "Though on the dark side it is exactly that—a distorted passage for its boy hero, who experiences first love, disillusionment and death,"[16] it is also in some strange way, joyous. The moment when Krishna and Manju dance in Rekha's bedroom leaps immediately to mind. It's that wonderful Satyajit Ray principle again: even when bad, life is good. In many of her films, Nair uses dance to reveal this happy facet of life, the freedom and joy of her *dramatis personae*.

And although Krishna clearly longs for the love of a mother, he also loves his freedom, and there's something about this vagabond existence that brings out his strength of character. All of these ideas have currency in the movie, and that's why it is not so easy to interpret the film in purely didactic terms. Life is a paradox. It can be good and bad simultaneously, and Nair as an artist seems comfortable accommodating that notion in her art.

Richard Corliss aptly wrote that *Salaam Bombay!* "sees the city as a school for life—life as it is for millions of Asian children," and that the film represents a "tightrope dance between sociology and sentiment."[17] Perhaps the realist in Mira Nair, the documentarian, wants merely to record an interesting facet of reality (hence the sociology), but her emotional, passionate side clearly identifies with the children, hence the sentiment.

Complexity is a core ingredient of Mira Nair's cinema. She often sets up her films as a dichotomy between two opposing forces. In *Monsoon Wedding* it is tradition versus modernity; in *Mississippi Masala* it is a battle between brown skin and black skin; in *Vanity Fair* and *Kama Sutra* it is a battle between two social classes (the poor and the rich; servants and royals, respectively), and as early as *Salaam Bombay!* it is possible to detect another such dichotomy. Here, however, it is reality versus illusion.

By day, the children struggle to make ends meet, by night the search is for safe places to sleep. They never know where their next meal is coming from. Yet on the other hand, these street children thrive on a strict diet of Bollywood films. These entertainments perk up their spirits, and bring them song and dance, but ultimately Bollywood only reveals to audiences the difference between what life is and the image of life being sold in the cinema. Nair expresses this theme by featuring a short scene set inside the cinema during a matinee. It is poignant to see the children together, thoroughly enjoying themselves and the experience. But the ridiculous, costumed shenanigans depicted on screen expose how the entertainment of this culture has no connection to the reality of this culture.

Salaam Bombay! is thus a film that, according to *Village Voice* writer Leslie Camhi, "shows characters caught in impossible compromises with fate, as they hold fast to their remaining illusions."[18] It also boasts social value within its own society, because it reveals the duality of the culture. Or, to put it in more colorful terms, as *Planet Bollywood's* Shahid Khan wrote, "In effect, *Salaam Bombay!* takes Bollywood conventions and pees on it."[19]

Though audiences have cheered *Salaam Bombay!* for the realism of its depiction of street life, perhaps its greatest value as a film is that its form reflects its meaningful content and it goes well beyond the rubric of "reality" to make an audience actually *feel*, not merely witness, life on the streets of Bombay.

Mira Nair's first feature is alive with motion and life, and yet it is, in the final analysis, the cessation of that motion, the stillness of its closing shot, that makes the film's point so succinctly. In that purposeful motionlessness, in that instant of realization, Krishna understands his lot in life. He can run, but he goes nowhere. He can revel in the fantasies of Bollywood projected in his cinema, but when he opens his eyes after the dreams on the silver screen, he will still have to wonder when he will eat again. He will still contemplate about from where—and with whom—he will next experience that most important aspect of human life. Love.

3

Mississippi Masala (1991) and
The Perez Family (1995)

MISSISSIPPI MASALA (1991)

SCS Films Inc. Presents in association with Odyssey, Cinecom International, and Film Four International, a Mirabai Films Production in association with Movie Works and Black River Productions, a film by Mira Nair, *Mississippi Masala*.

Crew:

Music	L. Subramaniam
Associate Producer	Lydia Dean Pilcher
Film Editor	Roberto Silvi
Production Designer	Mitch Epstein
Director of Photography	Ed Lachman
Co-Producer	Mitch Epstein
Executive Producer	Cherie Rodgers
Screenplay	Sooni Taraporevala
Producers	Michael Nozik, Mira Nair
Director	Mira Nair

Cast:

Demetrius	Denzel Washington
Jay	Roshan Seth
Mina	Sarita Choudhury
Kinnu	Sharmila Tagore
Tyrone	Charles S. Dutton
Williben	Joe Seneca
Anil	Ranjit Chowdhry
Pontiac	Mohan Gokhale
Kanti Napkin	Mohan Agashe
Dexter	Tico Wells
Aunt Rose	Yvette Hawkins
Jammubhai	Anjan Srivastava
Chanda	Dipti Sutha
Kusumben	Varsha Thaker
Harry Patel	Ashok Lath
Skillet	Willy Cobbs
Gossip #1	Mira Nair
Young Mina	Sahira Nair
Okelo	Kong Mbandu

THE PEREZ FAMILY (1995)

The Samuel Goldwyn Company presents a Samuel Goldwyn Company production, a Film by Mira Nair, *The Perez Family*.

Crew:

Associate Producer	Dinaz Stafford
Music Supervisor	Jellybean Benitez
Traditional Music	Arturo Sandoval
Costume Designer	Eduardo Castro
Music	Alan Silvestri
Production Designer	Mark Friedberg
Film Editor	Robert Estrin
Director of Photography	Stuart Dryburgh
Executive Producers	Julia Chasman, Robin Swicord
Based upon the novel by	Christine Bell
Screenplay	Robin Swicord
Producers	Michael Nozik, Lydia Dean Pilcher
Director	Mira Nair

Cast:

Dorita Evita Perez	Marisa Tormei
Juan Raul Perez	Alfred Molina
Carmela Perez	Anjelica Huston
Lt. John Pirelli	Chazz Palminteri
Teresa Perez	Trini Alvarado
Luz Pat	Celia Cruz
Indian Immigration Official	Ranjit Chowdhry
Angel Diaz	Diego Wallfraff
Officer Rhoades	Ellen Cleghorne
Felipe Perez	Angela Lanza
Armando "Papi" Perez	Lazaro Perez
Steve	Bill Sage
Orlando	Vincent Gallo
Woman Buying Flowers	Mira Nair

A SPICY MIX

Following the surprise success of *Salaam Bombay!*, many in America—and in Hollywood in particular—hoped to adopt Mira Nair. Perhaps remembering the philosopher Aristophanes' adage that a man's homeland is wherever he prospers, some film executives sought to bring this new talent full-throttle into the American filmmaking system. After all, she was now considered a hot "commodity."[1] But Nair was not so eager to be co-opted. She still desired control of her work, and still sought to choose what kind of films she would direct.

That kind of independence doesn't go down easy with some in Los Angeles. Many studio executives invited her to pitch stories, but just as many discovered that what she was selling wasn't what they were buying. Still, that didn't stop them from trying to steer her in a certain direction.

"After *Salaam Bombay!*, I could have picked up on any of several offers that came my way and lived happily ever after," Nair reported in 2001. "But somehow, honest commitment would have been missing. I needed a subject I could relate to."[2]

And that subject, not surprisingly, involved the Indian world again, this time its vast *diaspora*—the realm of exiles. In fact, Nair had begun to contemplate a film on that subject in the early 1980s after reading several nonfiction pieces about Indians expelled from Uganda by the warlord Idi Amin (1925–2003).[3] Amin had risen to power in a military coup d'etat in 1971, and subsequently controlled Uganda, formerly a British colony, for the majority of the decade.

Early in his reign, in 1972, General Amin decided, in the tradition of Adolf Hitler, that he required a scapegoat on whom he could pin all the country's woes. He promised his people an economic recovery, if only he could put the economy back in the hands of the "true" Ugandans and take it away from those who were "ruining it" for their own selfish ends, in this case, Asian residents. Consequently, more than fifty thousand Asian Ugandans were forcibly exiled from their homes in Africa.

Once again, Mira Nair's writing collaborator was Sooni Taraporevala. "Mira, I think, wanted to do something on Uganda, and she had read a story by V. S. Naipaul, *In a Free State*, which interested her," reports Taraporevala. "At the same time—I think it was quite synchronous—I was interested in writing, and I had taken that subject to her, an interracial love story based on a friend of ours who was Indian and who was going out with a black man. Now it's very common, but at the time, especially in America, you could count on the fingers of one hand the number of Indian-black couplings. There weren't any at all. And so, I think what happened, at least from my point of view, is that these things [ideas] got merged. That's how *Mississippi Masala* happened."

Together the duo researched the diaspora, and their scholarship led them to the deep American South. In March of 1989, on the first leg of this international diaspora tour, the duo manned a car and drove from South Carolina to Mississippi.[4] Their eyes confirmed the statistics they already understood: the motel trade in the Southern states was run primarily by emigré Indians, and then on the order of something like eighty percent.[5]

"The trip to the South was before Uganda, and it was really amazing, because a lot of what happened there is [material incorporated] for the script," Taraporevala relates. "The first day we set out, we had an accident. Mitch was driving, I think, Mira was in the back, and I was in the front. I can't remember the exact configuration, anyway, but we rammed into someone. The tow truck guy who came to pick us up talked about whiplash, and then I remembered another story of an Indian telling someone in India that in America, people sue all the time. So that accident is something that I used [in the screenplay].

"The motels were fantastic," Sooni continues. "The Indians we met there were fantastic. We met a lady who owned the liquor shop. We met a black carpet cleaner called Demetrius…and I was so thrilled when I met him and I said 'that's our main character!' I actually had to convince Mira and Michael Nozik, the producer, because they had wanted a preacher's son kind of character, and I said 'that's a bit of a cliché. This is new. This is contemporary; this is now.' So that's how Demetrius got his name and profession."

With their ingredients coming together, Taraporevala and Nair spent time in and around the Greenwood community while writing the script for *Mississippi Masala*, taking up residence in a local motel.

"Guys used to hit on us. 'Hey, you Mexican?' You know, all those lines," Nair told the *Village Voice*. "Sooni would write the scenes and we would call these guys into our motel room and ask them to stamp it, and they did."[6]

And Uganda? "That was a very eventful journey because Mira met Mahmoud [her future husband] when we went to Uganda. So that was very eventful..." Taraporevala repeats, without going into further detail.

Like their experience in the American South, the filmmakers also found interesting real-life characters in Africa whose stories would be incorporated into the film's story. One such person was a lawyer from Uganda who was suing the government to get his property returned, and his story became the background of one of the main characters, Jay.

The writers now had a people to write about (Indians), a story of exile (from Uganda), and a destination: Mississippi, U.S.A. The story they crafted became Nair's second feature film, and one that dramatizes the story of young Mina (Sarita Choudhury), who along with her parents, Jay (Roshan Seth) and Kinnu (Sharmila Tagore) are forcibly exiled from Uganda in 1972, because, in the words of Jay's black brother, Okelo (Kong Mbandu), "Africa is for Africans. *Black* Africans."

The family takes a home in the United States, running the rundown Monte Cristo Hotel in Greenwood, Mississippi, and Mina matures to become a free-spirited and beautiful woman. One day, when Mina is twenty-four, an unlikely traffic accident on the way home from a Piggly-Wiggly supermarket precipitates her introduction to a local black businessman named Demetrius (Denzel Washington). They fall in love, over the objections of both the black community in Greenwood and the Indian exile community living there.

While Jay fights to regain his lost property in Uganda and longs to make a visit to the land he has always considered his home, Mina and Demetrius each deal with racial prejudice in their own way. Demetrius is blacklisted in the business community for crossing racial lines, and realizes that his livelihood is endangered. He wants Mina to leave Greenwood with him, and Mina considers it, but her parents object to the plan. Finally, Mina makes a decision and embarks on a new life with Demetrius, one where the old definitions and taboos about skin color have no place. At the same time, Jay returns to Uganda for the first time in a generation, and experiences a reckoning about the course of his own life. In search of

Okelo, he learns that his brother died long, long ago, and that there is no longer the possibility of healing their breach.

Mississippi Masala's script deals explicitly with the question of "what and where is home?," and more to the point, focuses on Nair's seemingly favorite theme, "stories of people who live on the margins of society, people who are on the edge, or outside learning the language of being in between.[7]

"I have also been interested in the question of hierarchy of colour," she noted about the film's genesis. "We tend to think of racism mostly in the conventional Western situation of white versus black. We hardly ever ask what happens when one crosses the color line in a black versus brown situation."[8]

"For me, the film primarily was about race relations and the hierarchy of racism that exists among people of color," Taraporevala concurs.

The only problem with this thoughtfully constructed script was that it seemed nobody in Hollywood wanted to finance a film on this topic, at least not one in which a white lead wasn't featured. Prospective financiers lectured Nair about this point, and reportedly she came up with an agreeable compromise. She would cast Ben Kingsley—the Englishman of *Gandhi* fame—for the critical role of Jay.

Roshan Seth, who eventually starred as Jay, describes his personal perspective and memory of the film's formative period. "The film went through all kinds of contortion," he remembers. "She cast Ben Kingsley in it originally, and then he decided that he wasn't going to play Indian after *Gandhi*, and the Americans who had agreed to back the film, provided he was in it, pulled their money out.

"So I was really her second choice, or maybe even her umpteenth choice because I don't know who became between Ben and myself.

"And then," Seth continues, "that wasn't the end of the story, because after that, the Americans wanted to know who the *American* star was going to be if they were going to put money in it, and she said, 'There isn't one.' Then they said, 'Well, you have to have one,' so she put Denzel Washington in it [as Demetrius]."

At that time, Washington was still on an ascension into full-fledged stardom, having appeared in the television show *St. Elsewhere* (1982) and films including *Cry Freedom* (1987) and *Glory* (1989), but he was nonetheless deemed an acceptable choice. He was cast in the film, but then the

Hollywood actor also had his own set of concerns, according to Seth's recollections.

"He wanted to know what else his character did in the film, other than fall for an Indian woman, and Mira said, 'Well that's about the size of it,' and he said, 'That's not enough.' So his character was fattened up as it were, and the character that I was playing got relegated somewhat to the background."

"It [*Mississippi Masala*] also changed from the conception after actually researching what happened," agrees Taraporevala. "I think that when Mira conceived it, she conceived it more as a vehicle for the father (Seth). It was the father's story, etc. I think when I came in, and after the research, I sort of veered it more towards being a love story with the father's story kind of subordinate to the main love story."

She also stresses that it was her decision to develop Demetrius's side of the tale. "I think when I started writing it, the love story became the main story. I think that what I brought into it was the black characters besides Demetrius, because I said 'If it's *Romeo and Juliet*, then you have to know Juliet's family as well as Romeo's, not just one.' So there was a balance between the black family and the Indian family.

"There were two clear stories in that film: the love story, and the story about their family and their diaspora, and having to leave Uganda," Seth describes. "And a lot of people say to me that they preferred the political side of the story, the family plot."

Still, the concept of a film about the diaspora was one that really intrigued Seth, at least as it was initially planned "I may not be one hundred percent accurate about this, but Mira did tell me she wanted to do a political film—she said to me—on the 'Indian diaspora.' She wanted to do a political film, which excited me, because at that time in her life, she seemed to me to have a political edge to her thinking. I was interested in the diaspora since I saw and experienced it first hand when I was in England, where I began my career."

When asked to clarify about his experiences in the United Kingdom, Seth elaborates:

"What happened is that I began my career there, because I needed to work to complete my training as an actor, because it is a vocational training, and training is always related to the work. So if I just went there and went back to India, I wouldn't really absorb it. So what happened was that in the early 1970s, a lot of the African-Asians as they are called were kicked out of Uganda by Idi Amin, and a lot of them were refused entry into Britain in spite of the fact that they were British passport holders. So that made me very, very unhappy. I was deeply hurt to realize that it didn't matter what sort of passport you held, because ultimately, the color of your skin does matter.

"I have, on one or two occasions, [also] had some stupid yotz on buses and things pass remarks on to my mother who is dead now, poor thing, when she used to come visit. I've also had the odd occasion in the early days where people used to say, 'Sorry, the flat you've looked at to come rent has just been taken' when you know damn well it hasn't been taken. I've had one or two experiences like that. But by and large, because I'm not dark-skinned, or relatively *less* dark skinned, I fool people because they don't know quite where I come from. Yet the fact remains, we are all—Indians perhaps more than anyone else—deeply conscious of skin color. *Deeply.* It is amazing in India the kind of colloquial references to '*She's very fair.*' That's very common.

"All that interested me," Seth mulls.

Sarita Choudhury was a beautiful and talented newcomer, a former film student who grew up in Jamaica and Italy and had been doing modeling in London as late as 1990.

"I just wanted to meet Mira," Choudhury told *Entertainment Weekly* in early 1992, "I hoped I could work on the crew."[9] Instead, she joined the cast as its lead, Mina, and her debut performance in *Mississippi Masala* is one of fetching honesty and seductive innocence. She rehearsed with Denzel Washington in New York, and Taraporevala remembers being there.

"That was enormously helpful," she recalls. "And then I went to Greenwood, Mississippi, for the first two days of the shoot, and then I left to spend my newly acquired wealth!"

Ranjit Chowdhry, an Indian actor who has had a very successful career in India, Canada and the U.S., was cast in *Mississippi Masala* as well. A playwright as well as a performer, Chowdhry is familiar to Western audiences for his work in Deepa Mehta films including the award winning *Sam and Me* (1991). In the late 1990s, he also played a recurring character on television's *Cosby* and has taught screenwriting at the Summer Institute of

Film and Television in Ottawa. A gentleman with a charming sense of humor and a dry wit, Ranjit plays *Mississippi Masala*'s comical groom, Anil.

Chowdhry first met Nair at the Delhi film festival, back in the mid-1980s, he recalls. "She asked me to read for the part of the druggie [Chillum] in *Salaam Bombay!* I had no idea who she was, and she acted as if she'd already won the Camera D'Or, and been nominated for an Academy award. So I ignored her.

"Much later, while I was shooting for *Lonely in America* (1991), a film being directed by her then-editor, Barry Brown, she put me through several long auditions for *Mississippi Masala*," he remembers. "Mira's writer Sooni, is a long time friend of mine. I can read her work and say: 'well, she's written this for me,' but people here [in America] seem to love auditioning everyone for nearly everything, so one plays along. I feigned sheer delight when she [Mira] told me I'd won the part, then gave her a relentlessly hard time during the prep period to shift me to a smaller but much funnier part. Naturally, this did not happen."

In order to prepare for his role as Anil, Chowdhry also went on a trip with some of Nair's assistants to meet the locals who inspired a few of the film's characters. He remembers taking notes and "playing the part of an actor preparing, rather than actually preparing. That way, I could avoid long discussions about the work with her and maybe the producers. I think Sooni had it all on the page, the rest came through instinct, [and] teamwork with the other two actors and rehearsal."

And how did Chowdhry view his character? "Anil is an ineffectual racist who lives in mortal fear of being sued," he notes succinctly. "Plus [his] wife won't consummate the marriage. So there was some funny, sympathetic sides to the man. The racial stuff is not deeply ingrained."

GREENWOOD AND KAMPALA

With her cast of nearly eighty actors, and an international crew, Mira Nair began to shoot her sophomore effort, a five-and-a-half million dollar motion picture.[10]

In the U.S., *Mississippi Masala*'s crew filmed in Mississippi for the duration of the shoot, and the production team shuttled between Biloxi, Greenwood, Grenada, and Ocean Springs. The crew lodged together at a

Ramada Inn in Greenwood, and a thankful Mira Nair delivered six packs of beer to anyone who "had contributed a good idea that day."[11]

Seth, for one, enjoyed shooting in Mississippi. "That was an experience for me! That was the real experience! I was suddenly thrown back, and I saw the whole history of that country with the blacks and the cotton-picking singers, and the people sitting on their stoops, and the blues, and I really got it. I just somehow saw it and felt it, and it's still there. What's there is that life."

The only drawback, he says, was the food. "I couldn't get what I wanted to eat because everything was huge, and it was all fried in butter."

"A week into rehearsal and exploring Greenwood, Mississippi, I thought: 'So this is what someone was thinking and seeing when he said the South would rise again,'" quips Ranjit Chowdhry.

"After a week in Greenwood, Mississippi," he continues, "I realized how cannily and shrewdly observed Sooni's script was. Good cinema comes from a good story and a documentary milieu supporting it, and this one set us thinking about race, migration, exile, [and] community. And how seamlessly [all] this was integrated into a conventional love story that was as old as Shakespeare himself. At the time, I was living a rather insular life in Toronto, so all this had an effect on me. I think it was the start of me having some sort of worldview."

It was also on this leg of shooting, that Roshan Seth had the opportunity to shoot alongside Denzel Washington, particularly for a contentious confrontation scene over the fate of Mina in particular, and the specter of racism in general. It was a scene that, as conceived in the script, neither actor particularly liked.

"Denzel, even in that early part of his career was always apart from the rest of the company. He had a bigger caravan and special treatment, and he was already behaving like a star," Seth describes. "And that speech of Jay's was rewritten, partly by me. I don't think I wrote it well, but it was awful, and it was rewritten, and he didn't like it at all. He thought it was terribly pretentious. I suppose it was, because he knew much more about cinema scripts and all that, because he's grown up in America, and the Americans understand about cinema, and he's been calling the shots in many ways for a very long time.

"There was a slight undercurrent of unpleasantness," Seth recalls, "but it was all right. It helped the scene."

Chowdhry remembered one particular day on location that he considers interesting. "We were shooting on the graveled parking lot of the motel one very steamy morning. A scene begins with me running out yelling: 'What have you done to my car, what you done to my car...?' By the fifth take, I was expecting to move on to something else. [Instead] I heard the sound of expensive sandals crunching gravel coming straight to me.

"*Mira. Not happy*," he explains. "Somehow, I was not getting the right tone of whatever it was she wanted. So her set of directions included [the following]: 'Think of it as your dick. Think of: What have you done [as in *crushed*] to my dick, but say *car*.'

"I did."

Mississippi Masala's crew also filmed in Kampala, the capital of Uganda, in December of 1990. Although Nair knew little of that country before beginning her research on the project, she promptly fell in love with it. In fact, the house seen in the film as Jay's residence, which overlooks majestic Lake Victoria, the world's second largest freshwater lake, was actually a recent purchase.

"That is her home, it's extraordinary," Seth says of the patch of green trees, gentle slopes and crystal water. "It's beautiful. The light and the colors are so vivid. Uganda itself, I don't know. I can't claim to know it very much. I didn't respond to it in any positive sort of way, and I didn't respond to the few Indians I met there in any positive way, but that's okay. There's something about the colors and the land and the vividness of things that is extraordinary."

It was in Uganda that Nair met the man who would become her second husband, Mahmoud Mamdani, scholar and author of *From Citizen to Refugee*, a book about the Amin-directed exile of tens of thousands of Asians that informed the film.

It was also in Uganda that the movie's climactic scene was filmed, one involving Seth's character, Jay. After learning of his friend Okelo's grim fate, he would wander the streets for a time, and then be pulled into the joy and enthusiasm of several local street dancers.

In the script, Jay was to see this buoyant dance, this expression of freedom and hope, and be moved by it, but a bit of spontaneity resulted in an even more fruitful idea. A small child, carried on her father's shoulder would now touch Jay tenderly on the cheek, a physical, but tactile reminder of the human connection that reaches deep beneath such superficialities as skin color.

"That was my idea. I take credit for that!" Seth enthuses. "Mira didn't know how to end it, and I organized that. I spoke to a guy there with a little kid, and I told him at one point, 'Let her put her hand on my face, I will be distracted when she does that, and ask you if I can hold her.'"

The result, as viewers can attest, is quite moving.

"It's a great moment. A lot of people mention it," Seth says. "This is what happens when things [are allowed to] occur in an improvised sort of way. That dance was supposed to be a metaphor for all the things he feels about Africa, but it worked so much better with that little moment with the child."

MISSISSIPPI MASALA = SOPHOMORE SUCCESS

When *Mississippi Masala* played at the Sundance Film Festival in 1992, it won a standing ovation from the audience and also nabbed a Best Screenplay award for Taraporevala at the Venice Film Festival. A host of other awards followed, including a NAACP Image Award for Denzel Washington for Outstanding Lead Actor in a Motion Picture, an Independent Spirit Award nomination for Best Feature and a nomination for the Golden Lion at the Venice Film Festival. The film was released in France on September 18, 1991, and in the United States several months later, on February 5, 1992.

In limited release, courtesy of the Samuel Goldwyn Company, the film grossed a healthy seven-and-a-half million dollars, a sum well in excess of its budget.

"I loved it," Sooni Taraporevala says. "I was actually, at first, afraid that it might not work. Unlike *Salaam Bombay!*, the construction of it is quite different because every scene is a talky scene, you know? And that was what I was a bit afraid of, whether it would all hang together because it

Salaam Bombay! (1988) **TOP** The object of Krishna's affection, Solasaal (Chandra Sharma), is sold into sexual slavery. **BOTTOM LEFT** A Helping Hand: Krishna (Shafiq Syed; right) gives the strung-out Chillum (Raghubir Yadav; left) a shoulder to lean on. **RIGHT** Baba (Nana Patekar) and Rekha (Aneeta Kanwar) are about to share a forbidden kiss.

Mississippi Masala (1991) **OPPOSITE PAGE** Demetrius (Denzel Washington) and Mina (Sarita Choudhury) are a star-crossed, modern-day Romeo and Juliet. **BELOW TOP** Afterglow: Demetrius (Washington) and Mina (Choudhury) consummate their relationship in the quiet before a family storm.

The Perez Family (1995) **BELOW BOTTOM** Juan Perez (Alfred Molina) and Dorrie (Marisa Tomei) sell flowers on the streets of Miami to make a living and thereby earn American citizenship. **NEXT PAGE** Earth Mother: Marisa Tomei makes a sensual impression as Dorrie.

The Kama Sutra: A Tale of Love (1997)
TOP LEFT A portrait of the decadent King, Raj (Naveen Andrews). **RIGHT**: Sisters of the heart. Maya (Indira Varma; left) holds Tara (Sarita Choudhury; right) after the queen's suicide attempt. **BOTTOM** Stone and Flesh: Maya (Indira Varma) is Jai's ideal of beauty, and model for his sculpture.

My Own Country (1998) **TOP** Vickie (Glenne Headly) and Dr. Abraham Verghese (Naveen Andrews) share the screen in an adaptation of the best-selling non-fiction book, *My Own Country*. **BOTTOM** Brothers and sisters: Mattie (Marisa Tomei) helps her brother Gordon (Adam Tomei) through a diagnosis of AIDS. **OPPOSITE PAGE** Dr. Abraham Verghese (Naveen Andrews) precariously balances home life (and baby) with a busy patient load.

Hysterical Blindness (2002) **TOP** She's looking for love in all the wrong places. Debby (Uma Thurman) is front and center on the dating scene in the heart-wrenching *Hysterical Blindness*. **BOTTOM** Uma Thurman (left), director Mira Nair (center) and Juliette Lewis (right) discuss an emotional scene.

spans continents and time periods and all that stuff, and then with the flashbacks! But I was very happy it all hung together."

Critically, *Mississippi Masala* easily matched the enthusiasm generated by *Salaam Bombay!* even though the subject matter was very different.

"*Mississippi Masala* is a charming and exuberant interracial romance, it's like a neo-realist *West Side Story*," raved *Entertainment Weekly*'s Owen Gleiberman, who also championed Sarita Choudhury as a "startlingly ripe erotic presence."[12] Nair's second effort was also a film with "idiosyncratic charm, thanks to a strong cast and Sooni Taraporevala's character-driven screenplay"[13] by *People*'s way of thinking, and Stuart Klawans, writing for *The Nation*, enjoyed the film's "warmhearted optimism" and termed Mira Nair's second sortie "irresistible."[14]

Rolling Stone also hailed *Mississippi Masala* for its "erotic, funny and painful romance" and noted that the film offers "an intimately involving look at a clash of two cultures that are blind to what unites them."[15] Roger Ebert and Gene Siskel both gave the films an unqualified "thumbs up."

One person who didn't feel quite as enchanted with the finished film—perhaps because he had been afforded an early glimpse of what it might have been, was Roshan Seth. Notably, he is particularly hard on his own work in the film.

"I'm not sure I would play Jay the way I did," he ponders. "I'm not sure I knew what I was doing, even then. It was one of her [Nair's] early films, and I think I got the emphasis all wrong.

"I do see that something has come out," he acknowledges. "What tends to happen with my work is that I'm not quite aware. I don't think very deeply about what I'm doing, I just do it, and what emerges afterwards is a kind of residue. And in that residue, Jay comes across as a rather broken and weak man, and I don't see that this is wrong, because he gets such a shock when his friend, who is African, says to him 'You have to leave.' He doesn't understand that.

"But there was something there that was critically wrong," Seth explores. "He *should* have understood it, being an Indian, because Indians understand about race more than anybody else. There is something missing in that film at an early stage that I think would have given it an edge. It tended to be rather sweet on the family side, but I don't think it was necessarily like that [early on]."

In part, Seth points to the truncated relationship between Jay and Okelo, which was much more significantly featured in the script. And though several scenes were shot, they didn't make it into the final cut.

"I have a feeling, you see, that this is where the film has its weak point, because the idea of his friendship with Okelo is supposed to be much more than just friendship. The film skirted around that side of the narrative. But he [Jay] is actually brought up by Okelo's mother who is a black African, and there's a scene where he's playing by the riverside as a kid with Okelo.

"You see, this is missed. This is what happens when narratives are fooled around with. He and Okelo have grown up together as children and his mother, for all intents and purposes, is also Okelo's mother. So when Okelo says to him, 'You must leave' Jay can't understand it, because he says 'How can my own brother ask me to leave my mother?' So that doesn't come across, because that early part of the story was taken out to accommodate that silly love story," Seth laments.

"I think everybody missed it. It's just too subtle."

Still, Seth received tremendous notices for his work as Jay. "Roshan Seth has the sharp profile and deep eyes that beautifully capture Jay's sense of loss," wrote Richard Blake in *America*. "It's is a fine, delicate performance."[16]

Seth, for one, would like to see Nair return to the type of film that she originally envisioned. "I think she should do a political film. A really good film, like *Battle of Algiers*...I liked her early instincts. She should do a political film. That's her forte."

WHERE THE HEART IS

Mira Nair's second salvo into the universe of feature filmmaking is one that focuses on two interconnected issues: the importance of a home and the ongoing cycle of racial hatred that separates people from each other. These themes circle around one another in an interesting manner in *Mississippi Masala*. The loss of a home, as in the case of a forced expulsion, is caused by racial hatred...and yet the same act also *generates* racial hatred. Nair's ultimate point seems to be that Jay, Seth's character, has unwittingly become a victim of this cycle and only by seeing examples of that cycle being shattered, particularly in Mina's taboo-breaking relationship with Demetrius, can he shed its shackles.

In many ways, Jay is *Mississippi Masala*'s main character, and certainly its most interesting. It is his journey that feels the most important thematically, and Mina's subplot feels present mainly to reveal a positive example of how youth always boasts that wonderful ability to look beyond the mores and restrictions of the present and craft its own set of rules. As in *Salaam Bombay!*, we are in the realm where children represent the future; our teachers. But nonetheless, Jay is the focal point, because he is the one who understands fully what it means to lose a home, and then, at the end, to find it again.

Considering the importance of Jay's story arc, it is crucial to begin the film before his forced departure from Uganda, before his metaphorical and literal expulsion from paradise. Accordingly, *Mississippi Masala* begins in Kampala in November of 1972, in a time of chaos and ethnic hatreds gone berserk. After a nighttime debate between Okelo and Jay, and after the advent of a new day, Ed Lachman's camera pauses to take a long, slow pan across an incredible, natural vista. This unsoiled landscape is one of gorgeous flowers, placid waters, and utter serenity. From this vantage point of Jay's backyard, one can almost see across the breadth of the whole Earth, and there exists only beauty as far as the vision stretches.

This is an important shot, not just to establish location, but because it absolutely frames the film's debate in visual terms. For Jay, who has grown up in such an ennobling paradise, this is indeed a slice of heaven. It is the land that nurtured him and raised him, and looking at it in this fashion, nobody can blame him for holding onto it. But the audience must experience that desire firsthand, and that is one of the glories of film as a medium. It has the capacity and the responsibility to show us things we haven't seen before, and to depict those vistas in ways that impact our understanding of our existence. This shot manages that feat, and because the image is so powerful, audiences immediately sympathize with Jay.

Accordingly, the moment of expulsion is one of tremendous sadness. Wind blows lazily through an empty house, an omen of the impending departure. Standing over his ledge, Jay clutches a flower, grasping between his fingers a last, tactile slice of this beloved piece of Earth. Then, finally, it is time to leave…

The first pan—and then this scene in conjunction—depict the loss of something beautiful in wholly understandable visual terms. Idi Amin has scapegoated Asians and seized this beauty for himself, fostering a hatred that will linger inside Jay for many years. Because these images make Jay a comprehensible character to audiences, he becomes the vehicle through which racial hatred can finally be purged. In simpler words, we sympathize with his plight. The audience understands why he's a broken and bitter man. Nobody could lose such a beautiful home and not feel powerfully the loss of it.

The world where we encounter Jay again some years later, Greenwood, Mississippi, is quite different from that paradise on that hill in Uganda. Jay runs a dingy motel, and seems to live on the edge of poverty. The earth here is paved, flat, and almost washed out. Apathy and poverty have practically turned it into a wasteland, a direct contrast to the unsullied beauty around Lake Victoria. Living in America, in the American South, Jay is bothered that his intelligent and beautiful daughter Mina cleans bathrooms for a living. He is disturbed that he cannot afford to send her to college. He has gone from dwelling in a natural Eden to a used-up purgatory of sorts, a place that feels mired in the pre-Civil Rights era, where he resides as part of a social underclass, either despised or invisible. Jay has not accepted this "new" world and does not really live in it. His heart, his mind, still calls for Kampala, or rather his *memory* of it, and he constantly writes angry letters to Uganda's government and instigates lawsuits to recover that which Amin—a black man—has stolen from him.

Although Mina remembers Uganda from childhood, she is an entirely different brand of Indian, one who is limited neither by Ugandan perspectives, or for that matter, those of white Mississippi. She is able to understand and process the concept that race need not be a divisive force, especially among those struggling to overcome it. Mina also sees that racism comes in all colors, literally. In her family, there are jokes about a "darkie daughter," and sermons about clinging to traditions ("We should not forget our roots…our traditions…" urges one relative). A product of a new world, and an outsider in all of the traditional ones, Mina is able to take a critical leap beyond convention and reach out for love wherever she finds it, and that includes Demetrius, an African-American.

For Jay, the romantic situation with Demetrius and Mina is intolerable. He believes he understands the ways of the world, but in fact is merely repaying an evil with evil. Black Idi Amin hated Asians, and now he, an Asian, hates blacks, even if his racism is not overt. Perhaps because he is older than Mina, perhaps because he is still rooted in that house on the bluff in Uganda, Jay is not able to make the same leap beyond tradition as Mina does. "The world is not so quick to change," he says sadly, believing that a union of two people of different races can end only in disaster. He no doubt remembers Okelo's divisive words about Uganda being for Black Africans. Yet by his thinking, his daughter should not be with a "lower class" black man in America. Is there such a difference in opinions, Okelo's racism and his own? Is Jay a hypocrite to blame and then shun Okelo for beliefs that, in fact, mirror his own?

"Through the father's journey," writes Cecilie S. Berry in *Cineaste*, "Nair underscores her point that distinctions based on class and property are as much barriers to humanity as cultural or racial jingoism, and that the seduction of status can turn even an enlightened bourgeois liberal into a well-intentioned bigot."[17]

In *Mississippi Masala*, Mina and her father share a close relationship, a fact acknowledged subtly as they sit together in a diner to discuss the future. Just for a moment, Lachman's camera tilts down a tiny bit, quite unobtrusively. Revealed in the adjusted frame is a glimpse of their intertwined hands—touching gently on the tabletop. It's a tender connection that speaks volumes of their relationship. Not surprisingly, given this closeness, it is only once Mina has revealed her heart, and demonstrated her ability to move beyond established racial divides, that Jay begins to similarly adjust his views. His conversation with Demetrius has exposed him as holding racist beliefs, but Mina's act—disapprove of it as he may—has shown him what true courage is, a fact he acknowledges in his letter to her (read in touching voice-over) from Uganda.

When he returns to Uganda, Jay learns of Okelo's death, and comes to understand something of his brother, and the decisions that he forged twenty years ago. Without Okelo, Uganda is not so much the home that Jay remembered and longed for. Suddenly, he realizes it was foolish to hold onto a place, and more importantly, to the pain and hatred that came with the loss of it.

The last sequence in *Mississippi Masala* portrays Jay's final epiphany in beautiful, and visually poignant fashion. On the streets of Kampala, Jay becomes enmeshed with a group of black locals who start to dance, and one is carrying an angel-faced child. That baby touches Jay's face innocently, and in a flash, Jay realizes that blacks, whites, Indians, all races have something in common: their humanity and need to have a home.

"Through that embrace, a small hand put to a tear-stained cheek, Nair suggests that the father's place is not just in Mississippi, but in Uganda too," suggests Berry in *Cineaste*, "Not, however, in the hillside mansion where he once resided, but in the streets, in the mainstream of human existence, where joy and loss are accidents of life that all people share."[18]

This climax is a cathartic moment in the film, and one in which Jay's "transcendence lights up the screen,"[19] according to critic Peter Rainer in the *Los Angeles Times*. In that final moment of transformation, Jay understands that it is the people whom he shares life with that make a place home, not simply a parcel of land.

"'Home is where the heart is, and my heart is with you,' I think he says," remembers Roshan Seth. "It's a terrible line. It's a Hindi film line, but there you are. In that film, yes, his identity—because he has no identity—is with his family. He doesn't belong to America. He doesn't belong to Uganda. He doesn't belong anywhere. He belongs to his home. That is his world. I don't think Mira feels those things anymore, but maybe deep down…you know, once an exile, always an exile."

It may indeed be clichéd to state that "home is where the heart is," but the line is a final and efficient distillation of Jay's journey, and it represents a moment of terrific hope, even more so than Mina's promising beginning with Demetrius. This is so because Jay has moved beyond his hatred, whereas Mina never carried the hatred to begin with. She could always be courageous because she didn't buy into the old morals and tradition that "people stick to their own kind." But Jay is a survivor of racism, and still he has elected to give up that hate. It is a poignant conclusion to a film that, according to *Film Quarterly*, "offers fresh images of people previously ignored, denigrated or stereotyped by Hollywood."[20]

Peppering in the sweet romance between Demetrius and Mina succeeds in *Mississippi Masala* as an effective counterpoint, a glimpse at how things *could* be. Not that it is particularly realistic, even by Sooni Taraporevala's way of thinking.

"When I was in high school and we read *Romeo and Juliet*, I was a bit of a skeptic. I believed that had they not died, they would have broken up in a few years, you know?" She laughs. "It depends on your point of view."

So if Jay's life path is the difficult road of the exile, the hard reality of a man without a home, then Mina's story is a romantic dream, an imagination of what the future might look like. Jay's story would no doubt have benefitted from greater screen time, but the counterpoint had to be there for contrast; the old generation versus the new. It is for these reasons that the film's structure is a solid and illuminating one. At times, if it feels more mild than the political essay it might have been, that's an exigency of the business, and a very big (and common) problem for international films.

"In America I think it is often said to me that very little is known about India among the vast majority of Americans," Seth says. "That's probably true as far as America is concerned, because America is occupied with its own self, as indeed Indians are. But the Americans, perhaps to a greater degree than anybody else. So the Americans, to tell you the honest truth, couldn't give a damn about what's happening in India. And that's probably right. Why should they?

"It's very difficult to sell a film to an American audience that is about somewhere else that isn't recognizable to them," he continues. "I think the educated audience is very good about that, whether it is in France or Britain or America. In a city like New York, people are willing to embrace other cultures and other films and other stories just because they want to improve their minds.

"I don't think that is necessarily true of the vast majority of people who go to the cinema," Seth concludes.

In studying the Nair film canon, the movies that tend to stand out the most, *Salaam Bombay!*, *Monsoon Wedding*, and even *Hysterical Blindness*, are those that don't surrender even an inch regarding their subject matter. These stories are told with a refreshing candor and honesty, and frankly, a seeming lack of overt commercial "intent."

In some ways, *Mississippi Masala* feels almost like the lead-up to the glorious *Monsoon Wedding*, and is certainly within that inner ring of great Mira Nair motion pictures. Jay remains an unforgettable character who takes a meaningful journey, and those last five minutes on the streets of Kampala, of dancing and joy and human contact, are both touching and remarkable. Nair is especially good at finishing strong, always closing movies with a rush of cathartic emotions and memorable images, and that's a statement as true of *Mississippi Masala* as *Salaam Bombay!* The ending portends hope. Weaving a new patchwork quilt of interracial amity from the frayed threads of old hatreds and prejudice, perhaps the next generation can finally get a few things right.

COMING TO AMERICA

In 1990, the contemporary writer and humorist Christine Bell, author of *Saint*, published her latest novel, an ethnic comedy replete with tragic overtones, *The Perez Family*. Set in the year 1980, it portrayed events already depicted on film once before, in Brian De Palma's 1983 gangster film, *Scarface*, starring Al Pacino. In particular, the novel focused on the months after Fidel Castro released one hundred thousand political prisoners and criminals from captivity and shipped them off to the United States in boats. The event was known as the Mariel boat lift.

The main characters in *The Perez Family* all boasted the last name Perez, but Bell's unique twist was that they were totally unrelated except by predicament. The lead character was a former political prisoner, Juan Raul Perez, who had been separated from his family for twenty years. His wife, Carmela, waited patiently and a bit anxiously in Miami with their daughter, wondering when and if she would ever see her husband again.

Then there was another Perez among the newcomers, a young thug named Felipe who would become involved with seedy Miami drug trafficking upon gaining his freedom in the U.S. He represented a "son" of sorts in this ad hoc family. Filling the role of a grandfather was Cesar Armando Perez, an old and loyal soldier who would develop a fierce devotion to Juan Raul.

Finally, the focal point of this group of exiles was the book's most colorful and well-drawn character, Dorita "Dorrie" Perez, a brassy woman with a love of life, and passion for all things American, especially John Wayne and Elvis Presley. To escape the immigrant camp in the United States (located in the Orange Bowl stadium in Miami), Dorrie managed to pull all the like-named outcasts together as a "Perez family." Doing so by sheer force of personality, Dorrie understood that family units received first priority in the long line to American citizenship. However, holding the diverse exiles—all with competing interests—together, was no easy task.

Bell's novel focuses on the travails of this motley group, sometimes funny, sometimes quite moving. In the end, Juan Raul realizes that he cannot truly be reunited with his long-suffering wife Carmela—too many years apart and too much water under the bridge—and that, almost against his will, he has fallen in love with the irrepressible Dorrie. This final realization comes only after two unfortunate deaths in the Perez family.

Library Journal called Bell's book a "fast moving, hilarious epic" that was "full of surprises" and "quite out of the ordinary."[21] Rosellen Brown noted in *Massachusetts Review* that what was so "beguiling about the book before it succumbs to its excess of plot is the complexity of its tone, like a treble melody, sunny and optimistic, played against a profoundly somber bass."[22] The reviewers were overwhelmingly positive, and so *The Perez Family* seemed ripe for a movie adaptation.

Screenwriter Robin Swicord, an author and producer with a successful track record in Hollywood, who penned scripts for such hit mainstream films as *Little Women* (1994) and later, *Practical Magic* (1998), adapted the book and worked closely with producer Julia Chasman, who produced *Shag* (1989), and later went on to such projects as *Polish Wedding* (1998) and *Quills* (2000).

Swicord reportedly enjoyed an outstanding working relationship with novelist Bell, who escorted the erstwhile screenwriter on a research trip through Cuban Miami to help assure a faithful and honest translation of her work in print. A first draft was broached, one that featured both Spanish and English interludes, and in some cases utilized subtitles to maintain an authentically Cuban atmosphere.

On the business end, Chasman and Swicord reportedly advocated the film as a small-budgeted effort, and garnered the support of Sydney Pollack's production company, which opened the door to Universal Pictures. Shooting the film in Miami looked like it would be prohibitively expensive however, and the film was probably too small to be a Universal release, so the option eventually lapsed.

At that point, the Samuel Goldwyn Company picked up the option to produce *The Perez Family*, but there was a difference of opinion among camps almost immediately. Allegedly, the Goldwyn people didn't want to go with Chasman and Swicord's first choice as a director, young Alfonso Cuarón, whose films include *Solo con tu pareja* (1991), *Great Expectations* (1998), *Y tu mamá también* (2001) and *Harry Potter and the Prisoner of Azkaban* (2004).

Instead, the Goldwyn folk demanded a director who had just made them a great deal of money on another small picture, *Mississippi Masala*. It was an arranged marriage, and the groom to Swicord and Chasman's bride was none other than Mira Nair. Much was at stake in this union, because many at the Goldwyn Company reportedly referred to *The Perez Family* as their own version of *Moonstruck* (1986), the Cher-Nicolas Cage romantic vehicle that had achieved crossover success and become a multi-million dollar hit.

At eleven million dollars, *The Perez Family* represented Mira Nair's largest budgeted picture yet, and therefore the riskiest. It was also the first in which she functioned, essentially, as a hired gun. After all, this was a property she had not nourished or developed through her own auspices and network of associates, though—uncannily—it nonetheless seemed to feature all the elements that had figured prominently in her earlier features: a community of exiles; life on the streets; a search for a new place to call home; the quest to deal with modernity (in America) versus tradition (in Cuba).

CONTROVERSIAL CASTING

The Perez Family had its first public controversy the moment casting was announced. Among the big three stars—Marisa Tomei, Alfred Molina, and Anjelica Huston—there was not a Cuban among them, and that rubbed the exile community in Florida the wrong way.

Tomei, an Oscar winner for *My Cousin Vinny* (1992) gained twenty pounds to play the novel's Earth mother Dorrie,[23] and essayed the role with a Cuban accent that some critics would eventually compare (unfavorably) with Pacino's in *Scarface*. Despite the noticeable lack of Cubans in the cast, Nair announced to her crew before the commencement of shooting in

April of 1994 that she was "ready to make a very Cuban movie," and that she felt "the same energy" she had during *Salaam Bombay!*[24]

Also joining the cast in the small role of an immigration official was Ranjit Chowdhry, *Mississippi Masala*'s Anil. "*Perez* was Mira's first as a hired hand. I usually give her a pep talk on such occasions. 'Mira,' I say, 'from you I expect big things…and small roles,'" jokes Chowdhry.

"The role was written for a ditzy blond and they were hoping to get Carol Kane," he continues. "Don't know what happened about that, but I told Mira of an experience I'd had heading back to Canada when this obnoxious Sri Lankan immigration official gave me a very hard time, patronizing me for hours on end. Mira thought the immigrant as keeper of the borders was a novel idea, and we collaborated on changing the role. I felt I should be a sympathetic figure who helps Ms. Tomei circumvent all the Draconian, absurd rules of sponsorship. Some critics later felt that Mira, as helmer, was—through my character—advocating open borders."

FAMILY BUSINESS

The Perez Family lensed in Coral Gables, Florida, with some shooting completed in Miami's Little Havana. Mar Chiquita in Puerto Rico eventually doubled as Cuba. Chowdhry remembers that "nothing exceptional" really happened in Miami besides the "usual location vibe," but that working with Tomei was a joy. "Marisa is a consummate pro," he says.

The Perez Family also introduced a recurring collaborator to the Mira Nair moviemaking family, namely Stephanie Carroll, a set decorator working under production designer Mark Friedberg. This talent would ultimately return in that capacity on *Kama Sutra* and later graduate to production designer on *Monsoon Wedding*, *Hysterical Blindness* and *The Namesake*.

Carroll comes from a background in the study of literature, and traces her career in film back to Cambridge, Massachusetts, where she interned at the American Repertory Theatre and found herself moving unexpectedly into the art department.

"I truly believe that writing is very much like production design," suggests Carroll. "When I was writing, I was always thinking of the character and the color, and what the environment was like, and what motivated characters, and the emotions to me are designed in shapes and colors. That's what production design is for me. That how I came to production design—through the story and really through character.

"I had done other things in life, which I think is truly important for people in film. I see life experience lacking now in a lot of film school graduates. I think that theatre people also have a good background in design. There's a sensibility in theatre and life experience that makes the better filmmaker than just film school. That's my old-fashioned belief."

Carroll remembers that she enjoyed working with Friedberg on *The Perez Family*. "I was very collaborative with him," she recalls. "I was very involved in the design at that point with him too. That's how I met Mira, and then we did *Kama Sutra* in India."

Specifically, Carroll worked on Cuba. "We used Puerto Rico for Cuban cane fields. The film was about the Cuban boat lift in 1980, so we did a lot of research on that. We also dressed parts of Miami to look like that time when they [the exiles] came to live in the Orange Bowl.

"I [also] did Anjelica Huston's house," Carroll explains. "She had come over on the boat lift, so the house had to represent Cuban and American sensibilities. Which is obviously what I do a lot of with Mira—I put myself into other cultures. I'm not Indian; I'm not Cuban; but I enjoy that challenge."

It was during production and postproduction that stories about the making of *The Perez Family* begin to diverge. Behind the scenes, producers reportedly complained about some of Nair's selections, for instance her desire to impose a Felliniesque vision on the film (seen in the movie's opening dream sequence). Also, her refusal to include P.O.V. shots (which the director considers clichéd) was also reportedly a bone of contention among some. Even Nair's selection of a non-Cuban composer for the film's score was debated.

Representing another viewpoint, there were those who insisted that certain people, locations and cuts were actually imposed on Nair, who was navigating the slippery slope of corporate Hollywood for the first time on this project. In particular, the editing room was named as the place where the most wounding battles were fought.

"It's like horse-trading," Nair told the *Washington Post*. "They previewed it [*The Perez Family*] and began to think it was a broad comedy.

And I was saying 'Let's preserve the rhythm.'"[25] Several months before release, Nair also called *The Perez Family* "an unsentimental, deeply cinematic picture,"[26] so it was clear that different parties had differing perceptions of the multi-faceted Bell material. Comedy or drama? Farce or realistic depiction of exiles? *Moonstruck*, or something far different—and less romantic—tonally?

At a lengthy running-time of one hundred thirty-five minutes, *The Perez Family* had the misfortune of opening Friday, May 12, 1995, the same day as another Hispanic themed film, Gregory Nava's *Mi Familia*. That production ended up on several top ten lists for the year, but *The Perez Family*—advertised as a whimsical romantic comedy with ad lines like "On the way to finding a family, she found love," and "A family became strangers and strangers became a family"—was not so happily received.

After the back-to-back critical success of *Salaam Bombay!* and *Mississippi Masala*, it was no doubt a rude awakening when Nair's *The Perez Family* was released to very, very mixed reviews. Writing in the *New Republic*, Stanley Kauffmann, perhaps the U.S.'s pre-eminent critic, called the film "a slow, lumbering mess."[27] The *San Francisco Examiner* complained that "one emerges from the messy, belabored, badly edited and badly written *Perez Family* doubting Nair's competence."[28]

The negative reviews tended to fall into two distinct camps. The first complained about the lack of authenticity in the project, particularly the non-Hispanic casting, and the second took potshots at Marisa Tomei's efforts in the role of Dorita. On the former front, the *New Internationalist* complained that the film "could well leave you thinking that *cha cha cha* and swinging hips are all that can be said about Hispanic culture."[29]

In *Entertainment Weekly*, Lisa Schwarzbaum asked why "not one Cuban in a starring role?"[30] Finally, *Hispanic*'s Robert Macias went even further, terming *The Perez Family* the worst movie of the year, citing its "hokey" script, "uninspired" direction and the fact that most of the principal actors are non-Hispanics.[31]

Rolling Stone observed that the film was "crushed by miscasting," and that Tomei used the same "ju and me accent that tied a tin can to Al Pacino's turn in *Scarface*."[32] *People* opined that Tomei sounded "uncomfortably close to Charo"[33] in the role of Dorrie.

Nor did the film adaptation ultimately please the author of the source material, Christine Bell, who informed reporter Marc Stengel that as she was watching it she was thinking "'Wait. That doesn't happen next.' And there are a lot of technical twists and turns. For example I know that this street in the movie doesn't connect with that street. A person who dies in the book doesn't die in the movie; in fact that person isn't even shot. And that was a major part, you know—who lives and who dies."[34] Bell also said that though she respected Mira Nair, she felt the film was miscast, and had special difficulty with Tomei as Dorrie.

Though many, especially those in the Hispanic community, complained about the non-Hispanic casting and derided *The Perez Family* as "unauthentic,"[35] others did champion the film. Gene Siskel and Roger Ebert gave the films "two thumbs up." Richard Schickel of *Time* noted *The Perez Family* was a "juicy, messy, exotic and utterly delicious treat,"[36] and Mike LaSalle of the *San Francisco Chronicle* leapt to Tomei's defense. "There is only one way to play a Cuban spitfire," he opined, "And that's just to go ahead and do it. In *The Perez Family*, Marisa Tomei risks making a complete fool of herself, bumping and grinding, throwing herself at men with great Latin abandon...but Tomei more than survives it."[37]

As usual, the truth about *The Perez Family* probably fell somewhere between the two poles of critical response, and many critics were candid enough to make note of the film's strengths and weaknesses within their reviews, giving, perhaps, a more fair appraisal of the film than some of the out-and-out pans.

"The results are certainly giddy, but are they good?" Peter Rainer of the *Los Angeles Times* trenchantly asked. "Nair...is a gifted filmmaker," he went on, "but her best range doesn't get full play here. She has a strong eye for documentary detail, and she fills the screen with color but she can't reconcile her performers to her feeling for realism. She captures the florid, carnival atmosphere of Miami in glints and spurts. Whenever the performers take center stage, which is most of the time, the film turns into a play-act charade."[38]

"Mira Nair...has an eye for color and a sense of daring about story structure," noted John Anderson in *Newsday*. "She balances the disparate, parallel stories of Juan and Carmela and their hesitant romances—Juan with Dorita, Carmela with a friendly fed (Chazz Palmenteri)—smoothly.

But regardless of technique and Robin (*Little Women*) Swicord's snappy script, little about the characterizations are believable. They are, on occasion a little bit unsettling."[39]

"Some people may be put off by the movie's volatile shifts in mood, from comedy to pathos and back again" opined *New York*'s David Denby. "*The Perez Family* is melodramatically plotted and the ending is a shambles (a couple of transitional scenes appear to be missing). Nair needs to smooth a few things out, but she's become a comic-romantic director of great originality, a sort of spicier, more sensual Paul Mazursky. *The Perez Family* is held together by immense affection for its characters and its chaotic milieu. With any luck, this luscious and happily absurd movie will serve as the taking off point for a great career."[40]

"I'll add that everyone involved deserves the proverbial 'A' for effort, starting with Nair," added the *Christian Science Monitor*'s David Sterritt, who also commented that Nair was "heroically single-minded"[41] in her concern for characters not often shown on the big screen.

Financially, *The Perez Family* proved an unmitigated disaster. It recouped less than three million dollars against its eleven million dollar investment. For Nair, *The Perez Family* experience only left the director—in her own words—wanting "to flee into the real challenges of filmmaking, which happen when you make your own film."[42]

EARTH MOTHER

One thing that remains so remarkable about Mira Nair's film canon is the manner in which the director finds romance and beauty in the lives of people that audiences don't normally assume are romantic. Chaipau and Manju dance merrily to Bollywood tunes while rain incessantly pours outside Rekha's tiny room in *Salaam Bombay!* Men and women dance expressively in the streets of Kampala at the close of *Mississippi Masala*, and it is a moment of unfettered joy when Ria, Dubey and Alice all take up an exultant dance in the closing moments of *Monsoon Wedding*.

The joy of dance is no doubt a prominent feature in all of Mira Nair's films, and even in her less well-known works, including *The Perez Family*, it is present. It is the symbol that Nair utilizes to show that, in the spirit of

Satyajit Ray, even if life is sometimes bad, it can also be joyous and wonderful.

In *The Perez Family*, it is Dorita who is connected explicitly with the freedom and expression of dance. Early in the film, while aboard a small boat bound for Miami, she breaks into dance at just the right moment. Around her, in quick close-ups, we see the weary, hardened faces of her fellow travelers, as well as Juan Raul's somber affect. Then, anchored in the middle of the frame like the sun, Dorrie steps forward and begins to sway and move.

The others join her, and before long, their anxiety has passed and they are all dancing. Dorrie even cheers Juan Raul up some, grinding her luscious hips into close contact with the gloomy exile. The message is plain: this woman is a beacon of light and life in a world that desperately needs such joy. More to the point, Dorrie possesses an instinctual emotional intelligence, and knows how to break a bad mood, and cast her own seductive spell over others.

Later, even the staid Carmela is swayed by Dorrie. Glacial Carmela, accompanied by her F.B.I. suitor, gazes upon the young woman at a disco as Dorrie takes center stage on the dance floor. Carmela explicitly wishes that—*just once*—she too could be so expressive, so unrestrained, so free. It is thus in the act of dance, whether in a cheesy disco, the back of a cramped boat, in the hustle-and-bustle of busy Miami streets, or in the embrace of Juan Raul, that this character is at her most alive and vibrant. The audience is clearly meant to see her that way too, which is why Nair goes to such lengths to associate Dorrie with ravishing colors both in her choice of clothing and surroundings (which invariably include blossoming flowers and vibrantly painted murals). She is a force of color and light to be reckoned with.

Again, it might be prudent here to repeat that film is primarily a *visual* art form. Character need not be conveyed only by words and dialogue (as Sooni Taraporeval noted for us, as in a play, where everything is spoken). Instead, choices of composition, production design and framing make these the salient points in film, and in *The Perez Family*, Nair adheres to this philosophy by literally and metaphorically putting the beautiful Dorrie at center stage throughout—dancing and moving, keeping things alive and upbeat.

Dorrie is a special kind of woman, one, for lack of a better phrase, we might call an Earth mother. And no scene demonstrates this better than the lead-up to her arrival in America. Beforehand, we have seen close-ups of her sensual lips, and there is the feeling that although she is "like Cuba, used by many, conquered by no one," there is simultaneously the feeling that she is a ravishing beauty filled with light. A woman whose sensuality reaches down into her core and very being, and is somehow tied to nature, as if she is more than a personality, but a *force*. Or as Juan Raul tells Dorrie, "you always know exactly where you are on this Earth."[43] It is a quality of sexiness and groundedness and joy, all wrapped into one colorful package.

Nair's great gift as a director is her ability to convey key plot points and character information through such imagery and framing, and at many points, *The Perez Family* is indeed impressive in this regard. After Dorita joyfully kisses Juan Raul on the boat, she jumps spontaneously into the golden waves to swim the last few feet to shore, to reach freedom under her own steam.

Notably, Dorrie's dress folds up into the waves like the spreading petals of a flower as she warms herself in the sunny waters of Key West. It is as though freedom has actually made her blossom. This dynamic arrival on America's shore is representative of that trademark Mira Nair extended moment, an instance of importance slowed down until the viewer feels the full sensuality and joy inherent in it. As performed by Tomei, the moment is also incredibly feminine and sexy. In a slightly slowed down movement, Dorrie kneels in the gentle waves, her hands running up her sides to her long, curly hair, and then down to her breasts.

Given the impact of such moments, is not difficult to determine that Marisa Tomei's Dorrie represents another great Mira Nair heroine, on a par certainly with *Mississippi Masala*'s Mina, *Kama Sutra*'s Maya, and *Vanity Fair*'s Becky Sharp. She is a woman who is not shy about her sexuality, or for that matter, the life she desires. And like the best literary heroines, Dorrie is not one to be acted upon, but one who pushes and scrapes for everything she achieves. Dorrie is not only sexually aggressive (with the guard), but respectable too in that she won't let herself be treated like a whore. She is not coy (unlike the demure Carmela), but forthright and honest, and that is why she ultimately wins Juan Raul.

But more important than matters of sex or marriage, it is Dorita who has an agenda. She brings together others to achieve a desirable goal. She forges a family with Juan Raul, Felipe, and the Old Man, and therefore gets *all of them* out of the Orange Bowl more quickly, something that none of the men could have accomplished even if it had been on their radar, which it was not.

Yes, Perez is the name they have in common, but it is Dorita's drive to live in freedom that they adopt. Each member of the family benefits from her presence and orbits it like a planet. She is mother, caretaker, lover and provider. Some critics clearly had a problem with Tomei's performance, but in retrospect it seems one of the most outstanding elements of the film. Dorita is the glue that holds *The Perez Family* together for as long as it coheres, which, admittedly, is not quite its full one hundred thirty-five minutes.

Alas, other elements in *The Perez Family* are not so successful. The film is overlong for such scant material, and some sequences feel markedly out of tune with the film's subject matter and tone. Nair is true to the novel in some senses, but then abandons it in others.

For instance, the film opens with a gorgeous dream, the dream of a "long white beach" and "turquoise sea" as discussed in the book, but in the film, the vision is distinctly and unmistakably Felliniesque. In other words, it is surreal—and seems slightly self-indulgent—though expertly and beautifully staged.

Federico Fellini (1920–1993), the great Italian film director, is today renowned for his non-linear images, for frames where there is no clear boundary between fantasy and reality. His later films, full of surrealism, exaggeration and comic satire, are often seen as a response to the neo-realism of the early portion of his film career. Mira Nair is an acknowledged admirer of Fellini, but why, one might ask, is this Felliniesque approach utilized at the start of *The Perez Family*? How does it fit, thematically?

Here's how *Sight and Sound*'s Peter Matthews describes the sequence:

The Perez Family begins well with a magical title sequence depicting a golden-hued memory of Cuba. The setting is perhaps the '50s, but the impression is of some timeless idyll of gracious living remote from the din of cities and revolution. An affluent bourgeois clan, each member arrayed in dazzling white, is having a picnic on the beach and the camera tracks lovingly over the faces, food and children's games as if greedy to preserve the evanescent details. Yet the imagery is too honeyed and hallucinatory to be quite credible and the scene ends with a surreal shot of half a dozen of the revelers bathing fully-clothed in the sea.[44]

This description captures the utter loveliness of the imagery, but also the confusion it raises. Juan Raul has been incarcerated in Calvario Prison since 1960, so how could "his dream" possibly feature Felliniesque touches? He would never have seen a Fellini film, or if he did, they would have been of the old neo-realist school, not the later surreal style. Since this sequence is supposed to be occurring in Juan Raul's dreams, it is ostensibly created through his eyes, his mind. Does he think of his life in such terms? It is unclear.

So did Mira Nair pick a style for the dream out of a hat, simply because of her admiration for Fellini? That may well be, but the approach doesn't totally work for the film because Fellini is—first and foremost—a satirist. It is an approach at distinct odds with Mira Nair's dynamic passion as a filmmaker, and also the manner in which she views Dorrie—a hot sun whom the other *dramatis personae* become attracted to and ultimately orbit. So as beautiful as the imagery is, it feels off-kilter.

On another front all together, it seems fair to state that there are major differences between the novel and the movie, and one can see how that is certainly grating for some reviewers, though critics who complain too loudly should remember that film and literature are two totally different mediums.

But, in the novel, for instance, it is plain that Juan Raul is a newspaper man, one jailed because he supported Castro's opposition in print. This is never made clear in Nair's film.

Still, it is probably Dorrie, who has changed the most, at least physically, from one medium to the other. In the book, she is described as having "mother-Cuba hips." In other words, she's supposed to be a little big, a little wide. Tomei put on some weight for the role, but she's certainly not big by any stretch of the imagination, just more voluptuous than in her other films. Dottie is also forty-four years old in Bell's novel, and Tomei doesn't look a day over twenty-five, which seriously messes up the novel's time line when one begins to ponder the Castro Revolution in Cuba in 1960. The very background of the character is subverted by the change in the character's age.

At points, *The Perez Family* also evidences that unfortunate Hollywood trend of softening characters so that they become more palatable to the masses. Juan Perez (who is fifty-seven in the book, by the way, much older than Molina...), actively hates the boy who becomes "his son," Felipe. After the boy dies in Bell's novel, Juan curses him out because the boy stole his family's hard-earned money. He says that he hopes the boy "rots in Hell," and this is uttered after his death. That's a level of hostility the movie totally ignores, presumably so that *The Perez Family* can be safe, consumable, "romantic," *Moonstruck*-style material for the widest possible audience.

The screenplay also amps up the romance between Carmela and Det. Pirelli, a barely expressed relationship in the novel, so that we can have a happy ending and Carmela will not be left alone when Juan Raul chooses to be with Dorrie rather than the woman who waited twenty years for him. Again, this choice feels like a commercial one, a marketing decision that concluded both characters must have prospective spouses so that no one will be hurt or sad when the lights come back on.

Another change from the novel involves the guard who falls for Dorrie. In the book, he is Esteban Santiesteban and he has a much different role than the character in the movie. He is also rejected by Dorita in the book, but not under the circumstances in the film, which come mightily close to rape. In the book, Dorrie and Esteban don't repair to his apartment. He doesn't treat her like an object, but instead brings her flowers when he learns of Felipe's death.

In the book, he is also tortured by the fact that he believes Dorrie is a married woman and he is breaking up a happy family. In the film, none of those notes are struck. The guard disappears from the story altogether after trying to force Dorrie to have sex with him. Again, the tenor of this change seems to indicate that somebody wanted Dorrie to be scrappy, a fighter, and it was simply more in keeping with that image to have her fight back when pressed sexually, maintaining her character's dignity. No one can conclude she's a whore since she doesn't go all the way with the guard.

The greatest alteration from book to film involves Cesar Armando Perez, the old man who becomes the adoptive father of the Perez family. In the book, he is a crazy old soldier who becomes very attached to Juan Raul. In fact, he sees himself as Juan Raul's protector. In the book, the old man is shot and killed during the climactic confrontation at the music festival, a tragic note on which the book ends. However, in the movie, Cesar has been neutered. He's just colorful, rather than dangerous and a vigilante. He runs around places naked, climbs traffic lights and trees, and is good for a laugh now and then. He's cute—that's all. At the end of the film, he's astride a tree, looking off into the horizon, eternally searching for "his" Cuba.

In the book, "his" Cuba made Cesar Armando Perez a soldier, and ultimately led to his demise.

Still, these are perhaps small points to consider. Most people who saw the film had likely not read, nor heard of, Bell's book, and wouldn't be troubled by the changes from page to screen. When examined in the context of Nair's film canon, *The Perez Family* actually hits a number of familiar notes quite successfully. As in *Salaam Bombay!* there is a scene of the characters sitting to watch a film, highlighting that conflict between Hollywood illusion and grim reality. In Juan Raul and Carmela's daughter, Teresa (played by Trini Alvarado), we have another example of a "next generation" character akin to Mina in *Mississippi Masala*, navigating the byways of a new culture in her own fashion. And, of course, there's that reminder of exile, also an element of *Mississippi Masala*. Here, the film ends with a dynamic shot, an aerial thrust (by helicopter) towards Cuba, a land that will always be on the mind of Dorrie, Juan Raul and the Old Man, no matter how long they live in the States.

These familiar Nair touchstones are certainly welcome ones, as are her dynamic visuals. On the latter front, we are reminded by critic Michael Medved that Nair "has a prodigious flair for dazzling colors," and that "few filmmakers can so memorably convey the vibrant pulse of daily life with its spicy tastes and pungent smells."[45]

Writing for the *Tucson Weekly*, critic Zachary Woodruff wrote in a similar vein, that throughout *The Perez Family*, "Mira Nair fills each frame with gobs of culture. Within a single panning shot, you might see eye-popping flower arrangements, funky knick-knacks, interesting old people's faces, wildly colorful murals, exotic dances, bizarre mannerisms. It's an attractive spectacle..."[46]

For some, that attractive spectacle will no doubt suffice. For others, *The Perez Family* feels like Mira Nair's most unsatisfying feature. There are moments of her trademark genius throughout it, but they do not come often enough, or add up to such a pleasing totality as they do in her other films.

4

Kama Sutra: A Tale of Love (1997),
My Own Country (1998), and
The Laughing Club of India (1999)

KAMA SUTRA: A TALE OF LOVE (1997)

NDF International LTD. Pony Canyon Inc., Pandora Films in association with Channel Four Films present a Mirabai Films production, a Mira Nair film, *Kama Sutra: A Tale of Love*.

Crew:

Associate Producer	Dinaz Stafford
Co-Producer	Caroline Baron
Composer	Mychael Danna
Featured Musicians	Shubha Mudgal,
	L. Subramaniam,
	Ustad Vilayath Khan
Costume Designer	Eduardo Castro
Film Editor	Kristina Boden
Production Designer	Mark Friedberg
Director of Photography	Declan Quinn
Executive Producer	Michiyo Yoshizaki
Screenplay	Helena Kriel and Mira Nair
Producer	Lydia Dean Pilcher
Producer and director	Mira Nair

Cast:

Raj Sing	Naveen Andrews
Tara	Sarita Choudhury
Jai Kumar	Ramon Tikaram
Rasi Devi,	Rekha
Teacher of the Kama Sutra	
Maya	Indira Varma
Babu	Ranjit Chowdhry
Biki	Khalid Tyabji
Annabi	Arundhati Rao
Young Maya	Surabhi Bhansali
Young Tara	Garima Dhup
Rup	Achala Sachder
Bashir	Arjun Sajnani
Vazir	Avijit Dutt
Praveen	Prabeen Sing
Courtesan	Dinaz Stafford
Courtesan	Maya Krishna Rao

MY OWN COUNTRY (1998)

Showtime Presents a Main Title Pictures Production, a Mira Nair Film, *My Own Country*.

Crew:

Casting	Susan Forrest, Beth Klein
Costume Designer	Noreen Landry
Co-Executive Producer	Steven Hewitt
Music	Jeff Danna
Film Editor	Kristina Boden
Production Designer	Phillip Barker
Director of Photography	Dion Beeb
Executive Producer	Barbara Title
Producer	Mira Nair
Based on the book by	Abraham Verghese
Screenplay	Jim Leonard, Jr., Sooni Taraporevala
Director	Mira Nair

Cast:

Dr. Abraham Verghese	Naveen Andrews
Vicki Talley	Glenne Headly
Lloyd Flanders	Hal Holbrook
Hope Flanders	Swoosie Kurtz
Mattie Vines	Marisa Tomei
Gordon Vines	Adam Tomei
Rajani Verghese	Ellora Patnaik
Allen	Peter MacNeill
Chester	Sean Hewitt
Langdon	William Webster
Mrs. Vines	Sharon Dyer
Mr. Vines	David Fox
Carol	Colleen Williams
Vadivel	Ranjit Chowdhry
Saryu Joshi	Mira Nair

LESSONS IN LOVE

Mira Nair's fourth feature film, *Kama Sutra: A Tale of Love*, arose from the ashes of a previous unmade project, one which the filmmaker had hoped to produce as early as November 1992, during the same year as *Mississippi Masala*'s release. That film was *Tsotsi*, an adaptation of the novel by South Africa's pre-eminent playwright, Athol Fugard (1932–   ).

Written in 1960, but published in the early 1980s, the novel's title means "black hooligan," and the story concerns violent gangs that threaten the peace in the towns of South Africa. Fugard's novel received mixed notices when published (a grade of "B-minus" from the *New York Times*, for instance), but for several reasons, *Tsotsi* was a story Nair felt inspired to tell.[1]

Helping her to do so was a Johannesburg-born playwright and screen-writer with a degree in dramatic art theory and English literature, Helena Kriel. An eloquent and well-spoken author, Kriel has worked in films and television for many years in both her native South Africa and the United States, and her credits include original plays such as *Arachnid* and also adaptations of such literary work as Sena Jeter Naslund's best-selling novel *Ahab's Wife*, a film project currently in development.

"What happened is I had written a film which was an adaptation of an Athol Fugard novel called *Tsotsi*, which Mira was attached to direct," Kriel recalls. "I went to Uganda to work on *Tsotsi*, and we had a very nice, creative collaboration, and then Mira and her family moved to South Africa to start pre-production on the film, which unfortunately fell apart. I had moved there for the film as well, and Mira just said to me, 'Let's collabo-rate on something else,' and then said she'd always wanted to do a narrative love story using the principles of the *Kama Sutra*, so I stayed on in South Africa for the purpose of that collaboration."

The *Kama Sutra* might seem an unlikely source for a film project, cloaked as the work is, even today, in a degree of mystery. Written by Vatsyayana, the title, roughly translated, means "Aphorisms of Love" or "Lessons of Love." The *Kama Sutra* contains over a thousand verses, and features chapters on such subjects as sexual unions, attracting a wife, under-standing a wife—apparently two very different challenges—and also learn-ing about the wives of others. Another chapter focuses on courtesans.

Outside the text, however, relatively little is known of the mysterious author, including his first name. Even less is known about when he actually lived. Vatsyayana is believed to have written the *Kama Sutra* some time between the first and sixth centuries, a pretty wide historical span. Most often, it is said that he wrote around the year 300 AD.

"The research happened on various levels," Kriel states, describing the project's genesis. "There was obviously immense research into the *Kama Sutra* itself, and trying to understand what it meant and how we could communicate that, and what the history of it was, and how it had affected the sexual behaviors of India in that time.

"We are conditioned to believe that love is an external phenomenon," Kriel reflects, "that we fall in love with a person who is embodied in a male or female form outside of ourselves, and that's where it stays. You get into external dynamics with that person and build a home and have this relationship in the outside world with them, but the *Kama Sutra* is absolutely and essentially about turning your life into meditation; of taking that external love and turning it into an internal thing, developing an internality through the agent of the person that you love so that everything external goes inside again, and—through the combination of male and female inside—the self comes to spiritual realization."

MOVIE MOGHULS

The next stage of crafting this unusual screenplay involved finding a specific world in which to explore the concepts of Vatsyayana's philosophy. Here, Nair and Kriel settled on the age of the Mughal (sometimes "Mogul") Empire, a Muslim ruling group that reigned over a mostly Hindu India with a stable, centralized government from the 1500s to roughly 1707.

"We went into extensive research on the Moghul culture in India, and they were a very dynamic and interesting group of men who were quite enlightened in many ways and very decadent in other ways," Kriel describes. "It was this combination, this dialectic between the decadent and the enlightenment that became really fascinating. It was their whole politics around women, and around love, and around how dispensable women were, because they had harems of ten thousand women.

"So we really got into some interesting research about the Moghul kings of India. It was absolutely fascinating, and we read journal accounts and poetry that had been written about them, and had a look at the different architectural cities that they planned, and the astronomy and the astrology. They were quite an intoxicating group of people, and I found myself growing enamored of a certain Moghul king," Kriel continues.

But all this research involved one particular idea about that ancient world: how a woman could hope to achieve independence and power there. As Kriel puts it: "Out of ten thousand women, what would it take for one woman to strike [the fancy of] a king who had that kind of sexual diversity accessible to him?"

In answering that question, Kriel and Nair forged a tale of two women who would each catch the attention of a young, highly-sexualized Moghul king, though for different reasons.

Another subject that Nair and Kriel wished to highlight in their collaboration was art. "At the same time, we were exploring what it meant to be an artist," Kriel reveals. "We chose [Auguste] Rodin (1840–1917) as our [inspiration] because he did a lot of work with sculpture, and a lot of work with live, female models.

"We did tremendous research into Rodin, and then I also wanted to get into male sexuality. And being a woman, it was a certain kind of journey I had to take, so I began to read Henry Miller, and I really got under the skin of that powerful, rampant male sexuality through the works of Miller.

"It was an intoxicating process," Kriel says, summing up. "And then, of course, we had to find what our story was. We started off with a short story.

"The first sixth of the film was inspired by the short story that we found, which was about two young girls growing up in a palace, one being the daughter of the king and queen, and one being the servant girl, and the friendship that developed between the two of them," she remembers.

The tale which Kriel refers to is *Hand Me Downs* by Wajida Tabassum. It appeared in an anthology of stories about sisterhood through the ages called *Such Devoted Sisters*, published in 1994. The collection included twenty stories beside Tabassum's, but it was *Hand Me Downs* that caught Nair and Kriel's attention. It involved a competition between the two friends of different classes, and how, in the end, the wronged servant made certain that she wouldn't always be the one receiving hand me downs. Her gambit involved a visit to her friend's fiancé's bedchambers on the eve of their marriage.

"We took that as our starting point and developed this narrative about these two women who develop this friendship in childhood that becomes extremely complicated as they grow up."

Although there had been flashbacks to 1972 in *Mississippi Masala* and *The Perez Family* was set in 1980, *Kama Sutra* was to be Nair's first genuine period piece, a costume epic set totally in the historical world. Developing this complex tale would take the better part of three years, during which time Nair left South Africa and directed *The Perez Family*. But for long, unbroken periods, Nair and Kriel worked together in close quarters to refine their manuscript.

"Well, we lived together for about three months, so it was a very intense kind of collaboration that happened. We were cooking together, swimming together, sharing music and families together, and it was a very dynamic and fun period," Kriel explains. "It was quite crazy [and] at one point, we were living in a little one-bedroom apartment, writing in Durban, which is a very humid part of South Africa, in the middle of the summer.

"There was construction happening right outside the window, and her son (Zohran) was eighteen months old, and he'd been kind of displaced and was unsettled and crying, and we worked with all this din around us...and we used to go and swim. We developed this habit of long-distance swimming, and it was really amazing, and so helpful. Swimming was a kind of meditation."

Kriel remembers this period of development on *Kama Sutra* fondly. The best part was that she and Mira developed "an active friendship" that was "absolutely honest" and "very creative." One day really stands out in the writer's memory.

"I'm thinking of a particular day, where we had moved into the second house that we lived. Mira's whole family was there—her husband, son, her mother and two in-laws, and they were all living upstairs, and I was living downstairs," she describes. "The downstairs was my work area, and the upstairs was the family area, and Mira and I were in separate rooms downstairs, and I was researching Rodin and had this complete epiphany, this complete creative intoxication that he must have felt with himself and his work…the kind of powerful, creative energy I think he was channeling.

"It came to me in a very intense way. I wrote a scene, and I went to Mira, and she was writing a scene, and I looked at her, and it was suddenly all visceral…a kind of feeling that I had in that moment with Rodin and the work, and the family upstairs, and the lunch that we'd cooked, and the dinner we were going to cook, and the swim we were going to have, and her in the room, and I just went to her—and I don't remember the words that I used—but I think I said '*I'm completely in love, out-of-my-mind intoxicated.*'" Kriel remembers.

"It was a great sense of creative energy happening in such a powerful way with a collaborator that was a great partner and great fun. It was total euphoria."

PASSAGE TO INDIA

Although much had been accomplished, Kriel and Nair's research for *Kama Sutra* would soon turn outward from this idyllic realm of creative partnership described by Kriel. To fully understand the world of their heroines, Tara and Maya, and the universe she was creating in the manuscript, Kriel felt it necessary to visit India herself. She had never been there.

"I had always been very interested in Indian mysticism, and as a result of that, had been quietly involved with India in my imagination, in my spiritual life," Kriel explains. But now the time had come, after three years working on the screenplay, to change that.

"Mira and I worked together for the first ten days of that trip, and then I had another two weeks when I was going to be on my own, and she'd pretty much set up quite a detailed itinerary for me that involved scholars at different points, and hotels and taxis. Everything was organized."

But Kriel was uncertain if this was the right fashion by which to experience India, and inspire the next phase of her research.

"I realized that I had to get down and dirty and get scratched and uncomfortable, and that was how I wanted to creatively do the work," she explains. "I didn't want to be too comfortable [because] I just don't think creativity thrives on being too organized or too comfortable, so basically I said to Mira that I wanted to head off into India on my own, and I wanted to go to spots we had identified as important to what we were doing, but I didn't want to do it with guides and taxis and hotels or anything organized. I basically said 'Just let me go and be a vagabond.'"

Nair responded positively to the entreaty, while noting that she had already paid for everything, and that it would be a waste of money. Kriel answered that she would live on ten dollars a day, and that would keep expenses low.

"So that was our agreement," Kriel laughs. "She gave me ten dollars a day, and I headed off and got lost in India for about two weeks, and had an absolutely extraordinary time. [It was] very intense—quite overwhelming—at certain times, but it was exactly what I needed creatively, and I think that I gained access to the spirit and culture and color of the place in a more dynamic way than if I had gone the other way.

"I think that coming from South Africa, which is quite a colorful and vivid and chaotic country in itself, landing in India wasn't as much of a shock to me as it might be to someone coming from Europe or America, or the classic 'First World' in that sense," Kriel considers. "I just seemed to jump off into India, and there was never a false step that I made in my experience with it. I felt immediately at home, completely intrigued, and in love with it."

When it is pointed out to Ms. Kriel that her lead character, Maya, undergoes a similar journey in the film, thrust out of sanctuary on her own, beyond the walls of the palace, on a voyage of discovery, she laughs at the connection.

"It's not that I set out and said 'Oh, that would be good for Maya' and 'That would be good for the King,' but through the whole experience, you become very porous," she suggests. "Everything's affecting you and coloring you, and it all comes tumbling out in the work and through all of the characters.

"Maybe the lack of comfort I felt when I just went on that little journey on my own might have affected the lack of comfort that the character [Maya] had. But I had also left South Africa and come to America on my own, and was quite familiar with being an outcast, and having to slowly move my way into a foreign place and a foreign culture. So I think it was that more directly that affected my understanding of that character."

After Kriel's sojourn through India, the screenplay of *Kama Sutra: A Tale of Love* was completed, and a story of friendship emerged. The film tells the tale of two small children in sixteenth century India. Tara is a future queen and Maya a servant, but the girls are educated together, learning dance and other skills. Over the years, Tara begins to lord her status over Maya, who grows tired of receiving only Tara's hand me downs. Then, when they are young women, Tara is promised to a young, passionate king named Raj. He is more interested in pleasures of the flesh than matters of government, and on the night before his wedding, is willingly seduced by Maya. Tara learns of Maya's betrayal, and Maya is banished from the palace.

Outside the palace walls, Maya meets young Jai Kumar, a talented sculptor who believes that Maya can help him better understand the female form for his artwork, which he often sells to Raj. Maya is slow to respond to Jai's romantic advances, but eventually they begin a relationship. When Jai proves fickle, Maya leaves him and seeks out the tutelage of an instructor named Rasi Devi, who promises to make Maya a courtesan according to the philosophies and precepts of the *Kama Sutra*.

Maya eventually becomes the favored courtesan of King Raj, over the objections of Tara, but before long, Maya seeks a deeper love and reconciles with Jai. When Raj learns that he cannot have Maya body *and* soul, the impulsive and increasingly drug-addled king fights Jai, and orders the young sculptor executed. Meanwhile, Maya and Tara renew their friendship, and Maya instructs Tara in the ways of the *Kama Sutra* too so that she might better understand the art of love, and her own self. While Jai awaits his death, forces gather outside the kingdom. Raj has neglected matters of state too long, and now war is inevitable. Maya and Jai share a sad goodbye before his death, even as soldiers storm Raj's palace, and Tara's brother Biki becomes one of the new rulers. Sad but somehow stronger, Maya continues on her journey of insight.

One thing about this screenplay that was quite clear throughout all stages of preparation was that *Kama Sutra: A Tale of Love* would indeed be a highly sensual and erotic film, perhaps even one of the most sensual films ever produced. This was not a component that Mira Nair shied from, and in fact, she has been very outspoken on the need for more films—both in the West and the East—that would honestly debate issues of sexuality.

"I make films of issues that get under my skin, and I made this film almost directly to counter the perversity with which women are being presented on our screens, not just in India, but in the West as well," Nair told interviewer Yves Jaques. "I wanted very much to go back to a time in our country when sexuality and love were something to be taken very seriously, as an art, as a skill, as something sacred."[2]

This sort of manifesto not only informs *Kama Sutra*, but was par for the course for Nair, who remains a staunch women's advocate. In the book, *Women Filmmakers and Their Films*, contributor Cynthia Felando writes that Nair is "refreshingly unafraid to depict beautiful, lusty women who openly express their attraction to men,"[3] but her views on sexuality run much deeper than that too.

"I think that Mira is a sensual person who embodies the world in a very sensual way, and certainly sexuality is something she's interested in, and she embodies," suggests Kriel.

"The way sex is treated in film today is quite naive," the writer continues. "It's all tearing off each other's clothes in the kitchen because we haven't even made it to the bedroom, and then we're on top of the table, and the buttons are popping off. It doesn't go into all the interesting ideas to do with sex and sexuality and love.

"Why should a woman tow the line and be controlled and restricted?" Kriel asks. "And why shouldn't women reflect their birth right as these beautiful, sensual creatures? The *tantra*, which is one of the very big teachings of Indian mysticism, is all about the fact that it's actually the female energy that embodies the power of sexuality, and that the male needs to allow the force of the feminine—and sometimes the force of the female—to direct the sexual route rather than him and the direction of moving toward orgasm as the directing force.

"*That is Indian*," Kriel reiterates. "That is in the Indian teachings. And being Indian and coming out of that culture, why should she [Mira] accept that women should have to tow the line?"

Still, there are people in India, particularly in government who would not appreciate the eroticism layered into *Kama Sutra*. But according to Kriel, that fear never stopped Nair. "I think she was concerned about it, but you know, was not going to have that affect any of the creative decisions, and it certainly didn't."

The first salvo in the battle to preserve the tale of *Kama Sutra* as Kriel and Nair had imagined it, was fired not by bureaucrats and censors, however, but rather the film's financiers, some of whom grew concerned when they read the completed script. Not because the film focused on matters of sexuality, but because *Kama Sutra* featured the greatest of all movie taboos: *an unhappy ending.*

"There was a lot of debate about the ending," Kriel confirms. By picture's end, a liberated Maya has lost her lover, Jai Kumar, but goes on in peace, knowing she will always carry his love inside her; and that it has changed her forever.

"We were challenged all the way along by financiers and producers about making a happy ending, and having the two of them sort of vanish off into India together and be safe, but you know, I kept coming back to the fact that we wanted to deeply affect an audience. You affect an audience more deeply, I think [with an unhappy ending]. The ending is really how you send people out, and I was quite sure we wanted to send people out with a more complicated and classical ending when the one person dies."

This was part and parcel of the screenplay Nair and Kriel had constructed, and the original intent of the artists. So they weren't budging.

"I think that we wanted to craft a kind of classic love story and didn't want to bow to the dictates of Hollywood. We wanted to be very classic in our approach, and you know, love stories end badly. They just do," Kriel elaborates. "In terms of the Shakespearean construct of the story, someone dies at the end, and I think that's because we understand that in the end, love is complicated. It's not always so easy to resolve things when emotions are powerful and you throw that emotion against the context of a life."

In particular, Kriel felt that a happy ending with Maya and Jai walking off in the sunset together, hand in hand, would have betrayed the spiritual journey that Maya had undertaken throughout the film.

"Because the *Kama Sutra* is, in the end, a spiritual document and we were trying to tell a spiritual story, we needed to have that experience [Jai's death], and the realization that the power of love had to be taken inside herself. The final voice-over when Maya leaves the place where he has been killed was…one of these ancient teachings which is very much about establishing a balance within and establishing an internality that leads to a kind of integrated life."

By Kriel's estimation, Maya's final departure from the place of Jai's physical death also involved the total incorporation of him into her spirit. Understanding that tenet would give audiences a taste of what the duo hoped to communicate in the story.

With its script complete and the ending intact, *Kama Sutra: A Tale of Love* went into pre-production. Cast in the film as the young, arrogant moghul King was Naveen Andrews, a Shakespearean actor who had starred in *The English Patient* (1996) as Kip, the mine detonator. Today the accomplished and rugged actor is beloved by international audiences for his portrayal of Sayid in the smash ABC television series, *Lost* (2004–   ).

"I first met Mira for an earlier film," Andrews remembers. "She was going to do a film on the life of Buddha. I think it was about 1991, or something like that; I know I was pretty young at the time, only about twenty-one or twenty-two. I remember being extremely impressed with her because of *Salaam Bombay!*, which to me is a piece of art. I still love that film. It's fantastic, and it's the reason I wanted to work with her.

"Unfortunately, that film about Buddha didn't get made," Andrews explains. "They dropped it because I think Bertolucci was doing his film about *Little Buddha* (1993) at the same time. So the next time I saw her was for *Kama Sutra*. I think Susie Figgis was casting it, and I can remember having one meeting and getting the part."

And his impressions of the *Kama Sutra* script? "It was fantastic. It was totally outrageous for a start. It was the kind of part that any actor would kill to play. I was just intrigued to know how it would be done and how it would be shot, etc. And I really didn't get all that until I met Declan Quinn. To me, he's a big part of that film too. The way it's lit; the way it's shot."

In terms of preparation for the part of the oversexed King, Andrews notes that, well, a lot of it came from real life. "In terms of research, at that time in my life—I think I was twenty-six—I didn't have to do that much research, to be frank with you, in terms of the King's habits. It was pretty much where I was at that time. I must say, I enjoyed it for all the wrong reasons. I pretty much lived that way then, I think."

Nor did the accomplished young actor have trepidations about a film that was designed to be so powerfully sexual. "One of my favorite films was made by Nagisa Oshima, *In the Realm of the Senses* (1976). To me, that is a beautiful film. It involves sexuality, but that's not essentially what it's about. I thought the film was made about love, a destructive kind of love, but still love. That was made in 1976, and I thought it went a lot further than *Kama Sutra* for obvious reasons [actors in the Oshima picture actually have sexual intercourse with one another on camera]. So I had no trepidations at all."

And in fact, his previous film work prepared Andrews for shooting scenes of a sexual nature. "I don't want to sound like I'm an old hand at this kind of thing, but I'd done things that were actually a little more...full on. In *The Buddha of Suburbia*, which was directed by Roger Michell and written by Hanif Kureishi, who also did *My Beautiful Laundrette* (1985) and *Sammy and Rosie Get Laid* (1987), there was an orgy and a masturbation scene. There was a dog that jumped on my back and came on my back. And just lots of man-woman scenes as well...god knows how many of them there were! I'd done that about two years before I shot *Kama Sutra*, so by that time, it was just part of the work. You don't treat it as anything radically different. It's acting, and it's a part of the work."

Andrews and Nair, did, however, discuss the kind of the man he would be portraying. "One thing that we agreed on was that he would be debauched," Andrews recalls. "You know, kind of a Keith Richards from the early 1970s, even though that's a modern context."

Casting all the king's women turned out to be a more difficult job than selecting Naveen Andrews. For the critical role of Tara—she who would be queen—*Mississippi Masala*'s Mina, Sarita Choudhury, was retained, playing a role totally different from her earlier and very memorable creation. In fact, she had originally been cast as the other lover, the courtesan, Maya.

Two relative newcomers would play the doomed lovers: Ramon Tikaram as the hunky sculptor Jai, and model Indira Varma, whom critic Stanley Kauffmann described as "one of the most beautiful women" he'd ever seen, "on screen or stage, or anywhere."[4] She would essay the starring role of Maya.

Varma was only selected after Nair auditioned more than one thousand women in London, Los Angeles, and Chicago. According to Nair's DVD commentary on *Kama Sutra*, Varma appeared at the end of a marathon four day casting call (arranged by Susie Figgis), and had a bad bout of the flu. But when she returned the next morning to read a scene with Andrews,

Nair was hooked. Varma was selected not for the role of Maya at first, but Tara.

Another beautiful woman, and one originally sought by Nair for the role of Manju's mother in *Salaam Bombay!* was cast as the teacher of the *Kama Sutra*, the sensual Rekha (1954–   ). Known for her "legendary status," in India with a "*femme fatale* image,"5 this stunning and skilled actress had presided over a film career lasting more than twenty years, and she proved a perfect choice to guide Maya (and the audience) in the ways of lovemaking.

In preparations for their roles, both Varma and Choudhury attended a course in classical Indian dancing at a school in Bangalore. The women appearing in the film underwent a strenuous exercise regime during pre-production in an effort to be as much in shape as possible and offer the filmmakers and audience a glimpse of the classical, perfect female figure for this tale about love.

Ranjit Chowdhry was also cast in (another) small role, that of Babu. "My work in *Kama Sutra* was very brief," the actor reports. "As Mira said while introducing me to the festival audience in Toronto: 'his inner beauty can be seen in the film. His outer beauty remains on the cutting room floor.'"

Conceiving the period piece's look fell to Mark Friedberg, who had designed *The Perez Family*, and his assistant, set decorator Stephanie Carroll. For Carroll, this was her first visit to India.

"India was never a place I had gone in my life, so I went, and *Kama Sutra* was a great vehicle to take me there, because they had a lot of money and time [for pre-production]. It was a lot of money for India in 1994…but it was a sixteenth century period piece, so we needed a long time to do research, and luckily, we had a great crew.

"I traveled all over the country having things made," Carroll recalls. "I designed fabric, and had it made there. I actually had the money, because services are so cheap there—which I could never do in New York with that budget—to hire a man to cut down a big tree. I then stenciled the outline of Naveen Andrew's body, who was playing the king. The man then spent a couple of months carving for me a massage table with that image. My idea was that the king was so corrupt that he had his own massage table with his body imprint in it when he laid down. So that was featured."

Carroll enjoyed collaborating again with Nair. "Mira is very visual, which is why it is great to work with her. She is also very involved, and wants to be very involved in the decisions, we [Friedberg and Carroll] made and was never overbearing. It was very collaborative.

"In the 1500s, there weren't any photographs to tell us what the rooms would look like, or what the clothes were like," Carroll describes. "So we researched these miniature paintings in India, and went to look at them with our magnifying glasses. Some of the same furniture actually exists today: the *choki*, the checkered curtains…I used the same things. The research was quite interesting…"

HOT AND COLD

Kama Sutra: A Tale of Love was shot in Jaipur, the capital of Rajasthan, and in Kahuraho and the Rajgarh Fortress following monsoon season, in October of 1995. Production lasted ten weeks, and Nair has reported that she referenced the photography of Nan Goldin and Andy Goldworthy to inspire her compositions.

The first Mira Nair film shot by her recurring director of photography, Declan Quinn, *Kama Sutra* was reportedly budgeted at seven million dollars (though some sources list three), and, among other difficulties, a crew of three hundred had to deal extensively with the hot Indian sun because so much of the film was set outdoors. By contrast, the nights were often terribly cold.

"My work intersected with Naveen and Indira for one night," Ranjit Chowdhry explains. "Very rushed, very cold. We charged through the work and fell asleep en route to the hotel. I flew out the next day.

"We shot there in December, which is the coldest month," Carroll elaborates. "We started in the summer, which was the hottest season of all, and by the end of shooting, I was wearing blue jeans, which I hadn't seen in months. The thought of wearing blue jeans over there is nauseating because it's so hot, but I actually had to buy blue jeans because it got cold shooting at night there. And I think I may have worn my first cotton sweater over there. But for him [Ranjit], you have to understand, freezing is different, because he's Indian. Still, Delhi can get very cold. It can get down to forty degrees in the winter."

More memorable for Carroll than the temperature swings, however, was the opportunity to see so much of India's incredible history. "We shot at the erotic temples. They had been hidden by dense forests in the 1800s, and the British uncovered them," she explains. "They were pristine. They weren't damaged or looted or anything, so we shot in those."

In fact, the only damage to these impressive and ancient structures was of the natural variety. "We had a castle that we had to clean up," Carroll remembers. "We had to clean up all the bat-droppings. It was amazing having to do it with cornhusks, because it was an historical location and you couldn't use any kind of solvents on it, so we hired hundreds of people to go in there and clean the castle with cornhusks. But in India, bodies are cheap; work is cheap. They don't have the machines we do. They didn't even have scaffolding, so they built scaffolding out of bamboo."

"It was like a dream come true," Naveen Andrews suggests of the shooting period in Rajasthan. "I can remember going to India with my parents when I was fourteen or fifteen, and we were in the south some-where in this Maharajah's palace, and I remember having this fantasy about coming back to make a movie...and being a king. And that I had that dream come true in these circumstances—in a proper art film with Mira directing—was very romantic and highly charged. The whole atmosphere was highly charged. In fact, I think I enjoyed myself too much."

In particular, Andrews relished "the total freedom" with the character of the Moghul King. "I'd just finished doing Kip in *The English Patient*, and I felt that he was very held, reserved, not somebody who showed feeling that easily. It cost him a lot to manifest feeling. The way he dealt with his vocation, which was life-threatening on a daily basis, was through calm and aesthetic. He got through it by inner calmness, and this character [in *Kama Sutra*] was I felt—at that time—much closer to what I was like in life. So I felt tremendous freedom to go all the way."

He also felt he had a sympathetic director. "She understands actors a lot more than many directors do," he says. "I think she's a bit of an actor herself. She pops up—does bits—in her own films. I remember watching her and thinking that she enjoys acting. That's kind of attractive as well."

In a word, Mira Nair described the shooting of *Kama Sutra* as *grueling*. At one point during the shoot, a supporting actress playing Tara's mother was felled by a stroke during the shooting of a complex exterior sequence, and filming had to be delayed. Overall, the technical demands of the film were amazing: two thousand costumes (produced by forty-five tailors), intense shooting in and around ancient temples (and refurbishing interiors to make them look "lived in") and the recreation of sixteenth century wealth using the jewels owned by Nair's family (and kept in a lock-box).

Because of its racy content *Kama Sutra* had to be shot under the false title of "Tara and Maya" in an effort to cow local authorities. When bureaucrats visited the set, Nair reportedly had to quickly stage phony sequences for visiting officials in order to maintain the illusion. Also, during production, a European financial backer withdrew its participation, and—echoing the situation on *Salaam Bombay!* almost a decade early—Nair took matters into her own hands.

"I had to raise that money, and the phones wouldn't work," Nair told *Entertainment Weekly*. "We almost had to fly people to Delhi to make calls."6

It was also during the shooting that writer Helena Kriel faced her most daunting difficulty on the project: knowing when it was time to step back.

"The biggest challenge is that when you work in a very dynamic way with a director, you have this private world that you inhabit with them, and you are collaborators, and it's very heady and very exciting, and you're in this exciting bubble with each other. [But] when the film moves into production, you don't really move with the process," she considers.

"The director then takes the film on their shoulders and moves very dynamically, and the writers stay much more on the fringe of everything. I found that challenging, because I had a very strong vision after having worked very dynamically with Mira, so to have to relinquish that completely and then allow her—which, of course, is the way that it goes in film—to take it on and express it from herself, was a challenge. So, being on set and not being able to voice my responses and my opinions, and really just watching from the sidelines was challenging for me."

THE MUSIC OF LOVE

An artist who came aboard the project late in the process on *Kama Sutra* was composer Mychael Danna, who studied Musical Composition at the

University of Toronto, where he hooked up with undergraduate and future film auteur Atom Egoyan, and began writing theatre and film scores.

"I was an India-phile," Danna informs us. "When I worked on Atom's *Exotica* (1993), I gave into my Eastern obsession and traveled to India and recorded this score that used elements from the East and West, and [included] things that any Indian would have been familiar with, melodies and references.

"When she was making *Kama Sutra*, Mira wanted to do a score that had a modern inflection as well as referencing the historical period, and, of course, the South Asian setting. I think she may have felt that perhaps a white guy from Canada who had a sympathy and sensitivity to Indian culture and love for the music would be a good choice to score *Kama Sutra*."

Like Carroll, Danna reports that Mira Nair is a strong collaborator. "She's very knowledgeable about music, and she's very involved in it. I think she has very strong ideas about music, and that is often a really welcome and helpful characteristic from a director; someone who's so well-educated about music. And certainly in the Indian-based films, that was really fun, and I was able to bring a different perspective to her, and she was able to bring a different one to me—culturally and language-wise—and we had a big overlapping area. But we each had our own circles that we had our expertise in, and we both honored that and enjoyed the education both ways. That's the biggest difference between her and most directors I've worked with. She has that profound knowledge of Indian music."

Danna recalls the process of creating a score to complement *Kama Sutra*'s ravishing imagery. "I worked before with Indian musicians, and of course I had Mira, so we had a pretty good pool of people to work with, between the two of us. For instance, she was friends with the great Ustad Vilayat H. Khan, the sitar player. We were able to work with him, which was a stunning honor. She was friends with L. Subramaniam, and the vocalist Shubda Mudgal, who is another friend of hers from Delhi. And then I had this pool of musicians that I had worked with before: G. S. Sachev on the bansuri. He's one of the most important voices in the score of this film. And V. Selva Ganesh, who Mira and I have worked with many times since, [played] on the percussion instrument called the kanjira, which is basically like a small tambourine.

"Selva Ganesh does this incredible thing with this little six-inch-diameter tambourine which you really need to see to believe," Danna continues. "A lot of time, you'll hear these incredible drum flurries and you'll imagine several drummers with sticks, but it's just one hand on the kanjira. He can make that thing speak and sing; it's quite incredible."

The ultimate goal of *Kama Sutra*'s score, as Danna recalls, was to merge the modern "feminist" story of Tara and Maya with the ancient world, and that meant a fusion of styles.

"I think that where we started was this place of a historic setting, but it's a story that's very much modern day; it's something that we can relate to in modern day, and Mira's skilled in telling female stories. It's something you don't necessarily expect to see in that period, but in fact, it works so beautifully. So our goal was really to make the story relatable to us today, even though we're seeing images of people in these gorgeous settings and beautiful costumes from another place and another time. Mira wanted the music to communicate the inner truth and the universality of the themes."

The more contemporary elements of the score, in particular the electronic percussion, originated with Danna to "add the modern inflection" to the film's ancient world. But blending time periods wasn't the most difficult aspect of the job for the composer.

"The hardest thing was to write, and tear my eyes away from the screen! It [the film] was so beautiful to look at. There were so many beautiful faces to gaze upon," he recalls. "When you become involved with a film every day and every minute of every day, it becomes your life, so to dive head first into this pool of sensuality and stay there for a few months was definitely...it was a challenge."

Mira Nair's challenge, as it turned out, was getting her new film screened in India. In contemporary Indian cinema, there is a prohibition against depicting sexual content, even a kiss, and the film was consequently banned in Nair's home country. In particular, the censor board of India wanted forty specific cuts. They basically instructed the director to "remove all the sexuality from the film," according to Nair but she retorted that "this would no longer be the film that I made."[7]

Nair combated the censorship in court with a lawsuit (asserting harassment), thus engaging a lengthy court battle with the Indian government. The government's case came down to, basically, this line of defense:

"just because we have gone global, does that mean we embrace everything?"[8] That was its way of labeling *Kama Sutra* as pornography.

Nair's case was more about hypocrisy and double standards in India than about the particulars of *Kama Sutra*. When she went to see a Bollywood movie in Hindi, for instance, she saw sex as a ubiquitous influence, it just wasn't marketed as such. "The sex was so overt in the dance sequence,"[9] Nair considered, pointing to a scene wherein a woman was gyrating on the floor while a man straddled her. In all, Nair tallied two dozen pelvic thrusts in just that one sequence. Why was this sort of titillation appropriate, but *Kama Sutra*, which was actually *about* sex without exploiting it, not deemed so?

In the end, after more than two years of lobbying on Nair's part (from October 1996 to February 1998), the Indian courts ruled in Nair's favor. *Variety* reported that *Kama Sutra* had obtained government approval for public screening in India, though with cuts of the most explicit material. The cut material included Raj's first seduction of Maya before his wedding to Tara, a scene featuring Varma's full-frontal nudity.

Once the film was cleared for release, however, Nair still had to fight the apparently less-than-honorable tactics of the censor boards which delayed release by holding up the processing of certificates. Finally, two hundred prints of the film were released in India, where it was ultimately a huge success.

"Suffice it to say that this open and frankly sexual film called *Kama Sutra* was controversial in the land of the *Kama Sutra*," Ranjit Chowdhry notes with a sense of irony. "The image that stays with me is the final one when black-veiled men ride into town. To many, it seemed that the conquerors put a *pardah* (veil) over Indian sexuality, which to date remains very evident from the lifestyles and cinema of India."

Kama Sutra also faced a degree of censorship in the United States, though of a much less intrusive nature. Hoping to avoid a controversy, Trimark Pictures reportedly "toned down" the film before release,[10] and sent it to theatres sans an M.P.A.A. rating, thus avoiding the dreaded NC-17.

When released in the United States in February of 1997, *Kama Sutra* grossed over fifteen million dollars, a decent return on the film's investment. It played in multiplexes with ad lines including "Passion. Pleasure. Power," and "In a world ruled by pleasure, love is the ultimate seduction," but all the critics weren't necessarily seduced, and *Kama Sutra: A Tale of Love*, like *The Perez Family* before it, received mixed reviews.

Some in the press found much to appreciate in the effort. Writing for *Entertainment Weekly*, Owen Gleiberman noted that the film's mood of "overripe sensuality" hit the audience like "opium."[11] Kevin Thomas of the *Los Angeles Times* described the movie as "visually sumptuous beyond description."[12]

In that vein, the *New Statesman*'s Jonathan Coe wrote that "the pervading air of sensuality" was sustained by the work of production designer Mark Friedberg and the vibrant musical score of Mychael Danna. Indeed their efforts made him feel as though he was being "seduced, expertly and assiduously."[13]

Even conservative culture hawk and movie critic Michael Medved was moved to find some love, writing in the *New York Post* that *Kama Sutra* was "a triumphantly sensual film, not just in its frank approach toward passionate sexuality, but in its seductive celebration of the colors, clothes, feasts, music, architecture, landscape and sculpture of sixteenth century India."[14]

Bill Kelley of the *Sarasota Herald Tribune* called *Kama Sutra* contrived and noted that "there isn't a complete movie here,"[15] while *Maclean's* Brian D. Johnson graded the film a "D" and complained in the February 24, 1997 issue that it was "boring."[16]

On the fence was *Salon*, which wrote that "*Kama Sutra* is bogus history and cheesy storytelling, but what the hell, it's sexy."[17]

Despite mixed notices, the film performed well when released to secondary markets, where curiosity surely boosted sales figures. Still, in an interview with *Film Force* after *Monsoon Wedding*, Nair revealed that *Kama Sutra* was the one project that didn't live up to what she envisioned.[18] Others were harsher, terming it an aberration and the "low point"[19] in her film career.

In her interview with this author in 2005, Helena Kriel discussed the film's reception, and her feelings about the project today. "I think that what we set out to do was very ambitious, and I think that most films pick out two things to accomplish. We set out to accomplish five or six things. We wanted to communicate narratively in an epic way. We wanted to communicate socially. We wanted to communicate historically. We wanted to communicate sexually and erotically, and we wanted to communicate spiritually. So I think that it was a very adventurous and bold task that we undertook. Whether we succeeded on all these levels...clearly not, but I do think that we did succeed on a number of them, which is great, given how ambitious we were.

"I am very happy to have been creatively involved in the film, and certainly it has been a wonderful part of my collaborative and creative life, and I view the film very happily and very positively.

"I know that there was quite a lot of fall-out from the critics around it," Kriel continues, "but that doesn't interest me particularly, because I think that critics can be unnecessarily vicious, and often I don't agree with what they like. I don't think they have the right to stand as gods over the creative experience. So even though there was a certain challenge with some of the negative responses to the film, I still come away feeling positive about it, and certainly positive about working with Mira."

Naveen Andrews was also impressed. "The thing that struck me was the look of the film—it's beauty, the way it was shot. The cinematography is among the best I've ever seen, the music—I thought—was fantastic. It felt like a mood piece; that's how I picked it up. It kind of reminded me of the atmosphere in *Performance*, a Nicholas Roeg, Donald Cammell film from 1970. It would have been nice if we could have gone more in that direction, but just the fact that it has elements of that is enough for me."

Regarding responses to the film, Helena Kriel also suggests that some critics and audiences may have had a difficult time swallowing the film's controversial issues of sexuality without any "sugar coating. I think that critics—if we're talking about critics now—are not very educated in terms of interesting sexuality in film, and certainly there have been interesting French and Italian films that surface. I think that *Sideways* (2004) is an interesting film. It's very honest about male sexuality, but the thing is that it had humor going all the way through it. When you take something that's challenging and you couch it in humor, people have a way of accepting it. We weren't doing that. We were making no accommodation at all."

There is, perhaps, some nobility to be found in *Kama Sutra*'s effort to be truthful without leavening itself with distractions, and Kriel holds that from her personal experiences, the film has been received warmly.

"In fact, I was traveling in Peru," she remembers, "and I was in a busload of people and there was a woman in front of me who was talking about her divorce, and she was telling the person next to her that this movie, *Kama Sutra*, had helped her through it. This friend of mine who was sitting next to me overheard the conversation and said to her, 'Do you know that the woman behind you actually co-wrote the film?' and she was completely stunned, and we got into this whole discussion, and she said that she'd written the final voice-over from the film [taken from the *Zen Ch'an*] out for herself and put it on her computer, and then read that voice-over every day, and that it was the absolute core thing that helped her through her divorce. Then she went and announced it to the whole bus, and that, I think, is what I take away from my experience with the film.

"Really, what we set out to do was communicate how love is essentially not straightforward, and how you must survive it intact, blazing and whole and light, and being able to work from this so-called scene of the crime [Jai's tragic death] with a sense of—truly—the sky over you and the smell of the grass at your feet and a sense of lightness. And that she was able to use that through her divorce was for me…I couldn't ask more than that."

A SERVANT IS A MASTER IN DISGUISE

Kama Sutra: A Tale of Love opens with a beautiful shot of tiny hands intertwined beneath the water as rose petals float about, and refracted sunlight shines down hazily from above. As is par for the course in a Mira Nair film, the entire frame is alive with activity and texture, and here the image is both a pleasing and affecting one. The two figures holding hands are little girls, a princess and a servant, but in this place—and under the softly-lapping waves—those societal constructs don't matter. These young girls are best friends and enjoying carefree play in their bath. *Kama Sutra* concerns these women, Tara and Maya, as they grow up, lose their innocence, and discover that society has placed each one in a cage. As they mature, they fight with each other over social class, and even men, but what they must really fight is a culture that makes a woman either a princess or a whore; a daughter or a wife; and doesn't leave her room to discover what *she* desires to be.

That beautiful opening moment underwater feels like a bubble of life and freedom outside restrictive sixteenth century India, and it is a freedom that these two women rarely enjoy. To express this, the film follows parallel tracks as Maya the servant creates her own destiny because she doesn't like the hand society has dealt her, and Tara forges hers too, only belatedly, and with help from the former servant turned courtesan.

Kama Sutra's first minutes focus on the youthful rivalry of the two girls, first in dance, then in material wealth. Maya doesn't like wearing Tara's leftovers or "hand me downs," and Tara certainly lords it over Maya that she is a princess. When King Raj Singh (Andrews) arrives, and Maya catches his eye, Tara very publicly spits in Maya's face, a brutal and disrespectful act that raises the stakes between the women. Going far beyond what many viewers expect, Maya undertakes a mission adapted directly from Tabassum's short story. She goes to the king's bed chamber and—on the eve of Tara's wedding night—makes love to him. Now something that Maya has used is Tara's forever, in Maya's words.

Maya's act feels a bit spiteful, yet it is all part of this rivalry and the quest for Maya to discover her place. It is a necessary step in her maturation.

"Maya was always the vulnerable one," Helena Kriel considers "and Tara always had control, and Maya had to take things into her own hands. She had to stand up and say 'Enough.' Tara spits at her, and there are many incidents that happen before that act of betrayal on Maya's part where Tara is constantly manipulating her and being cruel to her. That's the first thing.

"The second thing is that I don't think we were exploring it in these very black and white terms about 'this one's the hero' and 'this one's the villain.' Love, I don't think, is black and white and I've always maintained that," Kriel explains. "I think that it was Maya taking the situation under her own control, even though she understood that there would potentially be a huge fallout from that. She was prepared to take that chance and make that choice, because I think that as a personality she was too wild, too rambunctious, too creative, too powerful, to accept what was handed down to her.

"You have to understand the story in cultural Indian terms," Kriel suggests. "This caste system is a thoroughly ingrained one, even though it's obviously abolished by law and everything. It still exists. It's very, very rare that you're born into the servant class and manage to graduate yourself out of that. It's still very entrenched in the whole culture of India, and I think it was a powerful story to take someone who was born as a servant and refuse to have that as her destiny. It was actually taking on everything that was encoded in her culture, and flies absolutely in the face of it. So, if you think of it in those terms, perhaps Maya was quite heroic. Even though what she does [to Tara] is complicated and not something that we would easily accept."

In fact, Maya has a great deal in common with another Mira Nair movie heroine, *Vanity Fair*'s Becky Sharp. Both emerge from the lower classes, both must depend on their wits and charms if they wish to succeed, and both desire a better position in life. What Becky never realizes, but which Maya does, however, is that social status is a trap. Though Lord Steyne warns Becky that there is nothing behind those social doors she wishes so desperately to pry open, Becky pursues social privilege anyway.

Maya undergoes a slightly different journey, however. She is educated in the ways of the *Kama Sutra* and some of the petty forces that drove her to revenge are cleansed from her person. She learns of the concept of wholeness, of togetherness, of love as both an act and an emotion. By the time she faces the ultimate terror of any person in love—losing that partner—she has learned perhaps the ultimate lesson too, to keep that love as a part of her, even though the physical being is gone. The film appropriately concludes with Maya declaring that her heart is "as open as the sky."

This line of dialogue has been misinterpreted by many critics who perhaps merely gaze at *Kama Sutra*'s luscious photography, rich colors, and supple flesh. These reviewers believe that Maya is somehow dismissing the death of her beloved Jai Kumar in this remark, but that is not the case. She has learned what she needed to learn from the experience, and Jai will always be a part of her, but Maya has done an important thing and *internalized* that love and made it part of her essence. If that sounds like New Age nonsense, don't blame the movie, blame a text written in 300 AD.

Tara's journey is a different one from Maya's. She is born with all the privileges of royalty: new clothes; the best instruction; every need fulfilled by servants. Yet she is not a complete or happy person in any sense of the word, as she learns when she crosses the threshold into adulthood. She is merely property to be transferred from one male owner to another. She knows nothing of love, or lovemaking, and so is a bitter person. But Maya, her spiritual if not literal sister, helps to educate her. At the end of the film, one feels Tara has learned too, and perhaps may even rule Raj Singh's kingdom with Biki, her brother, helping out.

Near *Kama Sutra's* conclusion, when Tara and Maya reconcile, some of the film's most cogent images are brought forward. Maya comes upon Tara in a palace pool after Tara has slit her wrists in desperation. Maya leaps into the water to help her friend, and suddenly there is a quick cut to a flashback, a view of the two childish hands touching one other beneath the surface of placid water, and their friendship is instantly reconnected. The rose petals in their earlier bathing scene, however, has become the crimson of Tara's blood, a sign of how badly things have gone for her. By visually referencing the first shots of the film, Nair reinforces the notion that Tara and Maya's friendship is a lasting one, even if turbulent at times.

After Maya has nursed Tara back to health, she is kind, and teaches Tara the ways of the *Kama Sutra.* In these scenes, they are violating the rules of society, and in a repeat of the film's opening images, they are often shot together in what might be interpreted as a "bubble world," one outside the confines of a repressed society. In one shot, Tara and Maya are back in the water of the pool. In another, they are depicted together in a close-shot and we see their reflections in a mirror—a surface which represents another pocket or alternate universe of sorts. Finally, their last shared composition is another tight one involving Tara and Maya beneath a tent of blankets, another domicile hidden from society. These places where they can share their togetherness are an indication that—in the "real" world of the sixteenth century—such sisterhood across the classes must be cloaked, or exist outside the norms of society.

Beneath a blanket, underwater, glimpsed in a mirror's glass and always so tightly framed, these shots suggest that Maya and Tara have almost seen their friendship squeezed out of life by repressive society, but for isolated moments, and yet in these bubble universes, the friendship survives.

Kama Sutra is an unceasingly beautiful film filled with meaningful imagery. We have witnessed in *Salaam Bombay!* and *Mississippi Masala* how Mira Nair is a strong closer, and how she pulls together all the film's themes in many of her concluding shots. Here, she does so yet again, primarily with canny visualizations. Our last views of Maya see her bundled up, bracing against a harsh, dusty wind. Also, she is depicted walking *against* the winds of war as troops storm Raj's palace and she heads in the opposite direction. These images are ones of bucking the tide, marching alone against a superior force, her society, but not being blown down by it.

Despite such efficient and meaningful imagery, one almost feels while watching *Kama Sutra* that the film's themes somehow get sidelined or minimized amidst a lot of the non-symbolic imagery. This is a film so beautiful, so opulent, so filled with dynamic, rich color, gorgeous locations and the bodies of some of the most attractive people ever seen on film, that it is hard to focus on the story. Nair has stated many times that she never wanted to create a staid period piece. *Kama Sutra* certainly isn't staid, but it does have something in common with many period pieces. It's overwhelming beauty causes, nay *invites* viewers, to step back and admire what's on display. The characters, their story, the machinations of the plot all become secondary considerations in this fashion and that's regrettable, because there is so much potential and beauty and spirituality in what has been imagined.

Sometimes, making a sumptuous and luxurious film comes at a high cost. In *Kama Sutra*, that price is that audiences will love the pretty pictures, be awed by the looks of the performers, and totally miss the film's carefully imagined point. For many viewers, that's precisely what occurs. Indeed, the film is all those things the critics have praised it as being: tantalizing, sensual, and languorous, yet those surface qualities undercut the very message of Kriel and Nair's story, that love must come from within, and ultimately transform what is within.

How else could the film have been done? With drab colors, ugly actors, and uninteresting sets? Not by a long shot. Kriel is on to something when she says that if *Kama Sutra* fails at points, it is because of ambition. And because it is incredibly—indelibly—gorgeous.

THE ONLY CHANCE TO PLAY HERO

In 1994, a riveting and heartbreaking account of one doctor's battle with the AIDS epidemic in the American South was published to wide acclaim and admiration. Titled *My Own Country: A Doctor's Story of a Town and Its People in the Age of AIDS*, this is the unforgettable true story of Dr. Abraham Verghese, an Ethiopian-born Indian physician and specialist in infectious diseases, recounted by the good doctor himself. Written with directness and compassion, and a flair for observing the myriad details of life around him, Dr. Verghese's book remains a riveting and dramatic read, exposing the story of the AIDS plague in a seemingly unlikely place, the rural Tennessee town of Johnson City, population fifty thousand, in the mid-1980s.

A sensitive and compassionate man, Dr. Verghese had dreamed of becoming a journalist since he was a youngster, but his parents encouraged him to go into medicine instead. He started medical school in Ethiopia at the age of sixteen, but was forced to abandon his schooling during his third year because of political strife and civil war. He emigrated to the United States with his family in 1974. "It was a terrible feeling," he told *Texas Monthly*'s Joe Holley, "being labeled an expatriate in your own country. I loved Ethiopia."[20]

After working nights as an orderly in nursing homes around the tri-state area, Verghese traveled to India and attended a Madras medical school for five years to earn his degree. By 1980, he and his family were back in the United States, and Verghese was growing more educated about his chosen field of specialty—infectious diseases—especially as the so-called gay plague of the early 1980s became known as AIDS. After a time at Boston University, Verghese began his tenure at a veterans hospital in Tennessee and started caring for AIDS patients. At first he encountered only a few such people, but then, all too soon, their numbers increased, until finally his caseload included eighty patients.

Dr. Verghese's book is an account of those lives that touched his during this span; their importance and dignity and impact. Yet *My Own Country* is also a personal story.

"The most frustrating thing is to have a disease where all you can do is hold your patients' hands," he has commented, but for Verghese, salvation came because he was forced in his association with AIDS patients to confront what it truly means to "be a doctor."[21]

My Own Country is also the journal of a self-described "foreigner" in the American South, a man without a home to return to, who ultimately finds acceptance from the sick men he treats, but ironically not from either the peers in his professional community nor his family, many of whom—including his wife—fear him as the town's so-called AIDS doctor.

"The tantalizing and fascinating paradox of *My Own Country*," writes Rajini Srikanth in his essay *Ethnic Outsider as the Ultimate Insider: The Paradox of Verghese's My Own Country*, "is its suggestion that sometimes to be the ethnic or racial outsider is to be the supreme insider."[22]

Dr. Verghese was interviewed for this text from his office at the University of Texas Health Science Center in San Antonio in early 2005, more than a decade since *My Own Country's* publication. Today, he is a widely-read author whose pieces have appeared in *The Atlantic*, *Esquire*, the *New York Times*, and *Granta*.

Verghese still remembers how he began writing his story, an odyssey which would ultimately consume three years of his life. "It was very exciting. I never thought I'd be writing non-fiction," he says. "I actually went to Iowa in 1992 to write fiction, and I was admitted to the Iowa Writers' Workshop. One of the stories that I published was called 'Lilacs.' It was an AIDS story, and it was published by the *New Yorker*. And when the editors of the *New Yorker* read a bit about my background, they seemed interested in a long non-fiction piece on AIDS in the heartland."

Dr. Verghese went on to diligently prepare a proposal for the piece the editors had proposed, using George Orwell's literary style as his guide, but when Verghese turned in it in, he discovered there had been a regime change at the periodical.

"As it turned out, when I put together a proposal, they turned it down for many reasons. The editor I was working with was leaving and another one was arriving, so I was left with essentially a book proposal," he laments. "And that was really how *My Own Country* came about. We shopped around the proposal and made the book."

While writing *My Own Country*, Dr. Verghese soon came to realize that his developing text wouldn't merely be a medical (or dispassionate) view of AIDS in the Bible Belt, but a peek into his own personal and professional life as well. Though he hadn't imagined it that way, he became the narrator of the tale. At first, that thought was a little shocking to him.

"I don't think I realized right off the bat that the book would be about me in that fashion," Verghese acknowledges. "I really thought it was going to be about the people in the town and the patients, and it came to me after awhile that clearly I was one of the characters in the book, in many ways. What became an interesting theme was to explore how I was reacting. I became sort of an eye for the reader to identify with. That may just be the nature of non-fiction. There always has to be an eye, but for me it almost became a narrative strategy with that book. Not consciously, but almost by lots of coaxing. The way my thinking changes becomes a significant part of the story," he suggests. "My own understanding becomes the reader's understanding, which I think is true of all non-fiction."

Coming from an accomplished wordsmith, *My Own Country* delivers more than a clinical recounting of dates and names. It is a moving, indeed compelling read that once started can't easily be put down. Verghese enhances the book with his near-perfect technique, including his choice to begin it with a powerful and succinct vignette, a look at a desperate and sick young man fleeing New York and driving home for distant Tennessee. No characters, including the narrator, have yet been introduced, and the vignette is penned in the present tense, granting it an uncomfortable immediacy.

"I'm not sure that I came to that chapter as a start right away," Dr. Verghese reveals. "I think that very often as you write a book, you come to the opening chapter later, and then you realize this is the opening and go back and make that happen. I liked the idea of starting in *media res*, in the midst of the action, as they say. We also start in the present tense. Just the sense of trying to invite the reader into a subject that may not be particularly inviting if you read the dust jacket; something that captures their attention and hopefully keeps them. That was the goal."

The resulting book—some four hundred thirty-two pages when completed—was published to terrific notices. It was nominated for the National Book Critics Circle Award, and Frank Rich of the *New York Times* termed it "one of the most affecting [books] the plague has created."[23] Others were equally complimentary. *Entertainment Weekly* noted that it was a difficult read because of its emotional subject matter, but ultimately "unforgettable" because of its "superb craft."[24] *U.S. News and World Report* found the effort both "groundbreaking" and "heartbreaking,"[25] and Dr. Verghese felt very gratified by this reception.

Far away, in Hollywood, others were also starting to take notice of *My Own Country*. Foremost among these was writer and producer Jim Leonard Jr., an experienced scribe who has worked on such television series as the sci-fi/horror anthology *Night Visions* (2001) and the American version of the British crime-drama, *Cracker* (1997).

"I think I read the book the year that it came out," Mr. Leonard remembers. "And I read it because my agent at that time had said 'There's a book that I think, just from the coverage of it, that you would be interested in adapting.' So he had told me the nature of it, and then I read the book quickly because it was such a good read. It's just a beautiful, beautiful book, and I really wanted to do it."

In fact, *My Own Country* touched a nerve with Mr. Leonard, as it has with so many other readers. AIDS had touched his life too.

"One of my closest friends had died of AIDS ten years previous to this," Leonard reports. "He had grown up in a small town in Indiana, and had dealt with a lot of the same issues as some of these characters had, in terms of not being terribly well-accepted, and that had affected me tremendously. He was the best man at my wedding, and had baptized my children, and was a very dear friend, and in many ways I wanted to do this to honor him. Also, I just loved the book. I couldn't read the book and not be moved by it."

Leonard began the process of adapting *My Own Country*, and it was no easy task. Not only was the book very long, but it featured more than two dozen characters, all of great importance to the narrative, and it is written, but for a few passages, in the first-person voice.

"I had my assistant at the time pull out—and she spent so much time doing this—all the dialogue, character-by-character," Leonard explains of his starting point. "I began to think about who was the most moving." Because there was so many characters, "there was no way to tell all these people's stories," Leonard acknowledges. "The key became extracting a few key stories and following those threads through.

"My first draft was huge," Leonard reports. "It was two hundred twenty pages, and then I had to narrow it down and keep trying to find the focus, and a way to keep Dr. Verghese [as a character]. [In the book] Dr. Verghese told almost nothing about his own marriage and his own family life. He was very protective and careful with that, and yet I knew that he had to be the main character and that you had to establish that, and it was very tricky."

Leonard also wanted to avoid the idea that the film might just be another "disease of the week"-type television production, and thought he could do so simply by presenting the material as it had been forged in the book. "At that time, there had not been that many films done about AIDS," he suggests. "Certainly, it was a very different take: backcountry people as the door to this disease."

Once finished with his adaptation, Leonard knew precisely where to take the manuscript. "I had written other material that Showtime responded to, and I was just extremely passionate about this book," he describes his pitch. "Showtime was really interested in it, and loved the book as well. I think it was my second or third draft that they were really thrilled with, and ready to go [with]."

Meanwhile, Dr. Verghese learned from his book agent of Showtime's interest. "I think that the expectation was that it would be very unlikely that they'd actually make it," he reports. "There are so many instances of people buying the rights and then nothing happens. I wasn't really paying attention to it, and then I got the word that they were actually going to make it, at which point what had been a very small payment became a much more significant payment."

Verghese had no interest in writing the screenplay. "I didn't care to for two reasons. First, I'm not a screenplay writer. And secondly I just thought it would be very hard for me to take my book and have to do the kind of pruning and spare narrative that you have to find to make that narrative work," he explains.

"I was just in the background. I made no stipulations, and at some point, the screenplay writer, Jim Leonard—a nice guy—showed me the script. He was doing a very good job of working very hard, but it seemed to me that it might be missing some of the insights and the richness of both my point of view and the richness of that particular culture."

Meanwhile, Jim Leonard was fully engaged in the hunt to find a director for the suddenly green-lit project. "They [Showtime] had liked some really interesting British directors, which made sense, because they were used to working on a Showtime-sized budget, and they'd done some really beautiful work. Their director choices were not bad; they were actually quite lovely," Leonard remembers, "but I had seen *Mississippi Masala* and some of Mira's other work, and I just thought she made such sense for this project on every level…"

"It was Jim—and I give him all credit for this—who really pushed Showtime to try to get Mira Nair," establishes Dr. Verghese. "Because it was really important that this was a story being told by an Indian-origin person. The view was not Indian, but it was certainly foreign. That was part of the charm of the book, I suppose. Here was an outsider getting to know the inside traits of a community and seeing it even better than the insiders see it. Sometimes it takes an outsider to see that stuff."

While Leonard lobbied for Mira Nair, he also happened to find his perfect Dr. Abraham Verghese at a multiplex, after viewing *The English Patient* (1996). He knew immediately that actor Naveen Andrews, who had already worked with Nair on *Kama Sutra*, was the man.

He telephoned Showtime about Andrews, and the organization "got in contact with him and loved him, but they were less convinced about Mira, who I did not know at all, although I had met Denzel Washington through my friend, Dan Pine, who I was working with at the time on some other projects. Dan and Denzel eventually did *The Manchurian Candidate* (2004) together, and they've done a number of things, and Denzel had nothing but good things to say about Mira.

"I campaigned for her very hard," Leonard recalls. "I think she was the right choice. Not the only choice, but the *perfect* choice, and Dr. Verghese was also familiar with her work and loved her as well."

But getting Nair's involvement was challenging, and Verghese understood her reluctance. "I'm sure she had some reservations, because this was a television movie which meant limits on budget and time, and a different format than what she was used to," he explains.

Still, Jim Leonard was not willing to accept "no" for an answer. "I had gotten her fax number in South Africa and I just faxed her repeatedly, until she or someone in her office called and said 'Please stop faxing me,'" Leonard says.

At this point, Leonard and Nair got in touch, and Leonard urged the director to read the book, and if possible, the screenplay. When she began to read coverage of the book, Nair gradually became more interested. Then Leonard urged Dr. Verghese to call her himself to cement her interest.

"She was not involved. She had not read the book," Verghese reminds us, setting the scene. "Jim had me speak to her on the phone while she was in South Africa, and she said 'I'm really busy with other stuff, [and] to be honest I haven't read the book. I've read of it, and I've read the reviews.' And I said, 'Before you make up your mind, would you read the book?' And so she read the book over a weekend and called me back and said she was going to make the movie; that she just loved the book. I think that was a tremendous moment for me. The sense that someone was inspired to make the movie who had not been inspired to do that before. That was really quite a big moment."

And so the deal was made.

"She came on board and I was elated," Leonard remembers. But soon things took another turn. "I think we had one conversation, and she said, basically, 'I want to go back to the book, and follow especially the early parts of the book more closely,'" Leonard remembers. "I said 'I attempted to do that in my first draft and Showtime said they didn't have the budget for it,' and she said, 'I think that may change, and I want to talk to my friend Sooni about how to do that, and it wasn't until later that I realized, 'Oh, she's talking about hiring another writer.'"

"Mira came to Bombay at the time they were offering her this," notes Sooni Taraporevala, "and she was very hesitant about whether to do it or not. She had the script with her, and the book, and I took a very quick read through the book and the script.

"I loved the book," Taraporevala continues, "and so what I did—with Mira's blessings—was I introduced the concept of the voice-over, and I basically reread through the book and we went back and forth about what we both liked in it." From there, it was a matter of making sure that those elements were included in the script.

Dr. Verghese confirms the shift in writing staff, at Nair's behest. "The first thing she [Mira] did was look at the screenplay, and she really wanted to rewrite it. Effectively, she and Sooni [Taraporevala] rewrote the screenplay, and this time I had a lot of input, and I wasn't shy about giving input. I didn't write it, but I read it very closely.

"I think Mira had just finished making *Kama Sutra* and that she had a sense if she had made a mistake on that movie, it was not to have really got the screenplay down perfectly before shooting. So she really invested a lot of energy making sure the screenplay was just perfect. Perfect for her, so she could shoot it," Verghese said.

For Leonard, it was difficult to see his involvement with the project come to an unanticipated end, but he sees the situation in perspective today, and ultimately as par for the course in moviemaking. "It's very common in film. Absolutely common," he notes, describing how directors often bring in new writers and other staff with whom they are already comfortable. "[Still] it's heartbreaking for a writer who is jettisoned, no matter who they may be.

"The important thing to me was that the book was honored, that Abraham was honored, and I think Abraham enjoyed the process and felt good about it," Leonard states. "I would just say that Showtime deserves a lot of credit for sticking with this project and going to the mat to make this happen."

And the differences Leonard ultimately saw between the two drafts? "I think I spent more time with the patients than she [Nair] ultimately did. She spent more time with him [Verghese] and his wife, and with his decision to arrive there and all that, and I just put him right into it."

"Jim's screenplay was a great start. It got us all going," adds Dr. Verghese. "But I felt very, very fortunate that Mira came aboard. I give a lot of credit to Jim for being the person to push for her presence."

With a director ensconced and a rewritten script prepared, Mira Nair set about the process of pre-production on *My Own Country*. She contacted Naveen Andrews about the lead role.

"Again, this time I think it was Mira who rang and said, 'I have this script and we can't think of anybody else to do it'—which is always flattering to an actor," says Andrews. "I believed it was true, so I said 'Great, I'd love to do it,' and then she said it was for Showtime, which meant that the schedule was like four weeks to shoot a whole movie. But the cast was Marisa Tomei, Swoosie Kurtz, Hal Holbrook and Glenne Headly—a really good cast—and once I read the book, I was very intrigued. I thought, 'It's going to be a lot of work to compress into four weeks, but I'm going to have a go see if I can do it,' and I'm really glad I did."

It was also during this pre-production period that Nair contacted Phillip Barker, an experienced production designer who has won widespread acclaim for his work on such films as Atom Egoyan's *The Sweet Hereafter* (1997).

When interviewed for this book in early 2005, Barker had just completed an assignment on Egoyan's latest film, *Where the Truth Lies*, a murder mystery about a duo of comedians not unlike Jerry Lewis and Dean Martin.

A lover of film and art-making since college, Barker draws creative inspiration from his father, who was a super-8 filmmaker in the 1970s. Barker is also renowned for his original "installations," outdoor projections of films onto buildings which incorporate live action, music and imagery. These stylish exhibits/pieces were seen throughout the 1980s in Holland, Spain and Canada, among other places.

"I had a call from Mira, who had just seen *The Sweet Hereafter* and was looking for someone who could bring a sort of realism to their film, a believable realism," Barker begins. "For her, I guess, it was her first TV film. She asked me to work on the film and, of course, I knew her work and was thrilled. *Salaam Bombay!* was the big film for me that I completely love, and I think I had just seen *Kama Sutra*, and I realized what a visual flair she had. I try to avoid TV films, but this was one of those experiences…it was undeniable that I wanted to do that film."

Fortunately, there was time for Barker and Nair to conduct some research on the project together. "We had a grace period of a couple of weeks before we started pre-production, where we went to Tennessee. Mira, the producer, and I met Abraham Verghese and he showed us around and introduced us to the people that are mentioned in the book, the people he worked with."

Verghese was happy to return to Tennessee and introduce Nair and Barker to the people he had written about, but it was still a bit strange to return under the circumstances of making a film.

"I'd already gone through that a little bit in terms of having been back there after the book got a lot of attention, and I'd been back there with *Good Morning America*," Verghese notes. "It was always strange, and this was also a little strange, but not quite as strange because we weren't going with lots of cameras and stuff. It was a sightseeing trip, and Mira was shooting some film with a simple camera, mostly just meeting people and getting the feel of it."

"It was totally amazing," Barker recalls of the trip. "I'd read the book by then, and I was meeting people he'd written about and was being invited into their homes in this small coal mining town. We met and had coffee and tea with his surviving patients, and the survivors of the family members that had died of AIDS. It was really affecting."

Because of the limits of a television budget, the scouting mission was an essential component of preparations. *My Own Country* would not be able to afford shooting in Tennessee. Instead, the crew was limited to Canada, but this trip gave the creators a chance to get a feel for the real town.

"When I think of it now, a lot of images come back to my mind about those homes we visited," says Barker. "Like often there would be shrines or altars to the deceased person. Often it was simply a collection of framed photographs around a television set. But we were helped by these people. It gave us a feeling of flavor."

The trick was matching and recreating that flavor in Canada. "We had to find these similar homes and exteriors, and with the meek budget, we had to do a lot," remembers Barker. "There was a lot of landscaping involved. Southern Tennessee flowers and plants and trees had to be added. The Canadian vegetation had to be removed, and then we had to import native vegetation from the southern states."

While Barker worked to recalibrate Canada to Bible Belt specifications, others in the cast and crew also did their due diligence. Naveen Andrews, playing Dr. Verghese, opted to study the real thing.

"Basically, I persuaded the network, Showtime, to let me go to El Paso, which was where Abraham was working, at Texas Tech, and be with him for about two weeks," Naveen Andrews relates. "I had recordings of him, but I got to hang out with him and go with him on his rounds and see how he interacted with patients. I also found out a bit about him personally, which is always invasive and you feel kind of embarrassed about doing it. But after all, you want to do a good performance, and we got that shit out of the way, and he wanted me to do a good job too, so it was essential that I go out there and meet him, and we actually ended up really getting on and being mates. It was great."

"Naveen came and stayed with me for a week, and learned to 'do me,' so to speak," Verghese elaborates. "Here he is, this English-born

Shakespearean actor learning to do my hybrid accent, and he did that very well. There are some people who see the movie and are convinced that it's my voice in the voice-over at the outset."

Also cast in the film were *The Perez Family* alumnus Marisa Tomei as Mattie Vines, and her brother Adam Tomei as Gordo Vines, Mattie's sibling. Hal Holbrook and Swoosie Kurtz were signed to play the Flanders, a tragic but "respectable" Christian couple who had contracted AIDS when the husband Lloyd (Holbrook) had a blood transfusion during an operation. Later, his wife Hope acquired the disease through sex.

Glenne Headly portrayed Vickey Talley, who also acquired the disease from her husband, a closeted bisexual named Clyde (Oliver Becker). Ranjit Chowdhry appeared in a small role early in the film, and Ellora Patnaik essayed the role of Dr. Verghese's wife, Rajani.

When describing the commencement of shooting *My Own Country*, Barker recalls that Nair set a wonderful tone from the start. "There was a mood of family," he explains. "It began right from the first day of shooting when Mira's mother—who often comes to the set and is around a lot when she films, at least in those days—blessed every member of the crew with a smudge [of red tika powder] on their foreheads."

Barker was also impressed that Dr. Verghese visited the set. "There was a feeling from the crew that we were doing something worthwhile, especially for a TV film. Most people who work on TV films are not that involved in the story, because the stories are not generally that good. It's a job. But working with the crew…it kind of transformed us."

But that doesn't mean it was easy. "It was a very hard shoot. Long hours. Difficult. But it made everybody stick together and hold on," says Barker.

And working with Mira Nair? "She's a passionate woman who really loves what she's doing and has a huge interest in many things. She really listened to what I had to say and was interested in my work. My impression was certainly that she is a warm and inviting woman whose passion for her work is a little bit threatening in the sense that I was obviously stepping into this huge amount of work. And knowing her films, this was a high standard to reach. My concern at the time, and throughout the film, was the amount of money we had to make it, knowing that she was used to a certain—not expense—but creative level in her films."

Barker goes into further detail. "She was working on a very different level and degree of perfection that was perhaps more than the production company was used to, so we were pushed quite a bit to get all the things Mira wanted. And we did a lot for so little.

"I remember, for instance, there was a scene that's a Thanksgiving dinner scene, and I believe it's the parents of a boy who has AIDS, and they're waiting for him to come home. And he never does come home, he has an accident. It was a simple scene of his family having Thanksgiving dinner. We had a set. We'd built a three-wall set of a dining room in a house, and all the props to go inside it: a table, paintings, chairs, a turkey dinner, and we tried to squeeze it [the scene] into the schedule four times, where we actually built the set. But there was no time to shoot it in the day, so we took the set down, put it in the truck, and drove off to the next day's shooting," Barker says. "And the next day's shooting was at a hospital, so we found an interior in the hospital and built the dining room again and set it up for Thanksgiving dinner, and hopefully we'd squeeze that shot in at the end of the day. It didn't happen. So we did it again…"

"Mira was like that," Barker explains. "She'd say, 'Come on, let's keep trying! Let's do it again.' So we set it up many times and never did we film it. But it was indicative of how Mira was intent on getting everything from this production, to her credit. I think that's why the film has a very lush, detailed look to it."

Not only did Mira Nair push the crew, she was a dedicated advocate for it. "It's insane, this time line of a TV film," Barker explains. "It was much less than we would normally have [on a film]. And we went over, I believe. I think we had an extra week because Mira was very good about convincing the producer to spend more money on the project. I remember that about her. She was the art department's friend. She would always fight for the times we needed to go over budget."

"It was very hard, the work," Andrews agrees. "It was exhausting, really exhausting. But you know what? Sometimes it's good to do a bit of hard work every now and then, you know?"

For Andrews, he found his greatest challenge on the film to show different shades of Abraham Verghese. "The challenge was to bring out what I personally knew about Abraham, and he was quite happy for me to show it, and yet because it was a movie of the week, you weren't able to do certain things…the use of profanity—things like that. So that was always going to be a challenge, to find what I knew was underneath.

"Abraham agreed with me at the time, and I'm sure he still does, but as a doctor you present his kind of facade to the world, and it's almost impenetrable," Andrews continues. "It involves charm, ease and a way of dealing with people. Behind that man is a living, human being who is susceptible to the slings and arrows that all of us are. Doctors are human beings, if you know what I mean, and to show those things within the constraints of the script, if you like, that was written for Showtime, was a challenge. But I thought that some of them did come out."

One of the few battles that Nair lost in crafting *My Own Country* involved Tennessee. She pushed hard to get a small team back in Tennessee to shoot some location establishing shots. The powers that be refused, but Barker is a super 8 mm filmmaker and takes the camera wherever he travels. And, indeed, on that first trip to Tennessee with Dr. Verghese, he brought it with him.

"It's like my diary. I just shoot stuff all the time. I shoot hundreds of rolls," Barker laughs. "I was just shooting. I was shooting the view from the airplane window, flying over the farms, out the back window of the car, going through the streets—filming homes and flavor and scenery. Sometimes I'd just aim the camera up into the air and shoot passing trees going overhead. I always do that, and from that it's like a sketchbook for myself in film, where I pull my ideas to make my own films from.

"I had maybe four rolls of super 8. I remember when she was finally denied the chance to go to Tennessee and film establishing shots, I thought, 'Hey, I've got this stuff,' and she said, 'This is perfect!' Not only was it establishing shots, but it had a flavor from the past; a grainy film look to it."

But before Barker turned in his rolls to Nair, he shot a little more. "I'd gone back to Toronto and I had these rolls of super 8 and I was taking them to get processed, and I had a bit of film left, so while I was driving to process the film, I stuck the super 8 film out my car window as I was driving and just shot wildly. I didn't even look through the viewfinder. I didn't even know that it was there when I gave Mira the film.

"She found it."

Indeed, Mira ended up utilizing those shots of green leaves going by overhead as *My Own Country*'s leitmotif, the viewpoint of a boy driving home to Tennessee, his body ravaged with AIDS. These shots appear in the film at least three times, and finally, in the climax, accompanying Verghese's final voice-over, where the meaning of the shots becomes plain...and touching.

Naveen Andrews' most vivid memory of Mira Nair springs from that final sequence in *My Own Country*, in which the audience sees Dr. Verghese leaving Tennessee—his home—for a new town and a new beginning.

"I'll tell you one thing that stuck with me that I've never forgotten. It was her doing that last shot of *My Own Country*. Abraham was driving in the car and his family was with him," he explains. "It's a shot through the windshield of the car, on him, as he's driving along. Mira just came up to the window of the car, because we were in the street, and it was one of those things where the car is being pulled and the camera is on a rig, and she just said, 'I haven't got any notes or direction. Just this.' And she leaned in and kissed me. Right on the lips.

"It was really nice, and she went back, and we did the shot, and that was it," Andrews reflects. "But there was a kind of purity about it. I don't know...it was like an elegy. It was the end of the film, and there was a certain mood and a kind of grace. If anything came through—not to make too much of it—it was maybe a bit of that. I remember that. It's about her, really."

Emotions of a different type emerged on the day that Dr. Verghese visited the set in Toronto, a strip mall that had been converted into a doctor's office for purposes of fiction, when tragedy struck.

"I went up there for one or two days of shooting and it just so happened on the day that I was there, an assistant director—a very young [pregnant] woman [named Sylvia]—suddenly collapsed in front of us," Dr. Verghese recalls somberly. "It was clear to me that she'd had a cerebral bleed. One of her pupils was blue."

Dr. Verghese treated her on the street pavement, aware that time was of the essence. "Blood was accumulating so rapidly," he later wrote, "that it had pushed the brain down, jamming the third cranial nerve on the left side and causing the pupil to lose its nerve supply and dilate."[26]

Fortunately, an ambulance arrived in time to get the young woman to the hospital for treatment.

"I wound up writing about that [incident], about life intruding on the movies, in an article in the *New Yorker* [entitled "Last Acts"]. Verghese describes. The piece, from September 22, 1997, meditates not on just this incident, but also on the deaths of Princess Diana and Mother Teresa during that time.

Following the completion of shooting, work on editing the film began, and there was a concerted effort to keep the film down to ninety minutes. Its running time was ultimately ninety-five minutes, and some things were lost in the process.

"I think that several scenes were cut because of the time constraints," Dr. Verghese points out. "I think there were a lot of scenes that were filmed that never got used, some with Swoosie Kurtz. The more leisurely pace of a movie might have allowed more exploration of things in depth, [but] I was in awe of the whole process. It was all new to me, the way it was edited and put together. I just liked every aspect of it. The quick flashback to Africa? That was something that Mira did, something that she took from a piece that I wrote for *The Atlantic*. She used that pretty much in doing that scene."

MY OWN SUCCESS

My Own Country premiered to high ratings on Showtime on Sunday, July 12, 1998 at 9:00 pm. Nominated for a GLAAD Media Award for Outstanding Television Movie and Miniseries, the *New York Times* reviewed the movie twice. Critics Jim Leonard (on July 13) and Ron Wertheimer (on July 18) each independently awarded the film a grade of "A."

Many other reviews tended to be only mildly enthusiastic. *The Advocate* wrote that the film's heart was "in the right place," but that the story had already been covered "frequently in newspapers, films and TV news magazines."[27] Writing for *People*, Terry Kelleher opined that it was a "worthy effort," but one that could have used "a script doctor."[28]

"I would have done it differently," says screenwriter Jim Leonard. "I loved the casting, I just would have done it a little differently. I felt like it was lacking in narrative at some points. [But] she's a very good filmmaker. There are some beautiful, beautiful moments in it."

"The difference is that some people use the book as a jumping off point to get somewhere else," Taraporevala continues. "We didn't use the book as a jumping off point. We gave the book the respect I think it deserved. I don't know how well it was received, actually. I think some people had problems with that approach. But you can't please everyone."

Ranjit Chowdhry, who shot just one day on the project in Toronto, remembers feeling "startled to see the finished product." He considers *My Own Country* a "very powerful film with superb performances."

To date this film unfortunately has still not been released on DVD.

BASED ON A TRUE STORY

Mira Nair's small-screen adaptation of Dr. Abraham Verghese's riveting *My Own Country* is, for the most part, a faithful retelling of his work, only some stories have been shortened or abbreviated for the sake of time. In this case, however, it is what has been added, not subtracted, that makes the effort a unique work of art. Those additions are, essentially, the powerful imagery of the book, brought to vibrant and intelligent life.

Whenever films (especially television films) about disease are broached, there's usually a ubiquitous somber tone, a sense of importance, and words like "bravery" and "nobility" seem to pop up with boring, predictable regularity. It's as though the seriousness of the topic precludes a filmmaker from embracing narrative and stylistic risks, lest a viewer or critic make the judgment that the subject matter—here literally that of life and death—has not been "respected."

However, Mira Nair's film does not shy away from such risks, relying on moments of visual daring and even, at times, lightness to relieve the oppressive sense that this work is about "an important thing" (which of course, it is).

An essential ingredient of Verghese's book is the chaotic humanity of the characters, especially the gay patients who have contracted the disease. These men don't apologize for who they are, and they are the sum total of their every life decision and choice, and in the book are depicted in every shade of reality. By turns, they seem humorous, bitter, determined, defeated, hopeless, outrageous, petty, in denial, triumphant, etc. They are far from the stereotypical ciphers of most "disease of the week" television productions whom we simply must pity because they have contracted a disease.

My Own Country succeeds because Nair is willing and able to capture something of this real life complexity in each of the vignettes involving patients. Using the technique of the flashback, she is able to grant the audience a sense of whom it is losing to HIV, and the fact that they are more than a pitiable creature to shake our heads at in despair. Remarkably, and gratifyingly, she does so via images, not merely through dialogue.

Gordo's story is a prime example. He is a closeted gay man, and yet that descriptor limits him only to his orientation and behavior. Nair's camera takes us back in time to show something of his special and unique spark, a moment when he is using his talent to please others. He is depicted singing on stage at night in a tux and a top hat. Two of the people in his life, his sister Mattie and his mother, are seen in one of those trademark Mira Nair "extended moments." They dance the night away, and it is the calm before the storm. There's so much resonance within this image, including Gordo's talent, Mattie and his Mom's love and enjoyment of his performance, and our own fear of what is come, and even his mother's denial. She can enjoy this moment for what it is, a tribute to his talents, but does not understand, perhaps, how his sexuality fits into his very persona. And that's why he disappears from his family's life for so long. They love him, he understands, but that's quite different from accepting him.

Later, in the same vignette, there is a surfeit of white light allowed into the shot, as if the film is overexposed, and the flashback takes on a dream-like, almost heavenly quality. It's another moment of joy for the family that reminds us of the earlier one, and another patented Mira Nair lyrical and impressionistic moment.

Noticeably, this vignette also opens with a long establishing view of a suburban neighborhood, and little water bubbles blow across the frame, floating about in what seems a touch of romance and hope, a dash of color and life in an otherwise routine setting (a metaphor, perhaps, for Gordo, also someone special amidst the routine of suburbia).

In each of these three instances, Nair could have opted for clinical detachment, for staid, tried-and-true camera techniques, but instead, her images express the *feelings* of the scene. Bubbles blowing lazily across a street to give us an idyllic view of childhood; a family reveling in a brother's performance, their enjoyment captured in slow motion; and finally the dream-like haze of a good memory before things turn irrevocably bad.

In the film's opening vignette involving the boy from New York and his arrival in the Tennessee hospital, Nair uses her frame to express something else, authentic horror. A spray of blood mars a shirt and as AIDS enters the picture, "fear spread like wildfire." Again, it would have been simple to compose shots in a strictly Euclidian way, reflecting this terror, but instead, Nair expresses visually the feelings of the medical techs, doctors and nurses who fear infection. Her camera pans slowly over their contorted faces— another extended moment, and the full impact of their fear is tangible.

It's illuminating that Nair is able to harness this image for two distinctly different purposes. On one hand, we sympathize with these terrorized faces, and the fear of infection (a fear that Verghese is also susceptible to), but on the other hand the faces also reveal a kind of irrational, paranoid fear that is somehow loathsome, prejudiced. Nair's camera presents these contradictory ideas in a single shot.

That ever-present Nair quality of mercy, perhaps inherited from her spiritual predecessor, Satyajit Ray, is evident in *My Own Country*, as Nair allows us to see both sides of Verghese's marriage. His wife is quite obviously unsupportive of his career choices, spurred on by the probing questions of her friends ("so how is your husband and his AIDS?"), but instead of depicting her with contempt for being a bigot, Nair is merciful in her treatment.

In a single pull-back (staged in the Verghese family foyer), Nair facilitates a view of this woman's essence as she dances. *All alone.* The camera pulls slowly away from her, giving a sense of the empty surroundings and isolation, and one suddenly comprehends how much she has given up, away from her family without even her husband to keep her company. Her hatred of AIDS results not just from prejudice, but from the fact that it is the disease that has become her husband's new (metaphorical) mistress.

Finally, Mira Nair's leitmotif, a hazy, slowed-down view of trees going by from above, has a devastating punch, connecting the beginning of the film to the finale. In the voice-over, Verghese notes that if that young man from New York were making his journey today, he would find a Tennessee more ready to accept him; certainly more able to treat his sickness. His voice-over takes us back to the film's opening moments, and the image metaphorically does the same thing. It is a beautiful and haunting image, a bookend both impressionistic and daring. Again the film could have easily survived without it, but the joy of virtually every Mira Nair production is in the manner she finds complementary images to reflect and augment the content.

This is an important conceit carefully layered throughout the film. Since one of *My Own Country*'s major themes is finding a home, and what it means to be an outsider in a community, the production team was encouraged to bring out that angle.

"That was definitely discussed," notes Phillip Barker. "There were to be two worlds going on; one of the West and one of the East, and that came through in the way the family house was decorated and the colors that I chose; [for instance] the definitely very warm marigold stained glass front door. It had a really Indian feeling to me, and in color and simplicity we tried to invoke interiors in India in that house.

"There was an analogy there," he continues. "The AIDS victims were outcasts, and there was an analogy to Abraham being an outcast because of his chosen profession, which is infectious diseases. You can almost see the brewing or continuing interest of that in Mira's other films, in the different structures within the Indian society. Certainly it's reflected in *Monsoon Wedding*."

Naveen Andrews agrees that Mira Nair's origins as a Western-educated Indian impact her art, and indeed, represents the subject of her art. She, Dr. Verghese, and even Andrews himself share this quality of being a part of many cultures.

"I can only relate it to my own experience, which is that I was born in England in 1969. I was the child of immigrants from India who got married in 1965 in England," he says. "I always thought that I was an aberration. The way I think intellectually is European, but my soul is Indian. There was always this dichotomy going on while I was growing up. You know, not really confusion, but just like, 'What is this thing that I am? Is it good or is it bad?' I knew it was different, but what the fuck was it? Is it going to kill me, or is it going to destroy me, or is it going to be an asset. I have to say now that I'm older—thirty-six—I've kind of accepted it. I may be an aberration, but I feel pretty good about it and wherever I am, it's something unique. I think Mira keys into that."

Indeed, the title *My Own Country* refers to Dr. Verghese's quest to find a place where he will be at home. For him, it is America, warts and all, that represents that ideal.

"That's what I love about America. They haven't got hang-ups like the fucking English," suggests Andrews. "I've lived in Los Angeles for the last seven years and I have to say this to you, I never considered myself English until I came to America. Americans see me as English in a way the English never did.

"I firmly believe that the American people...there's something great there; something good. I know that this country has a really checkered history, but at the same time, it's also produced James Brown and Muhammad Ali. They could not have up come anywhere else. People should remember that."

This theme—the search for home—truly separates *My Own Country* from the run-of-the-mill television film. This is not to suggest that it is a perfect film. It is very difficult to express on film the climactic notion of the book, that Verghese—in a fit of loneliness and despair—pulls everything together and comes up with an original and brilliantly researched discovery about the trends regarding AIDS in small, rural towns. There is a genuflection to this idea in the production, but it is a brief one. In fairness though, this is really just an example where the words—the theory itself—are easier to parse in print than translate into some compatible imagery.

That established, *My Own Country* also evidences the courage of its convictions, following through on one of the most controversial and least-talked about aspects of the book. In the book, Verghese has a discussion with his wife when she asks if he is sexually attracted to the gay men who are his patients. Verghese answers affirmatively, and makes the interesting argument that gay men might represent male sexual behavior and patterns in the most basic, unadulterated form. Because gay men do not have the "limiting" outside mores of female partners to worry about, they are able to express their needs in the way that they most desire and, in fact, may be the most natural for the male sex.

The adaptation of *My Own Country* preserves that deeply thoughtful conversation in its totality. Literally word for word, and that alone assures that it breaks new ground in its genre. The result is a film more often than not highly dramatic and involving. The view Verghese espouses is surely unpopular in these conservative times, when a politician such as U.S. Senator Rick Santorum wantonly equates homosexuality with bestiality, but the view is on display here, fearlessly unexpurgated.

"I really think that given the circumstances of shooting in a very short time, given the contingencies of a television movie as opposed to a feature film, Mira did a remarkable job," Dr. Verghese told this author in February of 2005.

"I thought I was incredibly lucky because it could have easily come out as a terrible movie with another director and another screenplay. It captured many of the moments that were very meaningful to me, so by that standard, it was very successful."

THE BEST MEDICINE:
THE LAUGHING CLUB OF INDIA

In 1999, Mira Nair returned to the world of documentaries for the first time in nearly fifteen years to craft a thirty-four minute film called *The Laughing Club of India*. Adam Bartos was her photographer on the project, Barry Alexander Brown (*Salaam Bombay!*) her editor, and Sabrina Dhawan—future writer of *Monsoon Wedding*—served as an assistant director and researcher for the film, which introduces viewers to a physician named Dr. Madam Kataria. He founded the original laughter club in March of 1995 after considering the *Reader's Digest* page whose header indicates "laughter is the best medicine."

Nair came to this unusual subject by accident, finding herself in a traffic jam in Bombay, and then encountering banners for "World Laughter Day."[29] She suggested to Bartos that the movement would make a unique subject for a documentary, and they were off to capture the phenomenon.

Shot in August 1999 the film reveals all the hallmarks of a Mira Nair motion picture. It opens with a long, sedate pan across an Indian metropolitan skyline, and then, dispensing quickly with formality, deposits the viewer onto street level, into the thriving life of the city which bustles with traffic, games of cricket, children playing, and men going off to work at an electric company. The quick cutting of the piece keeps it jaunty, and then before we know it, we're at a meeting of the electric company employees (in their blue overall uniforms) and it looks as though they are about to raise their hands in prayer.

Instead, they start laughing. Madly, uncontrollably and incessantly.

The camera then adopts a high angle, so audiences can detect the numbers of people involved during this strange ritual, and finally the documentary settles down into the meat and potatoes of the story, revealing first person accounts from participants who come from all walks of life, whether they be hairdressers or doctors.

The beauty of the laughter club, one participant notes, is that it is a thing with no form, no fee and no fuss. In other words, it's totally about freedom. Added to that, another participant—this one a female—makes note of the fact that Indians live carefully restricted lives, and this laughter club grants her the opportunity to express nonsense.

Watching *The Laughing Club of India*, one might even detect the seeds of *Monsoon Wedding*, Nair's next feature film. Her camera captures street billboards for cell phone services, Internet access and the like, and everything featured on camera is all about the hustle and bustle of a growing, modernized nation. In fact, gazing at this contemporary India, where everybody is on the run, one has to wonder if in the process of globalization, an American sickness has infected India, the need to always be at work.

The laughing club feels like an antidote to this increasingly fast-moving world, and Nair's camera catches children learning to laugh in school, and even snippets from Dr. Kataria's tour to New York City to sell laughter as a form of yoga and meditation.

The last portion of the documentary advances the notion that humor could be the cure-all for cancer, or a cough, but neither Nair nor Dr. Kataria—a practical fellow—seem to really give that thesis a lot of credence. Instead, they seem to view the laughing club in *social* terms. It brings people together who otherwise might be lonely, like the older woman whose birthday gets celebrated by a hundred of the participants. The clubs also provide some with a sense of hope. One member has a "sad heart," and has not left her house for six years following the death of her husband. But now she passes the time laughing instead of sitting alone and moping.

If God has given us problems, as one interviewee suggests in the documentary, then laughter is surely the way to face those problems head-on, and *The Laughing Club of India* considers this idea with a touch of grace. It bears the distinct stamp of Mira Nair, filled with dancing, motion, color and life.

The Laughing Club of India premiered on cable television's Cinemax on August 28, 2000, and won the special Jury Prize at the Festival International de Programmes Audio Visuels of the same year. It has been released on DVD with several other short documentaries under the umbrella name *Full Frame: Seven Complete Documentary Shorts*. And not surprisingly, Dr. Kataria's work goes on to this day. By 2005, there were eighteen hundred laughing clubs in India, and seven hundred more around the world, stretching from "Finland to the Philippines."[30]

"Life is such a comedy," states a character in *Monsoon Wedding*, and *The Laughing Club of India*—light as a feather but charming and witty—seems to understand that. It deals with topics like loneliness and loss, but shows how we can get past them. And in that sense, it is typical of Mira Nair's ethos. Even when life is bad, it is good.

5

Monsoon Wedding (2002), *Hysterical Blindness* (2002),
11'09'01 (2002), and *Vanity Fair* (2004)

MONSOON WEDDING (2002)

A USA Films release of an IFC Productions presentation of a Mirabai Films production in association with Keyfilms/Pandora Films/Paradise Films, *Monsoon Wedding*.

Crew:

Music	Mychael Danna
Line Producers	Shernaz Italia
	Freny Khodaiji
Associate producer	Robyn Aronstam
Costume Designer	Arjun Bhasin
Production Designer	Stephanie Carroll
Film Editor	Allyson C. Johnson
Director of Photography	Declan Quinn
Screenplay	Sabrina Dhawan
Executive Producers	Jonathan Sehring, Caroline Kaplan
Producers	Caroline Baron, Mira Nair
Director	Mira Nair

Cast:

Lalit Verma	Naseeruddin Shah
Pimmi Verma	Lillete Dubey
Ria Verma	Shefali Shetty
Aditi Verma	Vasundhara Das
Hemant Rai	Parvin Dabas
P. K. Dubey	Vijay Raaz
Alice	Tilotama Shome
Tej Puri	Rajat Kapoor
Chadha	Kulbhushan Kharbanda
Shashi Chadha	Kamini Khanna
Ayesha	Neha Dubey
Mohan Rai	Roshan Seth
Varan	Ishaan Nair
Rahul	Randeep Hooda
Tuppa Girl	Sabrina Dhawan

HYSTERICAL BLINDNESS (2002)

HBO Films presents a Karuna Dream/Blum Israel production of a Mira Nair film, *Hysterical Blindness*.

Crew:

Casting	Sheila Jaffe
	Georgianne Walker
Executive Music Producer	Alex Steyermark
Music Composed by	Lesley Barber
Film Editor	Kristina Boden
Production Designer	Stephanie Carroll
Costume Designer	Kasa Walicka Maimone
Director of Photography	Declan Quinn
Producer	Lydia Dean Pilcher
Associate Producer	Laura Cahill
Executive Producers	Uma Thurman, Jason Blum, Amy Israel
Screenplay	Laura Cahill (based on her play)
Director	Mira Nair

Cast:

Debby Miller	Uma Thurman
Virginia Miller	Gena Rowlands
Beth	Juliette Lewis
Rick	Justin Chambers
Nick	Ben Gazzara
Bobby	Anthony de Sando
Amber	Jolie Peters
Carol Ann	Callie Thorne
Fiancé	Jeff Aaron
Tanya	Laura Cahill
Michael	Alex Draper

VANITY FAIR (2004)

Focus Features presents a Tempesta Films Granada Film Production of a Mira Nair film, *Vanity Fair*.

Crew:

Casting	Mary Selway
Music	Mychael Danna
Film Editor	Allyson C. Johnson
Production Designer	Maria Djurkovic
Director of Photography	Declan Quinn
Associate Producers	Matthew Faulk, Mark Street
Executive Producers	Jonathan Lynn, Howard Cohen, Pippa Cross
Screenplay	Julian Fellowes, Matthew Faulk, Mark Skeet
Based on the novel by	William Makepeace Thackeray
Director	Mira Nair

Cast:

Becky Sharp	Reese Witherspoon
The Marquess of Steyne	Gabriel Byrne
Amelia Sedley	Romola Garai
William Dobbin	Rhys Ifans
George Osborne	Jonathan Rhys-Meyers
Sir Pitt Crawley	Bob Hoskins
Rawdon Crawley	James Purefoy
Mr. Osborne	Jim Broadbent
Young Becky	Angelica Mandy
Mrs. Pinkerton	Ruth Sheen
Mrs. Green	Lillete Dubey
Joseph Sedley	Tony Maudsley
Mrs. Sedley	Deborah Findlay
Mr. Sedley	John Franklyn-Robbins
Pitt Crawley	Douglas Hodge
Lady Southdown	Geraldine McEwan
Lady Jane Sheepshans	Natasha Little
Mrs. Matilda Crawley	Eileen Atkins

YOU ARE FORMALLY INVITED TO...

Mira Nair's greatest cinematic success since 1988's *Salaam Bombay!* remains *Monsoon Wedding*, the story of the Verma clan, a middle-class Punjabi family in New Delhi preparing for the wedding of its only daughter, the lovely Aditi (Vasundhara Das), to an Americanized Punjabi, Hemant Rai (Parvin Dabas). The film escorts viewers through four turbulent and exciting days of preparation as the large family gathers. Lalit Verma (Naseeruddin Shah), Aditi's father, worries about expenses, Aditi carries on a secret affair with a married man, and a dark family secret is exposed through the bravery of the lovely Ria (Shefali Shetti), an aspiring writer.

Our view of this busy, colorful, fast-moving middle-class world is contrasted with that of the Verma's harried tent-contractor, P. K. Dubey (Vijay Raaz), an independent entrepreneur who dwells in Old Delhi with his stockmarket-obsessed mother. While preparing and waterproofing Aditi's wedding tents, Dubey falls madly in love with the Verma's sweet, unassuming maid, Alice (Tilotama Shome). In the end, there are two joyous nuptials in the rain, two *Monsoon Wedding*s, to celebrate. It's a dazzling, affecting motion picture about family life that, as Professor Nair has stated, was made, at least metaphorically, at her own "dining room table,"[1] reflecting her family life in India.

Like many of Nair's earlier films, *Monsoon Wedding* underwent a dramatic development phase before production commenced, but the project originated with a young and intrepid Punjabi writer named Sabrina Dhawan. Considered by herself to be something of an anomaly in her Delhi-based family of physicians, Dhawan broke ranks with tradition because she wanted to work in the film industry.

"It wasn't one of those things where I knew what I wanted to do when I was really little," Dhawan reports. "Because I really thought I would be a doctor growing up, because that's like the family profession."

However, because of uncertainty about finding the right pathway to a successful filmmaking career, Dhawan did for a time attend medical college, but then quit the program after a month or so. Instead, she earned a Masters Degree in Communications Research from Leicester University in England. For three years following her education, she worked as a journalist in India, serving as a correspondent for *Newstrack*. She also worked at an advertising agency.

"In India, it's kind of overwhelming to get into film," Dhawan considers. "There's a big industry in Bombay, but you wouldn't even know how to get started there. So I felt like the best thing for me to do was to go to film school, and I was really interested in going to film school in America."

With this goal in mind, Sabrina Dhawan traveled to the United States in 1996 and enrolled at Columbia University's film school. It was there, in New York, that Dhawan commenced planning on a short Hindi language student film entitled *Saanjh*, or in English, *As Night Falls*. It was a difficult project to mount, but one that would eventually garner Dhawan a "Best of the Festival" prize at the Palm Springs International Short Film Festival in 2000.

"I wrote the short while I was in film school," she confirms. "When you do something as a student film, you really want to keep the production pretty simple because it's complicated and it's hard, plus—most importantly—you don't have much money, so you can't have special effects and things like that. You try to keep it simple. The short that I wrote is set on a train, and I knew it was really going to be hard, but I wanted to do it.

"So I was getting ready to go to India to shoot my short film, which was quite a journey in itself. Before I left, I bumped into Mira at Columbia University Film School," Dhawan reports. "When I say I bumped into her, it was quite literally that I bumped into her. I just saw her on the fifth floor of the film division and thought I should go say 'hello' to her and, anyway, I finally did. I mustered the courage to go up and say 'hello.'"

Dhawan introduced herself to Professor Nair, and to her delight, Nair had already learned of Dhawan through the outstanding reputation she had developed at Columbia. They spent a few minutes talking together, and then decided to adjourn for a cup of tea.

"We went to a café and had tea, and I gave her a copy of the script of the short film I was about to shoot, and she took a copy home and read it, and called me back the next morning to say that she really loved it," Dhawan remembers. "She said that it was amazing, and that if I ever wrote something, I should definitely show it to her, and we would work on something together."

It was this offer to collaborate that led, over a period of months, to the development of *Monsoon Wedding*. And even though Nair always maintains a busy—perhaps even hectic—schedule, she and the young student from Columbia found ways to stay in touch.

"When she read my short script, she was living in South Africa," Dhawan explains. "She was going to move, was in fact *about* to move to New York, but hadn't moved as yet, so we exchanged some e-mails, but [then] she was going to India to shoot a film that was set in Bombay called *Bombay 2000* or something, which then she didn't make. But she was in India and we communicated over e-mail, and we'd actually only met once at the time.

"Then I left for India and I worked for four months to get the short [*Saanjh*] together. It was very hard. You have no idea how hard it can really be when you have no money even to make a student film. And there was great difficulty shooting in India," Dhawan recalls.

"In New York, you can have friends from film school help you, and they understand at least as much as you do about running a film set because they've worked on student shorts, and they've been exposed to the same education. But in India…you're doing everything. You're the production manager, the location manager, the person giving out the food…so it's very trying.

"I was off dealing with getting my short made, so we [Mira and Dhawan] started talking [via e-mail] about how it would be nice to do something together and what could it be?," Dhawan continues. "I was keen to do something set in a middle-class family that also dealt with sexual abuse, set in Delhi. Mira wanted to do something during a wedding. So I put those two ideas together, but I couldn't start writing it then, because I was so busy with my short and Mira was in India getting her movie ready."

As fate would have it, Professor Nair moved to New York just as Dhawan returned from India and commenced editing *Saanjh*. Nair and Dhawan met intermittently to talk about different film projects, but nothing concrete.

"Then we went on to different things, and I was in a writing class and I just wrote the script [for *Monsoon Wedding*] very quickly, a first draft," Dhawan says. "I wrote it because I had to have something ready for the class, and I'd been thinking about the movie. The professor of that class told Mira that I had written the script, and Mira asked to see it."

The only problem was that Dhawan didn't really want Nair to see it, because she had written it in such a hurry, and it was only a first draft. Nair, however, insisted. What the director read she responded to instantly, because, as Dhawan has stated, it reveals the "other side"[2] of India, the modern, globalized, upwardly-mobile view.

"She's more than ten years younger than I am, and what was really startling to me about her perception of New Delhi was the whole new amorality of it, the sexuality of that younger lot," Nair later reported, highlighting some aspects of the script that had fascinated her. "I did not know what was going on in the bedrooms, back streets and universities as much as she did."[3]

In developing the script, Dhawan found Nair very supportive, and a collaborator who would not sacrifice the quality or honesty of the film to make it more "universally" appealing, as some people may have preferred. And she credits that decision for the film's ultimate success.

"It is the most remarkable thing," Dhawan says, considering the development of the script, and the qualities that have made *Monsoon Wedding* so popular both in India and abroad. "I teach at Columbia now at the same program I went through. It's something I tell my students, and it's something that I realize, and it's a law of screenwriting that I've discovered like a law of gravity that is absolutely and utterly true, which is: the more specific you are, the more universal you become.

"The thing is, I didn't have many masters to serve when I was writing it [the script]," she suggests. "I was writing it for myself, and I didn't think it would ever get made, much less made and be successful and be nominated for a Golden Globe and become the film that it became. So when you're not writing with the audience in mind, and you're not writing to sell a script for millions of dollars, you can write the truth. Even when Mira read it, the most important thing to both of us was 'Let's be honest.'"

That honesty came about in many difficult choices early on, Dhawan relates. "Certainly it came when we were thinking about language. If it was an all-English film, it would have a greater audience than a subtitled film, which don't do as well in America. But Mira said this wonderful thing to me. She said 'Just be honest.' So I said 'Okay.'

"Then, one time I got nervous about having a bride who has an affair the night before her wedding, because in India that wouldn't go down. I thought, 'God, they're going to kill me!'" Dhawan remembers. "But then I said, 'Just forget it, I'm going to be honest;' honest for *that* character.

"Once you are just specific enough to be absolutely honest to the character you are writing and the world you're in, everything else doesn't need translation, because people understand," Dhawan says. "It just becomes universal. People understand relationships. They understand what it means to want love, or feel insecure or be angry, so as long as you make them truthful and real, it doesn't matter what country you put them in. Or what time you put them in. You could put them in the fourteenth century and it would still resonate, or mean something today."

With the *Monsoon Wedding* script meeting both of their specifications, Nair soon informed Sabrina Dhawan that she believed she could get the film produced, and furthermore, the director believed she had a way (and style) in which to craft the film.

In particular, Nair's inspiration came from the Dogma 95 artistic manifesto, a pact in which a number of like-minded filmmakers, including *Dancer in the Dark* (2000) director Lars von Trier, pledged to adhere to ten cinematic commandments of "purity." Essentially, these were vows of chastity and economy, which promised that filmmakers would eschew Hollywood-style excesses and commit themselves to natural lighting and sound, and depend heavily on hand-held cameras. Essentially, it was a restoration of the neo-realist movement popularized by such international directors as Satyajit Ray (in *Pather Panchali*) and Vittorio De Sica in *The Bicycle Thief* (1948).

"At that time, Dogma films were the flavor of the year," Dhawan remembers. "They were really popular, and Mira wanted to do something which wouldn't cost a lot of money, where you could do something where you focused on story and performance and strip away the other elements of moviemaking, like big sets, and pare it down to its bare bones."

In fact, the tenets of the Dogma manifesto were ones that Mira Nair was quite familiar with, and which she often preached to her students at Columbia. To craft *Monsoon Wedding* in a short span of time, using minimal money and resources, was a way of challenging her students by example, a throwing down of the gauntlet, to put her money where her mouth was, so to speak. Nair also wanted the freedom to do something she wanted; the freedom, even, to fail, in that pursuit.

"When we first started thinking about shooting the movie, it was actually going to be done on digital video," Dhawan reveals. "And Arte [a French financier] was interested in doing it as a digital film. It was going to be something really small, something that could be shot in thirty days. That was the idea."

But, not surprisingly given the lush visuals of Mira Nair's film canon, there was a hitch. Although Nair wanted *Monsoon Wedding* to be her most personal cinematic work to date, as always she also wanted to capture the flamboyance and passion of Indian life, of *her* life. This was a quality that could easily be lost in the highly efficient, yet not particularly attractive or lush medium of digital video.

"Mira and I went to Delhi to go back to the country and get rein-spired," Dhawan describes. "We went to a wedding in Delhi as well, and Mira was shooting some things on her digital camera. But when she looked at it, the colors and the beauty and splendor of an Indian wedding could-n't be captured as well as it could on film. So we thought, 'Maybe we *should* do it on film,' but we still wanted to keep it quick and efficient and hand-held."

This course adjustment required one resource: *more money*. As she had on many other occasions before, Professor Nair—the business woman—quickly sought new financial aid for her project, and eventually brought the film's budget up to a still-meager one million dollars.

"IFC came in and were willing to give us more money so we could shoot on super 16 mm instead of digital, which is what we shot on," Dhawan remembers. But with more financial backers also came more creative partners, and that meant some trepidation about the film, which featured a subplot about child molestation. In the movie, Ria must free young Alia from the grasp of the same family friend who hurt her years earlier. This requires not merely Ria's great courage, but Lalit's as well, for he must confront the corruptor as the wedding begins, even though this "friend" has promised to help pay for the celebration and sponor Ria's education in America.

"When we were pitching the story, and then when I had a proper first draft and people read it, there was some concern that the tones wouldn't mix," Dhawan remembers. "You know, it was a lighter romantic film and this very dark element comes in, and how do you get an audience to bounce back from that revelation and then celebrate the wedding and feel happy in the end? So there was concern about that. It was unnerving to wonder whether it would really work."

And how did it come to work so well? According to Dhawan, Nair retained the subplot in its entirety, and the performances were so successful, so human, that audiences were already fully involved with the characters by the time the serious subplot was broached. Dhawan was glad it wasn't lost, not only because it made the movie "deeper" dramatically, but because it gave the family another challenge which would bring everybody—and their diverse plot strands—together.

"The family has a crisis, the family comes together, and it is a proud family. It's about this father who is an everyday kind of father who becomes this real life hero," Dhawan considers. "And then, I do think that the performances were so good that the elements come together in a way that made it possible."

Despite investor trepidation about the serious subplot, *Monsoon Wedding* was officially a go at a higher budget, but the strict restrictions on the shooting schedule would remain. This was a film that, by hell or high water, was going to be shot in a very short amount of time.

"Even though we had upgraded from digital video to film, for some reason, we still kept the shooting days at thirty," Dhawan ponders. This would prove a major difficulty because the script included nearly seventy characters and quite a few big set-ups. Some plot lines, including those featuring actor Roshan Seth, were pared down before shooting to make sure that the impossible could be accomplished.

"We cut down the script as much as we could before we started shooting," Dhawan describes. "Even the love story between the Australian cousin and the Indian cousin—the young kids—was also more fleshed out in the script than in the movie."

While Dhawan saw to the script and preparations were made for shooting to commence, Mira Nair continued seeing to the back-end of the filmmaking process, particularly editing. She wanted her editor on *Salaam Bombay!*, Barry Alexander Brown, to work on *Monsoon Wedding*, but there was a scheduling conflict.

Allyson C. Johnson, a graduate of the State University of New York at Purchase and an aspiring editor who had cut several documentaries, entered the scene. She had recently worked with Bill Moyers and for A&E Television and was currently apprenticing with Brown.

"Barry Brown was asked [by Mira Nair] to do *Monsoon Wedding*, and he was working on something else, and he and I had worked together a lot so he said [to Mira], 'Just give Allyson a try. I know she doesn't have a lot of feature experience, but I will be there if you have any questions at all. I will be there to come in and talk to you about things,'" Johnson remembers. "He was just wonderful. He was really my mentor in all of this."

Nair agreed, and an interview was arranged with Johnson. "I had one meeting with her before they went to shoot," Johnson recalls. "We talked a little bit about my work, and the way I work, and the kind of work I had done. Of course, a documentary background—with a director like Mira—really helps. She too comes out of documentaries and really respects that side of the business. Then it was funny, because she was off to India and I didn't see her again for months!"

Once she knew she had the job, Johnson had the opportunity to read the *Monsoon Wedding* script, and it was one that resonated with her. "You know, it's such a wonderful script. My family background is Bulgarian," she says. "I grew up with grandparents who had Bulgarian accents, though I was living in the United States. There's a very different feel when you have grandparents who come from another country, and I felt very close to the family that was in *Monsoon Wedding*, which is probably part of why it was so successful, because so many people can identify with that kind of large family unit. It was so rich with characters and it was just terrific, a great script from the very beginning."

While Johnson waited for the first footage to return from India, *Monsoon Wedding* began pre-production in New Delhi. The large cast, sixty-eight players in all, rehearsed for two weeks in a workshop so filming, once begun, could be achieved quickly. In Mira Nair's estimation, the rehearsal period was akin to a dance, a choreographing of all the movements in the film. At her side, she had cinematographer Declan Quinn, whose keen eye would capture the action.

Among the cast was the legendary actor Naseeruddin Shah, who had nearly played the role of the pimp Baba in *Salaam Bombay!* and probably remains best known to American audiences for his roles as Captain Nemo in *The League of Extraordinary Gentlemen* (2003) and that of a suspicious detective in the Michael Douglas/Gwyneth Paltrow thriller *A Perfect Murder* (1998). It was Shah who recommended Vijay Raaz for the critical role of the comical and touching P. K. Dubey, a character the world would soon fall in love with.[4]

Roshan Seth, late of *Mississippi Masala*, also had a small role. "I was so much on the edge of that film, I actually almost fell off," he jokes. "She [Mira] was desperate for me to be in it, because it was a difficult character. He was mean to his wife, who wants to have a good time. But again, like everything else, they got involved with the other side of the story, and those characters weren't well developed. It was just being there for a couple of shots and that's it. But I'm glad the film worked, and I rather liked it."

"Roshan's story was the one where most of it went," Dhawan acknowledges. "He played a bureaucrat, a very Anglicized man, and he belonged to this very anglicized world of Oxford and Shakespeare, but he had this problem that he used to beat his wife, and he had this wife who's an alcoholic."

The point of these characters in the original script had been to balance this (unflattering) portrayal of marriage with that of the Vermas, wherein everything seemed well and happy. Despite the thread's removal, one can still catch resonances of this subplot in the final cut. "There are little things left over from that story that manage to be in the film," Dhawan agrees. As for the rest? "It just wasn't essential enough, I guess, so it had to go."

A SHORT HONEYMOON

A veteran of *The Perez Family* and *Kama Sutra*, former set decorator Stephanie Carroll landed the assignment of production designer on *Monsoon Wedding*, and recalls falling in love with the script, and knowing just how to bring it to life.

"What was interesting about *Monsoon Wedding* is that I had never seen the modern India portrayed in films," she relates. "It's always kind of hokey, or people think of it as Bollywood, but there are very sophisticated people in India, and very wealthy and very educated people, and the world

Monsoon Wedding (2002) **TOP** Old India meets Modern India when Alice (Tilotama Shome; foreground) falls for hapless, lovelorn tent maker Dubey (Vijay Raaz; background). **LEFT** Here comes the groom. Hemant Rai (Parvin Dabas) cuts a dashing figure on horseback. **RIGHT** Meet the bride: The lovely Aditi Verma (Vasundhara Das) sheds a tear.

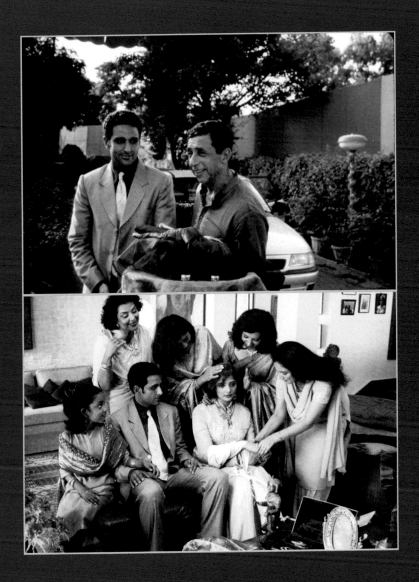

Monsoon Wedding **TOP** Groom-to-be Hemant (Dabas) meets the bride's harried father, Lalit Verma (Naseeruddin Shah). **BOTTOM** The wedding party, with Hemant (Dabas) and Aditi (Das) front and center.

OPPOSITE PAGE The married couple, Aditi (Vasundhara Das) and Hemant (Parvin Dabas) share a kiss, and a trademark Mira Nair "extended" moment during the climax.

Vanity Fair (2004) **THIS PAGE, TOP** Don't practice what she preaches. At the dinner table, Matilda Crawley (Eileen Atkins; left) suggests her love of romance, young love, and the tearing down of class barriers. But she doesn't mean it in her family, as social-climber Becky Sharp (Reese Witherspoon; right) soon discovers. **BOTTOM** The men in Becky Sharp's life. From left to right: Dobbin (Rhys Ifans); George Osborne (Jonathan Rhys Meyers) and Rawdon Crawley (James Purefoy).

OPPOSITE PAGE, TOP Seen here in sensuous close-up, Becky Sharp (Witherspoon) scandalizes English society by participating in Steyne's India-based dance performance. **BOTTOM** Having swung the doors of society wide open, Becky Sharp (Witherspoon) finds there isn't much of substance behind them.

Vanity Fair **BELOW** They make a handsome couple, but their credit card debt is through the roof. A portrait of social climbers Rawdon (Purefoy) and Becky (Witherspoon).

The Namesake (2006) **ABOVE** Ashima (Tabu, left) meets Maxine (Jacinda Barrett, right) as a nervous Goga...

The Namesake Ashima (Tabu) and Ashoke (Irfan Khan) arrive in the U.S. to start a new life with baby Gogol.

still doesn't seem to recognize that. Or, maybe they do now, but a few years ago, India wasn't as 'hot' as it was after *Monsoon Wedding*. It's like everyone goes to these shops now and dresses Indian and reads Indian authors.

"What was interesting for me to do on that film was to show contemporary India, but also retain the old sensibility. I had works of contemporary Indian artists on the walls [of the characters] and I loved that part of it. In every film, I do like to use the artists of the area, unknowns usually, but these artists were known in India, so that was a joy for me."

She also loved designing the wedding. "I had a touch of the modern, but also used traditional wedding colors, but in a different way," Carroll describes. "The tent I had made—I designed it—and now the tent maker is actually renting it out. My deal with him was that if he made the tent and all those decorations for me, he could keep it and rent it out as 'the *Monsoon Wedding*' tent. He asked me if I wanted a cut, and I probably should have taken it!," she jokes.

"But the real positive thing for me that I heard on set was from one of the actors who said how it was perfect, because the wedding was of India, but it also wasn't. It was an Indian wedding, but it had a little difference too; that whole modern aspect. That was great for me to hear, because that's what I was attempting to do. I didn't want to just go to a tent maker and put up the typical wedding tent. It had a twist to it."

As expected, the shooting in New Delhi in late summer of 2000 turned out to be something akin to pandemonium, despite the fine preparation of all those involved.

"There were a lot of challenges there, money-wise. We didn't have a lot of money and I was involved in every aspect. Even the trays that characters carried [in the film]—I made sure I saw them. Everything I'm very proud of. There's nothing in it I would change," Carroll remembers.

Still, the designer recalls one day where the scheduling almost scuttled a scene she desperately wanted to see in the film. "The big scene [in the film] for me is one which we almost didn't have enough time to do. Caroline Baron was the producer, and she just said 'We don't have time.' It was the scene where Alice comes out of the house and Dubey has the heart of flowers for her, with the candles behind him."

Realizing time was of the essence, Carroll reused a *Kama Sutra* set decorating piece to make Dubey's candelabra. "I had them weld together two pieces to make that large piece behind him with the candles. And we had the heart made there, and when the movie plays, everybody cries at that, so I was very happy. As a designer, my job is often to fight for what I think is important to the film, and that design aesthetic. It was like '*We have to shoot this!*' and we did.

"People stood up for that film," Carroll remembers with obvious pride. "It's important to be able to stand up for your work."

But the schedule didn't make that job any easier. And there was a domino effect to contend with if the film crew fell behind, even for a day.

"We had sixteen hour days, and because of the weather in August, it was extremely hot, and everything was going wrong, as it always does on a tough shoot," Sabrina Dhawan remembers. "[One day] they [the company] only managed to shoot three pages, and they were supposed to shoot eight pages, which meant the next day we had to do eight plus five, which is thirteen pages. That's an impossible thing to accomplish!

"So the night before that day, I had to sit along with Mira and find a way to collapse four scenes into one," Dhawan remembers, "and it became a matter of how can you quickly communicate information within the scene, [so that] the story not only makes sense, but it shines and is fun to watch?"

Other talents also found themselves under the gun. The renowned choreographer Farah Khan, perhaps the most influential such talent in contemporary Bollywood, was enlisted to create the film's climactic wedding dance. But the performance (by Neha Dubey, playing Ayesha) had to be shot in a mere three hours. The scene also required two hundred extras.

Back in the States, Johnson received footage of the work in progress, and began her work. "Normally I have the first cut of the movie when the director finishes shooting, but because part of the film was in Hindi, it was taking me a little longer," remembers Johnson, "and I needed Mira for some scenes that were all Hindi."

When shooting was completed, Johnson found that she had another problem. When she reviewed the remainder of *Monsoon Wedding*'s footage, she discovered that three hundred minutes of shooting had been damaged by a New York airport X-ray machine. The damaged footage amounted to five full days of shooting (one-sixth of the movie's shooting schedule!) and was mostly centered on the film's climactic dance sequence, filmed at a pool belonging to one of Mira Nair's friends.

"A lot of the damaged footage was during the pool scene, the big party scene," Johnson explains. "That particular scene we weren't able to reshoot because I believe the pool was only available for the period of time they did the original shoot. So that stuff we really had to use as little as possible.

"It basically looked like a big xerox," Johnson said of the damage. "The way you open a xerox machine, and then that white light goes by. There was a blue glow that would go from left to right on the screen every once and while. Depending how far into the reel the take was that you were using, that would tell you how fast the light was going to go by. We tried to use the least horrifying-looking footage. Because there were some things we just absolutely needed for the story.

"We were lucky enough that it was a party scene, so that if you saw something like a light go by, you weren't really sure if it was a light at the party, or if there was something wrong," Johnson says. "The biggest problem, I think, was the grain, because it caused the footage to be very grainy in certain parts of it. But again, it was such a busy kind of scene that we were able to cut the things that didn't have that damage, and then the audience kind of forgot about it."

But that wasn't the end of the crisis. It was obvious some form of reshoot was going to be required. "Part of the problem was that I was working in New York, and they were shooting in India and it took literally weeks to get the footage back. So by the time we even knew that there was a problem with the footage, the entire crew had disassembled," Johnson recollects. "The actors had gone their own ways, and in order to get everybody back it was a big deal."

But with insurance money garnered from the X-ray incident, Mira Nair was able to restage some of the lost scenes on a hurried reshoot spree in India three months later. Four scenes were redone, and the money from the accident actually afforded Nair the opportunity to feature a Hollywood-style deluge for several shots, bringing the monsoon of the film's title to vivid life.

With all the footage ready, the final edit was made, and Allyson Johnson had the chance to shape the film with Mira Nair. It was an interesting challenge. Nair's films are renowned for their "density in the frame,"[5] and *Monsoon Wedding* was no different. In fact, Nair had set out to chore-ograph "the sparkle of chaos," and have "every frame pulsing with life."[6] The hand-held approach of Declan Quinn granted her this level of boister-ous, over-populated, bursting life with many shots moving and weaving about large groups of family members, often in confined spaces.

Choreographing chaos (and capturing it with the eye of a camera) is one thing, but how do you *edit* chaos? That was the learning curve for Johnson.

"That's a big question. I can talk a little bit about the process of working with Declan Quinn, who's just a brilliant DP, and amazing at handheld camera work," she notes. "It's almost as if he knows exactly what's going to happen, even if something's improvised. He kind of knows in advance. That allows the editor to really have something to work with. There's nothing worse than wishing that the camera had gotten someone saying a certain line, and Declan was always able to keep the camera alive with movement, and also have great framing for me to cut with."

Still, with so many cast members, various takes and the like, conti-nuity could have been a stumbling block. For Johnson, however, this wasn't the case.

"When I first started in editing, I was almost overly concerned where people's hands were from one cut to another, and I find now that I have some experience that depending on how bad the match is, there are ways to cut where you can cover it up," she suggests. "If you're cutting on a movement, you don't really see—the eye doesn't really catch—that the hand was a little further off in one direction. You find a distraction for the audience somewhere else in the shot, so they're not looking at the fact that someone is looking up instead of down. Things of that sort.

"For me, at this point, I feel that the performance is so important that if the performance is good, people won't be bothered by that sort of thing," Johnson continues. "The scenes were very rich with improv, espe-cially in a scene like the dinner scene. So there was a lot to choose from, and there were a lot of different parts of the table that could be cut to if there was something really egregious. There are always ways around it. *Monsoon Wedding* was constant movement, and having the singing and dancing in that film also kept everything alive. And the characters were just so rich that it wasn't really too difficult to keep that wonderful feeling. The actors were just incredible."

It was also in the editing room that Johnson received some firsthand experience in the crafting of Mira Nair's signature "extended moments," those sensual seconds when a kiss, an embrace, or even a loving gaze is lingered upon and audiences swoon with the emotion of the moment. In *Monsoon Wedding* these extended, lush details came up throughout the film. They were a stylistic touch, and, as it turned out in some instances, such as Aditi and Hemant's romantic kiss, also a bit of a necessity.

"Some of that, some of the double and triple cuts come from just not having any other footage," Johnson laughs. "You're forced to think of another way to do it. We don't have, you know, five different angles. We had a hand-held camera that was kind of moving around this couple [for the kiss] and [we thought], 'What can we do to lengthen the moment and make it sensuous?' And a lot of those multiple cuts come from that type of thing, and Mira's encouragement to just tease, and take a moment that's so great and not let it go.

"She really taught me how not to get nervous that we're waiting that extra moment," Johnson explains. "It's her encouragement too. Before I met her, I don't think as an editor I was daring enough to do things like that. With every director, I feel like I learn something new about a different way to do things. We work together to make a style of the two of us, or a new style for the film."

Slow-motion photography is another way to hold and sustain a sensuous moment. "We don't really like to slow things down after the shot," Allyson reveals. "A lot of the slow-mo stuff you saw in *Monsoon Wedding* was slowed down in the camera [during shooting], which is a preferable way to do things. I think there may be a couple of shots that we ended up doing slow-motion after the fact [particularly Ria's leap into the rain at the climax]. The marigolds scene was already slow-motioned in the camera."

Another secret of Mira Nair's style is a rapid *pace*, and again, Johnson provides insight. "Pacing is very important, and Mira really loves very quick-moving things. So a lot of the film was very fast-paced. In order to get the whole story in, we had to move it along. We couldn't have a three hour movie. Part of it was trying to fit story in, [but] part of it was just Mira wanting the film to move—which it does—and then take a few scenes and just slow it down and take your time with the love scenes and the kisses and things of that nature."

Editing the picture, however, something got left out, a fact which would come to affect the colorful end credits sequence, which Johnson also edited.

"Mira and I had actually left out the wedding scene, the actual ceremony," says Johnson. "And she was very concerned about not having it in the film. She called me up after we had completed the film, and said, 'I want to put the wedding ceremony into the end credits.' Then we had to cut the end credits. It was supposed to be one continuous piece with these colors moving back and forth and everything, and so we ended up putting footage in between. That's how it came about. It wasn't planned that way, but it's nice having footage in the end credits, because so many people these days just get up and leave. So when you actually have footage in there you tend to stay a little longer."

Johnson also fulfilled another important role on *Monsoon Wedding*, one that would also help advance Professor Nair's vision. She became the sound editor.

"Well, first of all, I was a sound editor probably because I didn't know any better and didn't realize what a huge job that is," she jokes. But Johnson was also a music major in college, in clarinet performance, so the assignment seemed to readily fit with her CV.

"Because of my musical background, I thought, 'of course I can do this.' But it really is a huge job, and since *Monsoon Wedding* the movies [that she has worked on] have had enough money to hire a professional music editor, which is great.

"Part of the problem is that I was not only cutting the actual scenes, but cutting music to match the scenes," Johnson details. "You know, 'Do I cut the music first or do I cut the scene first?' And you end up doing a combination of the two, because you can. Whereas if you had a music editor, I would send the piece to the music editor and say, 'Hey, we like this part, we like this part, and it has to be this long,' and deal with it that way. It's always a back and forth, but it's tough when you have the ability to do it right then and there."

What she found, however, was that Nair was not only adept with visuals, but—the tradition of all true auteurs—music as well. "Mira is very,

very involved in the music," Johnson establishes. "She's very musical, and very particular about the songs that she uses, and she has this long-standing relationship with Mychael Danna, and he really knows the types of things that she wants. So the process really was that she would come in with a lot of Indian music that she really liked, or other pieces for temp music, and that sets the pace for the scene. After that, Mychael Danna comes in and composes for certain scenes. *Monsoon Wedding* actually had a lot of non-composed scenes with existing music in it, just because Mira wanted to get the feel of certain things from India."

"The funny thing about that film," composer Mychael Danna remembers, "is that Mira originally did not plan on having a score for it. She was just going to use songs, and [sometimes] the characters would sing. So she called me up and said, 'I have this little Punjabi movie which I don't really think needs any music, but why don't you take a look at it?' So I looked at it, and I called her back and just went, 'This is a little masterpiece, and I agree with you that it doesn't need a lot of score, but I would love to do some scoring on it. I just think it would give it a little bit of structure.'

"Certainly," Danna ponders, "the kineticism of it is brilliant and we didn't want to lose that, but there are some moments where there are pauses for reflection, and just small things that could be very nicely elaborated on slightly with music. That's what we did, and it happened insanely fast.

"I literally got the phone call and spent one week writing," Danna elaborates, "which is the shortest writing schedule I've ever had by far. So [I spent] one week writing, and I went to India for one week, and Mira was there shooting, but we hardly saw each other because she was doing reshoots. And then I came back [to the United States] and spent one further week, so the entire score—including a trip to India and recording all these musicians—was done in three weeks. It was insane. It was a crazy, crazy schedule, but I'm really proud of that score. I love the film. It's just one of those crazy things that's just very, very Mira. The entire situation. The entire film and the method of it is just very, very Mira, in the best possible way."

While working on the score, Danna also spent time with Professor Nair on the "pop" songs that would be included in the film. "Mira is very, very knowledgeable about Indian music and poetry, and is very sensitive to lyrics as well as the music, so she was very involved in choosing songs," he explains. "I had some input, and there were definitely moments when she would ask me what I thought, but certainly her knowledge is unimpeachable on that score. I think there are songs [in the film] that had meaning for her, as well as meaning within the film."

That meaning and feel in the music, not incidentally, is pure Bollywood. Indeed, *Monsoon Wedding* has been called a Bollywood film, but that isn't necessarily a classification writer Sabrina Dhawan agrees with. "When people talk about *Monsoon Wedding* as being a Bollywood film or a Bollywood crossover film, it doesn't make much sense, because in many ways it's like an American independent film, only it's about another culture. It comes from the same school as independent filmmaking. Bollywood films are three hours long, they have intermissions. They're very different.

"I think sometimes that within the film there are a lot of *references* to Bollywood," she clarifies. "A lot of the music actually comes from Bollywood films, a lot of the costumes too. But then, that is also a reflection of India, and particularly Punjabi marriages. If you were to do a movie about a wedding with any kind of truth to it, or to make it authentic, it's natural that it would reflect Bollywood."

Dhawan is also the first to admit that Bollywood's influence on *Monsoon Wedding* may be a subconscious one, simply because of the dominance of the form in India.

"There are so many different cultures in India, and the one link that all these cultures have is that they are all deeply influenced by Bollywood cinema," she considers. "People from the south and the north have a different mother tongue, but the reason they understand each other is that they all watch Bollywood films, and so there's this understood language, predominantly Hindi. A lot of Indian kids born overseas…the only thing they know about India, the only way they ever learn about Indian language is through Bollywood films, from watching movies. Bollywood is such an influence in our lives that if you were to make something contemporary set in an urban Indian world, especially when it's set during a wedding, it's inevitable there would be some Bollywood in it."

Nair seemed to concur, noting in an interview that *Monsoon Wedding* was responsible for "embracing and loving" Bollywood, yet "not done" in the way of those films.[7]

BOX OFFICE DELUGE

Monsoon Wedding had a staggered opening internationally, starting with Italy on August 30, 2001, and Canada in September. In fact, it played at the Toronto Film Festival on September 12, just a day after the terrorist attacks on New York City and Washington D.C. that changed our world so drastically.

"It's tragic how it came into the world," notes Mychael Danna. "The premiere was supposed to be September 11, 2001.

"The energy of the film is so opposite to the evil of September 11…just the life-loving qualities and the life energies of *Monsoon Wedding*," Danna considers. "I guess, in retrospect, it [the day] is symbolic of the two opposite sides of human nature. It seemed like on that day, the dark forces definitely won out."

Despite the grim date of the film's debut, *Monsoon Wedding* did not disappear. Even before the film opened in the United States (on February 22, 2002), the buzz and critical acclaim for Mira Nair's latest work began building. *Monsoon Wedding* nabbed the 58th Venice International Film Festival's Golden Lion Prize in 2001, the first Indian-made film since Satyajit Ray's *The Unvanquished* (1957) to claim that honor. Only the second female director in history to claim the prize, Nair accepted the award in person, noting that it was for "beloved India," her "continuing inspiration."[8] The film also played to packed houses in the United Kingdom when it opened there on January 4, 2002, vaulting into the top twenty film list.[9] In the United States, *Monsoon Wedding* did brisk business, eventually earning nearly fourteen million dollars against its initial million dollar investment. It was one of the highest grossing foreign films in history.

The critics were as effusive as general audiences. Writing for *Newsweek*, critic David Ansen wrote that Nair's "stereotype-shattering movie—like the polymorphous culture it illuminates—borrows from Bollywood, Hollywood, *cinema verité*, and comes up with something entirely its own."[10] *Variety*'s Deborah Young called it "Splashy, noisy and downright fun," noting that "*Monsoon Wedding* is an unrepentantly cross-cultural crowd-pleaser."[11]

Reviewer Joseph Cunneen felt impressed too, and told his readers in *National Catholic Reporter* that "The most colorful and entertaining movie invitation in recent months is to New Delhi to attend *Monsoon Wedding*."[12]

The film's sudden widespread popularity came as something of a shock to its makers. "It wasn't until I saw *Monsoon Wedding* that I realized Mira has found something to do with a docu-fictionalized drama, if you know what I mean," suggests Roshan Seth. "When I read the script, I thought it was a documentary record of a Punjabi wedding, and I didn't see how it was going to work, and of course I was completely wrong with that film because it did work. It was a great success."

"I was very surprised, of course. It's a small film, and it is certainly low budget, and it has no stars," Sabrina Dhawan remarks. "It took me at least a year or two for it to sink in, the level of success the film had."

Johnson feels the same way. "For a film that was made so quickly and with such a small amount of money, for it to have its own legs and take off, it was just great. It was one of those word-of-mouth things. People would just come out of the theatre and say, 'Oh my god, I have to see that again,' or go home and call their friends and say, 'You have to see this movie.' We were in shock. It was fantastic. But it doesn't happen very often, especially when you're up against films these days that have a lot of money behind them."

"I absolutely adored *Monsoon Wedding*," says Julian Fellowes, adapter of *Vanity Fair*. "What I felt about it was that Mira was able to combine the minutiae of character narrative while giving you a sense of the whole world that was involved, and it all fit together. I thought it was brilliant. I thought that's exactly the feel that was needed. When I watched it, I thought, 'I don't know anything about modern India but I bet it's like this.' You have such a sense of the truth of the film that you don't need knowledge, really, to back it up."

"We had a million dollars on that movie," Stephanie Carroll points out. "That's nothing for what we accomplished, I think."

"The whole film was really, in a way, just a shot-from-the-hip kind of project," Danna muses. "It happened quite quickly. It was shot quickly, and it was cut quickly. It tapped into this energy of Mira's which is so in tune with the subject of the film. I think it's one of those cases where it was just the perfect director and the perfect material, and all the energies clicked, and it's just a beautiful film. It's one of my favorite things that I've ever worked on."

When the critics had their say and all the receipts were counted, it was clear that Mira Nair had crafted in *Monsoon Wedding* her best and most beloved film since her feature debut in 1988. It was so successful, in fact, that reports indicated that *Monsoon Wedding* would soon be bound for Broadway. News leaked that a musical adaptation of the property was due in 2004, with Mira Nair directing. Nair noted that Dhawan's narrative had all the right "ingredients," even though it hadn't occurred to her that it could be a successful musical.[13] However, as of this writing, the notion of *Monsoon Wedding* as musical theatre was still only in the planning stages.

A CELEBRATION OF DIFFERENCES

Gazing at *Monsoon Wedding* today, it is clearly a film that challenges "our assumptions about Indian culture,"[14] as critic Cynthia Karena notes. It's a meditation about the heart (and national identity) of modern-day globalized India, "nothing short of an ode," in the words of the *American Prospect's* Adina Hoffman, to India's "particular brand of freewheeling hybridization."[15]

In the film, Nair "fondly depicts a country where old and new cultures exist side by side," writes Moira McDonald, "where traditional music can be drowned out by ringing cell phones."[16]

These reviews point out many fine thematic qualities of *Monsoon Wedding*, but it is also interesting to note how the film develops these ideas. In particular, it adroitly utilizes the all-encompassing umbrella of the family wedding—a joining of two unlike groups—as its central metaphor. Though this is a commonly used plot device throughout cinema history, such as in Robert Altman's *The Wedding* (1978), here the two forces being joined in holy matrimony are not merely unlike would-be spouses, the thoroughly modern Aditi and Hemant, but actually competing notions of modernity and tradition as a whole in India.

"So much of the movie is about globalized, modern India," agrees Sabrina Dhawan. "It's a society which is globalizing, but is holding onto tradition as well, and [the film] looks at India in a way that it hasn't been seen before; a world of cell phones and pagers where Indian tradition and Western tradition are sort of co-existing, in seeming harmony."

To highlight aspects of this newly evolved India and its two competing components, Dhawan designed the film to feature a love story between two characters who would each symbolize something, the new and the old respectively.

"More than any other character, P. K. Dubey symbolizes new India, this new, upcoming middle class," she says. "In the old system, you were content to be in the class you were born into. That's why America was the promised land, because you can rise above the station you were bequeathed. In India, you could not. What globalization has done now is made it possible—if you have entrepreneurial spirit, by whatever means you choose to do it—that [you can] actually go from being lower-middle-class to middle-class to upper-middle-class. You can be upwardly mobile, and P. K. Dubey is that person. He comes from the traditional world in Old Delhi, but now he owns a cell phone and pager and there are three people who work for him. He's a real symbol of a growing middle-class India."

Dubey's very demeanor, says Dhawan, is part of modern India. "He's someone who isn't apologetic for who he is. He doesn't apologize. He doesn't lack self-confidence, which is another thing that if you came from the lower class, you always deferred in a more servile way to the people who belong to a higher class."

In the film, Dubey falls in love with the beautiful and sweet Alice, the Verma family maid. She is designed as Dubey's symbolic opposite. "Alice is this person who is from the old world, the maid," Dhawan explains. "She is pretty much treated in the way that maids were treated in the old world, because in India that hasn't changed, even though we've globalized and modernized.

"In America, if you have domestic help, they can sit on the same chair as you do, or use the same bathroom as you do. In India that never happens. They eat in the kitchen separately from you. They don't sit at the dining room table with you. They have a separate bathroom."

Dhawan considers this dynamic for a moment, and reveals that the character of Alice comes from her own family experience. "I [my family] had a maid named Alice. When you grow up and you think about it, you just feel that you suddenly appreciate what you took for granted growing up. They have this other life that you've never considered, and that was something I wanted to explore.

"So you have P. K. Dubey who is the shining example of new, middle-class India and there's Alice, who's this kind of shameful reminder of how we've modernized in some ways, but we still haven't reconsidered the way we treat domestic help," describes Dhawan. "So when you're drawing this portrait of modern India, then those two characters, *those two different sides of globalization*, become really important. But of course, the two worlds come together, which is why they [the characters] must fall in love."

This oft-called "Upstairs/Downstairs element" of the film "illuminates within *Monsoon Wedding*, the vast class and religious diversity that makes up India today,"[17] according to writer Kyle Boltin. But what remains so delightful about how this sweet romance of unlike people plays out on screen is that the film's form reflects the content. A beautiful image, that of the marigold, is the *leitmotif*, the thing in common between Dubey and Alice, the bridge that helps them to see each other and discover the love.

"The reason that I wanted to put that in the movie is that I knew there was going to be a love story between the tent contractor and the maid, and I wanted there to be some kind of foreshadowing of what was to come, of two people who were very different and belonged to different worlds, but had this one shared thing—they both liked to eat marigold flowers," says Dhawan. "It was foreshadowing their coming together later."

Ironically, it is this lovely image that has become, perhaps, *Monsoon Wedding's* unofficial trademark. In particular, audiences around the world seem amused and touched by the sight of the eating of the beautiful saffron marigolds.

"It's so funny because when you're writing, it's hard to tell what image or moment will resonate with people. The only reason I put it in is because I used to do that!" Dhawan reveals. "My cousins and I would do that. We would get bored because Indian weddings are so long, so we would just hang around and play with the marigold flowers and arrangements, and throw them at each other and then go eat the flowers. They taste kind of bland. They don't really taste of anything."

But *Monsoon Wedding's* look at globalization in India also accomplishes something else. Through the rubric of globalization and competing modernity and tradition, the film's characters actually become more recognizable, more appealing, and more human. At every critical juncture, this argument over which kind of world to embrace leads a character into a crisis.

Aditi's young brother Varun Verma (played by Mira Nair's nephew, Ishaan Nair), for instance, does not represent Lalit's image of what a young Indian man should be. He stays home and watches television, wants to dance with his cousin, and even study in school to become a cook. This is not at all the kind of future that Lalit would plan for him. Instead, he expects to send him to a boarding school, where Varun can become a proper Indian male; re-educated it seems, to express the right aspirations and dreams. No son of Lalit's, he says, will be a cook.

In America, children often must deal with discouragement from parents, but there seems more at stake here, a vision of what it means to be an Indian man in the twenty-first century. It is a battle that Varun must face, and fight through.

The brief conflict between Aditi and Hemant is another obvious example how the "strain" of globalization is exploited to present appealing characters. Aditi conducts an affair with a married man, which is shocking, one supposes, to India's traditionalists. Even more shocking, it would follow, is Hemant's quick reconciliation with Aditi. This is a bold acknowledgment that tradition—and such concepts of premarital sex and a bride's virginity—no longer carry the currency they once did.

Again, this is a conflict that Americans can immediately identify with, but also one which addresses specifically the nature of modern-day India and its struggle to deal with changing social values. The flip side of this issue is that two such modern young people are also adhering to tradition at the same time they flout it, conforming to their parents' convention of arranged marriages.

By allowing its *dramatis personae* to face issues related directly to the modernity vs. tradition battle, *Monsoon Wedding* presents its characters as "appealingly human," and so it is possible to be "swept into the film's colorful world."[18] This is simply another way of affirming what Sabrina Dhawan refers to as a intractable law of screenwriting, that the more specific a problem, the more universal it becomes.

When considering *Monsoon Wedding*, one cannot quarrel with the assessment of critic Tom Aitken, who notes that when "the tumult and the shouting die," viewers are left with a sense of "how tough and resilient"[19] family love truly is. It is a remarkable accomplishment that a film shot in Hindi, featuring nearly seventy characters, feels so immediate, and perhaps more importantly *true*, to people living halfway across the world. The focus on the crisis of globalization and the all-encompassing umbrella of the wedding make *Monsoon Wedding* a potently involving and ravishingly intimate film. Nair's frequent "extending of the moment" and Declan Quinn's probing, *cinema verité* approach with the hand-held camera only make the material feel that much closer.

If "America has already come to India,"and in a "big way,"[20] as the *New Yorker*'s Anthony Lane suggests, than *Monsoon Wedding* is an important part of that journey, no doubt. Perhaps, as a film it does function as a "a multi-cultural tapestry which exposes the absurd fundamentalist claim that the population must rally to a nonexistent 'traditional India,'"[21] but more importantly than that agenda, it is a motion picture in which "when everyone comes together for a strained family portrait at the end," audiences know—and feel—precisely "what's lurking behind each of their fixed smiles."[22]

It takes a special breed of director to make a film that feels universal to multiple cultures. The joy inherent in *Monsoon Wedding* doesn't merely arise from Sabrina Dhawan's accomplished dialogue and provocative story, but from Mira Nair's style in the telling of the tale, her ability to enhance audience connections to characters through her choices of shots, through her composition of each frame, though her extension of important moments.

"With Mira, we work frame-by-frame," Stephanie Carroll confirms, "looking at each set and looking at each shot. When Dubey the tent-maker is looking in the window at Alice, the servant who is trying on her bosses's jewelry, I had an orange curtain there—which framed him—and we had a flower in his hand, and then with the window we had this kind of wavy glass," she points out.

This rich imagery for that one shot—a window representing separation, a flower symbolizing love, an orange drape blanketing him—shows the depth of detail in each *Monsoon Wedding* moment, and how many frames could stand alone as lovely photographs in their own right, but ones that *mean* something; suggesting emotion, desperation, unrequited love, or desire.

"Every frame, Mira and I would design to fit the emotions of what was happening," Carroll says. "We do that in every film together…"

HYSTERICAL BLINDNESS (2002)

In the early 1990s, a young New Jersey playwright named Laura Cahill put pen to paper to compose her newest work, a drama called *Hysterical Blindness*. Powerful and disturbing, the play concerns two Jersey girls in the 1980s, Deb and Beth, and their endless nights in a Bayonne bar seeking love, but finding only demeaning flings with men out to play the field. As a counterpoint, the play also details a tender and sweet relationship between Debby's mom, Virginia, and a new older man in her life, the gentle and kind Nick. Deb has a one-night stand with a local player named Rick, who isn't really interested in a committed relationship, and Deb is crushed by the experience. Then, there is an unexpected tragedy.

Like many great works of art, *Hysterical Blindness* arises from the context of its creator's life. In particular, Cahill had become fascinated with the people around her in towns like Bloomfield, Belleville, Clifton and Bayonne, New Jersey, and was inspired to write about them.

"I was really writing about my friends in New Jersey that I grew up with," she explains. "When we became adults, I had friends who were dating, and their mothers were dating, and that overlapped, and that was interesting to me. That's a big part of what gave me the idea for *Hysterical Blindness*. Mostly just the monologue that starts the play, with her [Debby] going blind at work.

"I had friends who were very histrionic," she continues. "I had friends who had clerical jobs—like I did myself—who could make drama out of nothing. And that was what I was going for with that monologue. *How dramatic could my day be at this terrible job?* I'm fascinated by the things people say, and how people act in certain situations, and the lies that they tell, and the lies that they tell themselves. People are just interesting to me, and that's what I write about."

In the original draft of the play, the action focused on Deb, her best friend Beth, and Deb's "hook-up," Rick. This version was performed at the Naked Angels theatre in New York City in 1994.

"It went really well," Cahill remembers. "I had three really wonderful actors, and the play was funny. It was the funniest version that we did. It was the kind of thing where the audience laughed from beginning to end."

By the play's next performance in 1997, Virginia and Nick had been layered in, and the story had a more serious bent. "It was a deeper version," Cahill notes.

On both occasions, *Hysterical Blindness* had an influential young actor sitting in its audience, Ethan Hawke, who has starred in *Before Sunrise* (1995), *Gattaca* (1998), and *Assault on Precinct 13* (2005).

"Ethan had been there in 1994. Ethan had been there when I did readings of the play before it was produced," Cahill notes. "The second time I did a reading of it was at his theatre company, and he was there. He's always been really supportive of my writing."

During the 1997 performance, Ethan Hawke brought along his then-girlfriend, future–*Kill Bill* superstar Uma Thurman, to see Cahill's work. Thurman and Hawke left after the theatrical presentation shell-shocked and overwhelmed by its intensity and honesty.

"I went to see the play," Uma Thurman told Donna Freydkin at *USA Today*, "and I was totally surprised and moved by it. It stayed in my head."23

"After Ethan saw the play in 1997, he called me the next morning and talked about what kind of a movie it would make, and who would do it, and things like that," Cahill describes. "We just talked about it, really. Then I went to Indiana to work on another play of mine, and I got a call from Ethan at the hotel, which came as a complete surprise, and he said, 'Let's make a movie. Uma has been thinking and talking about it, and we really want to do it. Instead of talking about it, we're going to do it.'"

So Cahill, Hawke and Thurman rendezvoused back in New York and began working out the business details of the movie, which included a deal for Cahill to adapt the screenplay for the movie. Cahill worked very closely with Thurman during this stage.

"We would sit and read the script together. She'd be Debby and I'd be Beth," says Cahill. "We did that for many nights and many times over the next couple of years. Uma would go away to make a movie and then come back, and by the end of two years we had a whole script."

In fact, Thurman and Cahill took the film to Miramax, and staged a cast reading in the screening room there. It was a high-tension moment for Cahill, but one that Thurman helped her get through.

"We had a really good cast," Cahill details, "but I didn't think the script sounded good at all. I went into the ladies room directly after the reading and I was like, 'Oh God, it was terrible!' but then Uma came bounding in and said, 'It was great!'"

The script next landed in the hands of *Hysterical Blindness*'s first producer (and a friend of Cahill and Thurman's) named Jason Blum, who sent the script out to various organizations, including HBO.

"We decided at the very last minute that Uma should play Debby," Cahill continues. "She never had any intention of being in *Hysterical Blindness*, she was just producing it, so it was really a last-minute decision, and it was a great one. I was so excited that Uma would play the part, and really fast after that we had HBO, and made it quickly."

However, as *Hysterical Blindness* commenced pre-production, it still didn't have a director. "I wanted Mira to be involved," Cahill says. "We had lists, and Uma and Jason and I were talking and e-mailing and everybody was talking about a director. Mira was on the first list that I got, and I wanted Mira."

Alas, Nair, at the time, was in India re-shooting a portion of *Monsoon Wedding* due to the damage of some film by an X-ray machine at an airport.

"She was in India, but nobody told me that," Cahill laughs. "So I kept pushing and pushing because I thought she was in New York and it would be easy to get her. Uma was also a big fan of Mira's work and decided that she would be the best person, so we really went after her."

In particular, Thurman placed an international call to Bombay and asked Nair to look at the screenplay. Nair's longtime producer and friend Lydia Pilcher sent Mira the script, and Nair liked what she saw.

Though drastically different in approach from much of the material she had developed herself, *Hysterical Blindness* offered the filmmaker the opportunity to explore a gritty, seamy world, and one that had thematic strands in common with her other works. And not unlike *Salaam Bombay!* and some of her other films, *Hysterical Blindness* highlighted a story about the relationship between a mother and daughter, something that Nair related strongly to.

"The first time that we talked, there were a lot of people in the room; we were in Uma's apartment," Cahill sets the scene. "We were all there when Mira came in, and she told me what she liked about the script. She told me what she thought was funny about it, and that made me love her even more, because she got all my jokes. And the things that she brought up were important things to me, but not the most obvious ones, so I was really happy."

After that first meeting, Cahill began to refashion the screenplay again. "Mira and I met alone to talk about the script, and her big thing was trying to get me to pull the drama from every scene. That's where Mira and I are very different, because I write dialogue and you have to get what is going on sort of between-the-lines, whereas Mira wants to pull everything out—to go very deep by the end of each scene. She had to push me a little to get me to do that."

And for this, Cahill is grateful. "It was good," she says. "It's really served me well in coming out to Hollywood to write studio movies. It helped, because she taught me to do something that I really purposely had never done before. So she was helpful with that, and in a few scenes it was easy to do. Sometimes, it was hard, and I was banging my head against the wall, but when she directed the movie, she kind of did it herself."

Opening up the play to film also benefitted the material, according to Cahill. "Other plays that I've written take place in one room, but *Hysterical Blindness* had a lot of locations, and locations that you can't create well on stage, so [for the film] I could go anywhere I wanted and that was freeing and very easy.

"The hardest part [of the adaptation process] was shortening the scenes. I did one version after Mira came on board and I tried to make it very movie-like," Cahill notes, "and Mira got a hold of the play and called me on the phone. She had highlighted all the lines from the play she wanted back in the script.

"I write plays because I love dialogue," Cahill reflects, "That's why I'm writing—to capture things people say, and in a movie, it's more about the story. So adapting my play, the story was told in the dialogue and to expand on it visually was hard. That was the challenge, and we restructured from the play to the movie. We turned some events at the end around."

The adaptation process also gave Cahill the chance to include scenes she had always envisioned, but found much too cumbersome for the stage. One of these involved Deb's desperate bid for Rick's love by promising to cook him a dinner of filet mignon.

"I had always wanted that in the play, actually. I always wanted that scene, but it never made it in because it was really just too hard to pull off on stage: Deb cooking filet mignon alone. It was hard to make that work. I was really glad to be able to put that in the movie."

The newly adapted screenplay by Cahill, like her play, was set in 1987. The details in the play were authentic, including references to New Jersey shopping icons like Shop-Rite and Service Merchandise, but some of these local nuances were dropped from the film to focus on other things.

In the play Rick is a more fully-developed character. He describes his vocation—he collects garbage off construction sites—and he likes high-end stereo equipment.

The Nick character was treated slightly differently in the original play. There are clues about his illness leading up his death. For instance, he tells Ginny that he doesn't feel so good. In the play, it is learned that he dies at Dunkin' Donuts, another detail that changes in the film. But overall, these alterations are very minor ones, and the movie adheres closely to the spirit and intent of Cahill's stage drama.

SHOOTING BLIND

The casting of *Hysterical Blindness* would prove to serendipitous, for not only did Nair acquire the talent of one A-list Hollywood actress in Uma Thurman, but she also hired another, the incredibly versatile Juliette Lewis, who in her career has done everything from Woody Allen films like *Husbands and Wives* (1991) to the Oliver Stone fantasy/satire *Natural Born Killers* (1994). Lewis would take on the difficult role of Beth, best friend to Debby, a single mother and compatriot in the trenches of the bar scene. The production also retained the services of two pros from New York film-making and the Cassavetes clan, the immensely talented Gena Rowlands and Ben Gazzara, for the roles of Virginia and Nicky.

Interviewed in January of 2005, Ms. Rowlands recalls how she came to be involved in *Hysterical Blindness*:

"I had met Mira at the Cannes film festival a few years ago, but at the time we said, 'Let's look for something we can work on together,' and then I didn't think anymore about it. When she got the script for *Hysterical Blindness* at HBO, she called me, and I loved it."

In particular the versatile actress felt that the role of Ginny was one which she could really sink her teeth into. "Well, I thought she was a woman who had been badly let down by her husband and didn't really understand it," Rowland considers. "She was of that age when women didn't have a lot of professions or training so when their husbands just walked out on them, they were in terrible trouble. I did admire the way that she learned to be a waitress and she stuck by her daughter—what a handful! And yet as different as they were, there was—I thought—a great feeling of support between them when push came to shove."

Rowlands was also quite satisfied to be working with Ben Gazzara again. "I love him," she says. "Ben and I have done a lot of things together, and he's such a very old friend. I always look forward to doing anything if he's a part of it."

It helped to have an old friend close by, no doubt, when approaching some of the heart-rending scenes in *Hysterical Blindness*, including one involving death. When asked how she prepared for such work, Rowlands thinks on it for a moment, and then answers. "You prepare all the scenes— or I do, at any rate—more or less the same way. You think about them. Thinking about them is a very big part of rehearsal. Not necessarily *talking* about them, but thinking, and then relating things to your own life, and the people that you've seen who had their husband die, or be in an accident, or something that they couldn't haven't been prepared for. You just think it out and feel it out.

"It's a tough picture," she adds. And one that she feels benefitted from Mira Nair's direction, and willingness to trust her performers. "Mira is inclined to let you go your own way, and then make suggestions on that," Rowlands explains. "And they are always good suggestions. She's just a very creative woman."

Hysterical Blindness was shot as a "guerilla project, down and dirty in just twenty days on a budget of six million dollars"[24] during the summer of 2001. The work went on for seventeen-hours-a-day often, and a large percentage of the telepic was lensed at the Military Ocean

Terminal in Bayonne, New Jersey, a port constructed in the 1930s but gated off from the town and closed as a federal base during the budget cuts of the 1990s.[25]

"Again, on *Hysterical Blindness*, there was not a lot of money to accomplish what we had to do," production designer Stephanie Carroll describes. "Mira was editing *Monsoon Wedding* at the same time this had to happen. So it was good that we had the same DP, Declan Quinn, who did *Monsoon Wedding*, because there was a language and a trust between the three of us that helped. Because we didn't have a lot of prep time.

"I had to trust the cinematographer would do a good job with my work, because whatever I do has to be photographed well, or no one sees it. And the same is true for him. He has to have something he wants to photograph," she notes.

The Ollie's bar exterior was shot in Paterson, New Jersey, and the film completed on schedule. Stylistically—as one might expect—Nair added her own unique touches.

"I put the bridges in the background of many shots to show Debby never looked outside her own world,"[26] she wrote in the *New York Times Magazine*. In toto, the experience was a positive one, and Nair had only words of praise for her top-flight cast. "Uma Thurman gives the most fearless performance," she said, "and Gena Rowlands is a person I had worshiped and very much love."[27]

Cahill had the chance to observe shooting, at least for a while. "Because we had worked on the script together for a couple of years, Uma and I had planned to go through the process [of shooting] together," the writer reports. "Playing Debby was a very different thing for her to do, and it was very close to her heart, and she wanted me there, but I had morning sickness and I couldn't sit on a movie set. It was like the last place I wanted to be, so I did go several times, but I missed most of it."

But what she didn't miss was the dedication of the cast and crew. "Declan [Quinn] is brilliant," she says. "He made the film very beautiful. Whenever you see bar scenes in movies, they don't feel like real bars, because bars have a certain feeling and look to them, and he was absolutely able to make it look and sound real to me."

HYSTERICAL RATINGS

Nair's second television film, *Hysterical Blindness* aired on HBO a mere eight months after the release of *Monsoon Wedding*. It ran at 9:30 p.m. (after an episode of *Sex and the City*) on August 25. It racked up a strong 11.4 rating,[28] making it one of the highest rated cable premieres of 2002. In general, critics were impressed, though some were taken aback by the bleakness and desperation of the material. *Variety* termed it a "numbingly obvious confection of laughter and tears that's utterly condescending to its one-note characters,"[29] this was the minority opinion. Reviewers such as Roger Ebert (who had seen the film at Sundance) gave it a thumbs up and *People* concluded that *Hysterical Blindness* was truly "something to see."[30]

Rowlands still remembers how deeply she was affected by viewing the completed film. "I was devastated by it," she says. "It was a tough picture, and I thought that Uma Thurman and Juliette Lewis were so marvelous in that, in their concept of their characters…and brave. Very brave. I admire both of them. I do say it was hard to watch, but you felt good that you did."

"I thought it was beautiful," Laura Cahill adds. "Mira really pulled together an entire vision, and I thought it had layers and layers. Uma and Juliette were amazing."

Hysterical Blindness was not forgotten during awards season, either. The television-movie won Emmy awards for best supporting actor and actress in a miniseries or motion picture, for Ben Gazzara and Gena Rowlands. Cahill was nominated for outstanding writing, and Declan Quinn for outstanding cinematography. Cahill was also nominated for an Independent Spirit Award for best first screenplay, and Uma Thurman took home a Golden Globe award for her performance.

LOVE IS A BATTLEFIELD

Vision is the concept at the heart of Mira Nair's adaptation of Laura Cahill's drama, *Hysterical Blindness*. From the very first shot—a blur coming into focus—and a profile view of Uma's Thurman left eye, the film obsesses on the concept of sight, and in particular, how one character, Thurman's Deb, views herself and the world around her.

In the film, Deb finds herself the victim of *Hysterical Blindness*, a psychological condition in which a person finds that he or she really can't see. It could be brought on by any number of things, including stress and anxiety, and it is usually temporary, but Deb actually seems to suffer from a more permanent form of metaphorical blindness.

Every weekend, and some weeknights too, she and her best friend Beth sit endlessly at a bar called Ollie's and wait, essentially to be rescued. They hope they are going to find a man in this dive, one who will love them, treat them well, and eventually marry them, thus freeing them from this life of bar-hopping and one night stands. The folly is, of course, that Bayonne, New Jersey, is a fairly small town, and that the kind of fellas who hang out at bars aren't usually the ones looking to find a commitment, let alone a wife. Indeed, these may be the very men who, down the road, abandon their families, as Virginia and Deb have been abandoned. They are there for one reason: to pick up women for sex, yet Debby and Beth don't seem to understand this. They'll sleep with guys and then hope against hope that he'll "like" them enough to see them again and marry them. Of course, they were never seen as wife potential in the first place, but, as the film tells us, they just don't see it.

To make viewers aware that Debby suffers from tunnel vision, if not outright blindness, Mira Nair fills the frame throughout *Hysterical Blindness* with views of the larger world, one where there are opportunities, new horizons and men different from those who frequent Ollie's.

Shortly after the opening sequence, Declan Quinn's camera captures a view of Debby and Beth driving over a bridge, and a slight adjustment upwards reveals the amazing breadth and size of the Manhattan skyline in the distance. There's a whole world out there, yet Deb doesn't think about moving to New York, about leaving her "home" in Bayonne. In this Mira Nair film, it's pretty clear that home is something of a trap, a stagnation.

It isn't just the skyline that looms. Nair also provides no less than a dozen views of bridges, the gateways to opportunities and new beginnings that for, whatever reason, Debby seems incapable of considering, let alone acknowledging. When Deb and Beth leave Beth's house, the camera tilts up and zooms forward, and there's a bridge looming over everything. Later, we see Ginny's diner, and it is positioned almost precisely under a bridge—a perspective seen more than once in the film, though none of the characters seem to notice.

There's even a shot of three bridges receding in the distance as Deb drives to work at the office. Other gateways out of Bayonne are rampant too, including a shot of Rick's car running parallel to railroad tracks, indicating that there is indeed a bigger world out there.

Because she can't see that her world is larger than Bayonne, Debby gets anxious, she goes blind, she's defensive and bitter. Bobby the bartender finally almost gilds the lily by telling Deb that maybe her problem is that *sometimes she doesn't see things so clearly*. Via Mira Nair's imagery, and the recurrent symbols of portals out of Bayonne, that's a point that's already been struck visually.

"It was really brilliant," Cahill says of Nair's visual conceit. "I can't think of anybody else coming up with that, with the things she came up with out of the script."

And what does Debby see, if she can't see Bayonne's escape hatches? Only her own desperation. That she can't sit alone at a bar. That her dad left when she was a kid. That Rick doesn't want to buy her an engagement ring and marry her. All she can see are the things that she doesn't have and the things she wants so much, not the things that the world at large can bring her. But the wonderful thing about *Hysterical Blindness* is that the film doesn't try to make pat psychology out of Debby's strange lassitude and inability to see the world beyond. Instead, it only hints at a variety of explanations.

"Why is Debby like this? That's the question that every actor would ask, every time we would work on this," says Laura Cahill. "That's really a hard question to answer, because when I write, I don't usually know. I just have these characters and these things about life that are real to me, but I don't know for sure why they do the things they do. I just write what they do. I know it comes from some pain somewhere, but I don't completely know because I don't construct the characters or make them up. They're real to me.

"I think that Debby did have a hard life," she considers. "She comes from a world where there's not much money, and has these boring clerical jobs that she doesn't do very well. Her father left when she was thirteen without explanation. He mother doesn't drive and works in a diner, and so

Debby has a tough life. I think she wants something that's exciting and something that's going to make her feel good. She wants it desperately, so she loses sight of what the real rules of life are, maybe.

"I don't think she ever goes blind at work," suggests Cahill. "She just makes herself feel that she went blind at work. She wants to feel important and she definitely wants attention. I had friends like that who had a problem every single day—especially when you're in your twenties—and Debby was kind of like that."

Like *Mississippi Masala*, *Hysterical Blindness* is also a film about the generations, and the cycles each one blindly repeats, and also the opportunity to escape them. Virginia's subplot involves her relationship with a kind man named Nick, a man who eventually dies. One senses that Ginny is just as sad as her daughter, if not as overtly desperate. She is a counterpoint to Debby, from the generation that wouldn't frequent bars, but was still otherwise dependent on the man in her life. Ironically, she and Debby undergo the same pursuit in this film—finding a relationship, thereby navigating the thematic road of counterpoint.

"It was a counterpoint. Yes I think so," says Gena Rowlands. "I don't see how they [Virginia and Debby] could be more different. Things were different when Benny and I were young, and now there are just so many things that, even if we weren't discussing, we were calling on, to make that relationship work for those characters. We're not very expressive, and there was a certain almost-shyness, because I think it's been a long time since they've fallen in love and he's lost his wife, and her husband walked out, and they don't necessarily know the new rules. Or they're tentative about them."

"It was really important to me to show the different value systems of the different ages of the women," Cahill agrees. "Like the mother, Virginia, was much more cautious and careful, and wanted to do things a certain way. Her daughter just didn't have any rules. She would do anything."

Then, finally, there is a youngest generation in the film, one represented by young Amber, Beth's daughter. She seems to have a better head on her shoulders than Beth and Debby, and the possibility is held out that she could be the first one to leave Bayonne. She will not have a child out of wedlock like her mom, or find herself trapped because there is no man in her life.

The film ends with all three generations together celebrating on a hot summer day, a sprinkler blasting Debby, Beth and Amber while Ginny watches. It feels like a new beginning and thanks to the use of "Girls Just Want to Have Fun" on the soundtrack, there's a valedictory note here, a sense that all the characters will survive.

"Mira wanted to bring Virginia into that [last] scene," Cahill notes, "to create this image of three generations of women who had found their place and were going to be okay."

Certainly, they have taken steps to improve their lives. They haven't left Bayonne, but they have made a change. They've done something for themselves rather than for the men in their lives: they've purchased new furniture. That may sound like a small or insignificant thing, but it isn't. It's a tentative confronting of their situation.

"It's a sign of hope, of change. Even this tiny little change that so many people would take for granted—going out and getting furniture," Cahill agrees. "To them, it's a huge deal. The furniture in Virginia's house has been exactly the same since the day she was married, and he left a long time ago, and she meets this man, and has hope that she is going to get out of this life and do something for herself. But when he's gone, the one thing that Nick left for her is the belief that she can make the change herself. She just doesn't have to hold on and wait for her life to begin again.

"Even though Nick is gone, she's going forward," Cahill points out. "I wanted people to feel that Virginia was going some place, not just leave her there in despair. That she was better for knowing Nick."

"It [the ending] was very hopeful," Rowlands agrees, "and there was a very good feeling between the mother and daughter. They can live without men, if necessary, and still have a wonderful life. Which is not to say they won't fall in love.

"Everybody has a chance at happiness," she continues. "The fact that they've been hurt and that they acted in ways that weren't in their best interest...you learn from those things, and you get stronger. And I thought that there was a nice settling-in quality among the women—and the little girl too—at the end of the film, a more comfortable feeling between them, and I thought they could help each other and express things to each other, and that the young girls needn't be so desperate."

The wonderful thing about *Hysterical Blindness* is that in its own inimitable way, it's really, like the best of Nair's films, a local story too, just as local as was *Monsoon Wedding*.

This author was raised near Bloomfield, New Jersey, in the 1980s, dated there, worked there and lived there, and can attest to the accuracy and authenticity of Cahill's words and characters. But even better, Mira Nair doesn't hit a false note in exploring a world far from Bombay or Delhi. She captures perfectly this microcosm and its denizens, and brings to the picture her own sense of imagery, symbolism and meaning in a way that enhances the material and makes it infinitely richer.

By being honest with the material, as Sabrina Dhawan would no doubt remind us, Mira Nair has revealed to audiences a local story that is ultimately universal. We can all identify with the desire to be wanted, and the inertia that sometimes keeps us from getting what we so desperately desire. This movie captures that desperation and offers the bravest and best performance in Uma Thurman's career.

Perhaps the most vivid moment in *Hysterical Blindness* is not a view of a bridge or another portal from Bayonne, but that of a desperate, lonely woman dancing in a bar—in a circle—all by her lonesome, almost in a frenzy. Although the dance has always been included in all versions of Cahill's play, it is also an important component of Mira Nair's cinema.

In her work, dance can provide a moment of catharsis (*Salaam Bombay!*, *Mississippi Masala*) or celebration (*Monsoon Wedding*), can reveal the nature of a character (*The Perez Family* and Dorrie), or even act as a point of entry into another world (*Vanity Fair*), but in *Hysterical Blindness* it serves another purpose: revealing an anxious, jittery character moving and spinning but—like Krishna in *Salaam Bombay!*—going absolutely nowhere.

"It's funny, because there are dances in almost all my plays," Laura Cahill considers. "The dance is in the play, and whoever played Debby always danced, but did it very, very differently. Other actresses who played her did it in an awkward I-don't-really-know-how-to-dance-but-I'm-trying-to-impress-you way, which is funny and heartbreaking too. But Uma can dance, and when she did it, it just had so much depth and feeling to it. It just really rocked me when I saw it."

Imagined by Cahill, staged by Nair, and performed by Thurman, Debby's dance in *Hysterical Blindness* perfectly encapsulates the character's trap of desperation. Accompanied by Pat Benatar's "Invincible," this dance reminds audiences that the search for happiness, and especially for love, sometimes really does feels like a "do or die" situation.

11'09'01 (2002)

Between production on *Hysterical Blindness* and its airdate, the world underwent a dramatic and terrifying change. On Tuesday morning, September 11, 2001, nineteen radical Islamic fundamentalists seized control of four American airliners and used them as weapons to destroy the World Trade Center in New York City, and attack the Pentagon in Washington D.C. The last hijacked plane was downed before reaching its target, likely the United States capitol. America was suddenly at war with a new kind of enemy, and that enemy had brown skin.

In the days following September 11, 2001, some Americans acted on their worst instincts and targeted anybody who, in their eyes, appeared to be an Arab. It was an ugly side of the culture, but the aftermath of the attack had caused a sea change in many people's thinking. The age of President George W. Bush's (seemingly endless) War on Terror was upon us, and meant in some cases that people—*even American citizens*—could be rounded up and detained in perpetuity without a trial, without even the pressing of specific charges. In years to come, these kind of atrocities may be remembered in the same breath as the Japanese internment camps of World War II, but even in 2006, much of Red-State America remains too close to the terror of 9/11 to see that some actions taken in our names after those terrible terrorist attacks were, perhaps, overreactions.

Sometime after the devastating attacks of the 11th of September, producer (and Frenchman) Alain Brigand considered some of these hot-button issues and laid out an interesting challenge to international film-makers. He wanted eleven directors—ten of them non-American—to craft short films on some aspect of the tragedy that affected them. The finished piece was to serve as an essay on "subjective conscience" and a tribute to "freedom of expression," which, of course, is what the War on Terror is really all about—the fight to maintain our freedoms.

As the DVD release of *11'09"01* establishes, the film aimed to "evoke the sheer scale" of the global shock wave that followed 9/11, "testify" to the resonance of the event, and "better convey" the human dimension of the tragedy. The film also sought to "give voice to all…"

For the directors, Brigand's only stylistic and technical stipulation was that each film had to run precisely eleven minutes, nine seconds, and one extra frame. Among those who participated in the enterprise were: Sean Penn (United States), Alejandro Gonzalez Inarittu (Mexico), Samira Makhmalbaf (Iran), Ken Loach (United Kingdom), Shohei Imamura (Japan), Claude Lelouch (France), Youssef Chahine (Egypt), Danis Tanovic (Bosnia-Herzegovina), Amos Gitai (Israel), Idrissa Quedraogdo (Burkina Faso), and Mira Nair, representing India.

Nair's short film for the project involved the new prejudice, the concept of Islamophobia and was based on a true story from that nightmarish day in September. Her segment, a so-called staged documentary[31] revealed "the agony of a Pakistani-American mother whose missing son, Salman, was accused of terrorism,"[32] when in fact, "as a police cadet and emergency volunteer, he had hurried to the Twin Towers to help in the rescue effort, and had died in the buildings' collapse."[33]

After a title card establishing that this short is "based on a true story," Nair's piece opens with a view of the New York skyline. From there, her camera pans across the "walls of the missing" that became so common in Manhattan after the disaster. The word "HEROES" blares across one newspaper headline. The film then cuts to Salman Hamdani's mother, a deeply religious woman with an expressive, tender face, as she prays for the safe return of her son.

Nearly as troubling as her son's disappearance is the question of his fate. Has Salman been taken by the F.B.I. and held without warrant and charged as a "terrorist?" Or is he lost all together, having somehow died in the disaster? While John Ashcroft and George Bush appear on CNN news clips on a television in her modest home, Mrs. Hamdani is questioned by agents of the F.B.I. about every aspect of her son's history.

"He's a big *Star Trek* fan," she reports.

"*Star Wars*," her other son, corrects.

"He is an American citizen," Mrs. Hamdani repeats again and again, her pleas and arguments ignored by the suspicious officials who judge any

Arab-looking person a threat to national security in the days after the crisis.

Mrs. Hamdani writes letters to Mayor Giuliani, even as newspapers refer to her missing son as a possible terrorist.

Salman's final fate is not known for certain until six months after 9/11. While the "tribute of light" shines from Ground Zero in Manhattan, it is learned that twenty-three-year old Salman's remains have been identified. Salman raced into the WTC to save people—his countrymen—not hurt them.

Mrs. Hamdani tearfully eulogizes her son at his funeral, noting that "Allah gives honors to those he chooses, or humiliation." Her son is a hero, but what, in the final analysis, does that description really mean? Is Salman's death Mrs. Hamdani's reward for raising a compassionate human being?

The devastating final shot of the short film reveals Mrs. Hamdani standing near railroad tracks, a train approaching slowly in the distance. Alas, the train will never again carry Salman home; yet she stands there, as if still expecting him; still hoping her son will one day return.

Typical of Mira Nair's sensitive approach, her tale in *11'09'01* is as much a human drama as a political one. As in *Monsoon Wedding* (which we see briefly in a television clip in the background), the family remains the epicenter of Nair's filmic universe. In this case, the focus rests on a worried and grieving mother.

Nair effortlessly captures the nuances of Mrs. Hamdani's "new" life after 9/11, from prayer to meal preparation, to a terrifying encounter at a train station—in which she imagines seeing her son on a passing train. Nair's work universally tugs equally at both the heart and the mind, and this effort is no exception, making the viewer feel the absence of Salman as a tangible, unceasing pain.

"I think that every filmmaker had the same amount of money," notes Stephanie Carroll, who served as Nair's production designer on the project and recalls its genesis.

"I can't remember how small it was, but that [production] was really a labor of love, and an important political statement to make. I am quite proud to have worked on that."

Carroll remembers that, as usual in the canon of Mira Nair, homework was a central part of her job.

"That involved a lot of research, because I really knew nothing about Muslims, and it was quite a political subject here [in New York] when you brought it up, or tried to do research. It was hard looking at some of the images we had to recreate, and the story was heartbreaking."

Allyson C. Johnson edited Nair's contribution to the film. In some senses, an editor was even more important on this film than a regular feature film, since the final results had to conform to the eleven minute/nine seconds/one frame edict of the producer.

"The biggest challenge was that the script was more like a seventeen page script," Johnson remembers. "It's good to start out with something that's longer, because you get to take the best of the best."

And was it difficult to keep the film within its allotted time frame?

"There are always ways of filling in the seconds when you have to be precise like that," considers Johnson, "but I don't think we ever made a shot an extra fifteen frames just because it had to be a certain length. We worked through the whole thing and made it as good as we possibly could, and then we were—luckily—pretty close to the time."

Beyond Nair's contribution to the film, results were mixed. Sean Penn's piece, starring a vulnerable, touching Ernest Borgnine, was a one-man show about a widower living in a dingy apartment. His wife's beloved flowers began to grow again after the towers fell, and their shadow was no longer present. Although Borgnine was quite moving in the piece, otherwise the work illuminated little about the human impact of September 11.

Likewise, Egyptian director Youssef Chahine's piece seems a tad off-kilter. The piece stars the director himself, as he encounters the phantasm of an American marine who was killed in a terrorist attack, in the barracks explosion in Beirut in 1983.

Chahine visits Arlington National Cemetery after discussing with the dead soldier the mentality of Arab suicide bombers. He explains that suicide bombers believe American citizens are as guilty as our government because they have a voice and vote in their own government. Therefore, civilians are acceptable as targets of war.

This seems a facile and self-serving argument. In fairness then, one must also conclude that Palestinians chose violence and suicide bombings over peace for many years, since their governing Authority did not renounce such tactics. Are Palestinian citizens "fair game" then, the way

American citizens are in this jihad? There are shades of gray here that the Chahine piece doesn't acknowledge.

One of the most beautiful pieces in *11'09'01* comes from Claude Lelouche, and concerns a deaf woman who writes a deeply-felt letter to her lover, a tour-guide for the hard-of-hearing, while he is away at the Trade Center. In the background, she emotionally composes her piece about the end of their relationship, while in the foreground of the frame, images of towers falling go unnoticed.

Then, at the end of the piece, her lover returns, covered in dust and grime, having barely survived the disaster…and the souls reconnect, having experienced something larger than the schism in their relationship.

Probably the most controversial piece in *11'09'01* was created by the United Kingdom's Ken Loach. Again, it involves letter writing. This time, an exile from Chile, now living in London, claims that America's interference in Chilean democracy resulted in death camps, torture and thirty thousand deaths on another Tuesday, September 11, one in 1973. Although this segment was viewed by many as the most anti-American piece in the film, it offers a critical perspective. To Americans, the attack on the World Trade Centers seemed to come out of the blue, unprovoked. Loach's film suggests that America's policies are behind such hatred for the West, and gives critical examples.

"I don't see why we should stand by and let a country go communist due to the irresponsibility of a people," said Henry Kissinger, thereby negating the "good" principle of democracy, if it results in an outcome the United States does not approve of.

Then, the film cuts to frightening footage of a CIA-led, Nixon-approved coup d'etat in Chile, paid for with ten million dollars, American cash. On television today, the audience hears Bush's call to fight the "enemies of freedom." The exile reminds us that America was actually one of George Bush's enemies of freedom in Chile all those years ago by refusing to accept the outcome of another country's democratic election. The result was a string of unbelievable atrocities, in which all resisters to the new fascist order of General Pinochet were termed "terrorists."

Reviews of Brigand's omnibus were decidedly mixed. Some reviewers felt the film was fervently anti-American, though in truth it just seemed determined to reveal an *international* view of the tragedy rather than a purely American perspective.

Others lauded the picture as being morally valuable and courageous. *The Newhouse News Service* called *11'09'01* "illuminating" and the *Toronto Star*'s Peter Howell considered it "genuinely empathetic."

Because the collection of short films ran into some political problems with America's vocal right wing and GOP echo chamber, it did not find an American distributor for more than a year. Empire Pictures ultimately released the one hundred thirty-five minute film in 2002.

"I wish it had better distribution," Carroll laments. "A lot of people haven't seen it...I don't know anybody who's seen it. I just wish [the country] had been a little more open to artistic expression. That's what it was."

11'09'01 was not made available on DVD until the end of 2004, more than three years after the tragedy that forever altered the path of America in the twenty-first century.

SHE WALKS IN BEAUTY

Following the unprecedented success of *Monsoon Wedding* upon its 2002 release, Mira Nair found her profile in Hollywood higher, perhaps, than it had been throughout her entire career crafting feature films. Not only did *Entertainment Weekly* name her (alongside Alfonso Cuarón) one of Hollywood's top ten "Entertainers of the Year," but two other serendipitous events coincided.

The first involved actress Reese Witherspoon of *Election* (1999), *Legally Blonde* (2001), and *Sweet Home Alabama* (2002), who wanted to meet with Nair in person to discuss a future collaboration. The second event would form the meat of that suggested collaboration. In particular, Focus Films, which had distributed *Monsoon Wedding* (under the banner of U.S.A. Films) offered Nair the opportunity to direct an adaptation of William Makepeace Thackeray's (1811–1863) timeless novel of social engineering in nineteenth century England, *Vanity Fair*.

This expansive, epic novel tells the life story of one determined young lass named Becky Sharp, a woman of undistinguished lineage in England in the early-to-mid-1800s, who—over time—attempts to reach the pinnacle of London society. After Becky fails to marry her friend Amelia's middle-class brother, Jos, she becomes the governess to the upper-crust Crawley family at Queen's Crawley, a stepping stone she uses to marry into the family. Yet even this is not enough for Becky as she aspires to ever greater heights, with enemies on all sides. In the end, for every gain, there will also be a sacrifice.

Thackeray was a man born into the gentleman class who had seen his financial wealth shredded during an economic downturn, and thus had to make a living to support his wife and daughters, a preoccupation that led him to a career in writing.

Before conceiving *Vanity Fair*, Thackeray was often considered a humorist of little consequence, frequently writing articles for magazines of the day, but *Vanity Fair* not only granted him stability in a financial sense— as well as the approbation of contemporaries like George Eliot and Charlotte Bronte—but the platform by which to comment on the society that had made him, due to economics, an exile.

Vanity Fair, which had been published in serial fashion from 1847–1848, reflected Thackeray's misgivings about England's class society, and so by many is considered one of the first truly "modern" novels. It's a satire featuring "no hero," *Vanity Fair* has also—in some controversial corners—been considered a proto-feminist work, and all of these aspects, from exiles and social commentary to female advocacy, appealed to Professor Nair.

As it turns out, Nair already boasted a long-standing affinity for *Vanity Fair*. When she attended the Miranda House, an Irish-Catholic school in Simla, a sixteen-year old Nair became acquainted with *Vanity Fair* and its ageless protagonist, the manipulative but spirited Becky Sharp.

"She was somebody who didn't care for the cards that society had dealt her and she made her own deck," Nair said of Sharp in 2004, noting that she was the greatest female character in literature, and that she "basically carved her way in a time when it was much harder to carve your way as a young woman on the other side of tracks."[34]

Thackeray's sharp view of the social conventions of his time was an approach that Nair felt mirrored her own. She described it in the film's DVD commentary as the "*cinema verité* of its day." In particular, because Thackeray had been born and raised outside England, in Calcutta, he wasn't shy about revealing the divides between classes. When he moved to

England as a young man, he was an outsider and thus able (not unlike *My Own Country*'s Dr. Abraham Verghese) to view the society from a different perspective than the native residents. The notion of outsider commenting on society was something Nair "identified with in a big way."[35]

But Nair imagined her *Vanity Fair* as something far different from the typical and often staid Merchant and Ivory period, costume piece. For one thing, she wanted to stress that the world of the British upper class—decadent and idle—was erected on the backs of the colonies, first and foremost, India. "Who better understands the colonial mentality than the colonized?" she told critic Carrie Rickey upon the film's release, describing a controversial decision to include so many obvious Indian touches in the film, including a new ending set there, and even a sexy Indian dance performed by Sharp in the home of the evil Lord Steyne.

To Nair, this acknowledgment of Indian influence on England was not in any fashion a perversion of the novel's intent or ethos. "People who don't know the novel may think, 'Oh here's an Indian director, she's imposed her India on it,' but the politics, the aesthetics—it was all given to me [in the novel]."[36]

Perhaps more alarmingly to purists—and there are always purists – Nair began to reconceive Becky as a modern woman. In her mind, Sharp was not a conniving manipulator, but a girl just forging her path under difficult conditions and using the rules of society (which were stacked against her) to attain its highest peak. Becky's edge could be softened, and the character could be made more sympathetic, and plucky Reese Witherspoon was thus the perfect talent to imagine her.

In the words of Witherspoon, it was Nair's intention to "turn the whole thing on its ear," because "attributes like ambition or desire were perceived as wicked then, now they're not."[37]

The first order of business after casting Witherspoon was to assemble a screenplay that would bring together all the elements of the classic in a fresh way, one that satisfied Nair's need for color, passion, flamboyance and a consistent theme. Originally assigned that task were writers Matthew Faulk and Mark Skeet, co-writers on such projects as the 2000 television miniseries, *Jason and the Argonauts*.

They had toiled on the script for nearly a decade,[38] but when Nair read it, she reported feeling "more attracted to the novel than the screenplay."[39] This consideration led to the hiring of Julian Fellowes, author of 2001's much-celebrated and honored drama *Gosford Park*. His screenplay for that Robert Altman film had won an Academy Award for best screenplay, as well as recognition from the Writers Guild of America, the New York Film Critics Circle and the National Society of Film Critics. He was a perfect choice.

The author of a bestselling 2005 novel named *Snobs*, about a woman who marries into the upper class only to find that she doesn't care for it, Julian Fellowes was interviewed for this book in early March of 2005, and takes us through the formative stages of *Vanity Fair*.

"I had originally been approached to do a rewrite, and I wasn't terribly interested in doing it, so I said no," Fellowes explains. "And then Mira was appointed director, and she really wanted to begin again. This is not to say anything against the script of Matthew and Mark, who are both charming and very talented. It wasn't that. It was just that she wanted to begin the process, really, when she came aboard, and she wanted me to do it. And with that understanding, it turned into a very different thing, and I very much came on at the behest of Mira. Then—together—we went through to see if we had the same *Vanity Fair* in mind.

"Then I flew to New York and we had a sort of extraordinary— romantic, really—Labor Day weekend," Fellowes explains. "Her family was in Kampala, mine was in London, and we just sort of wandered the streets of New York going to movies and going out to dinner and talking about how we wanted to do the film. It was wonderful actually. It was a wonderful, George Peppard/Audrey Hepburn way to start it off."

What they discovered on that weekend was that they shared a vision of the project. "I think we both knew that we were both in love with Becky," says Fellowes. "And never for a moment did we want to do a film about a woman you don't like or don't find attractive. That was absolutely from the start. Not that Becky had no flaws. Not that she didn't eventually get played out, but that there was something bewitching about her. Quite honestly, I don't believe it's possible to watch a two hour film when you don't like the central character. That may be a very bourgeois comment to make, but nevertheless, them's my sentiments. That was one of the things we were criticized for later."

But leaving that battle aside for the moment, Fellowes and Nair discussed the script in late 2002, and soon commenced an e-mail correspondence lasting well into May of 2003, when shooting was scheduled to commence. Their journal was featured verbatim in *Vanity Fair: Bringing Thackeray's Timeless Novel to the Screen.*

The substance of this electronic diary was the development of the script, and Nair's choices on what elements from the book were to be reinserted (notably the prominence of the William Dobbin character, Amelia's long-suffering sweetheart).

Fellowes discusses the difficulties of paring a nine hundred page book down to a two hour shooting script. "We decided that the main story would be Becky Sharp," he notes. "We also decided that our Rawdon would be a more romantic figure than the book's Rawdon. On the whole, we would stick to the narrative facts. We didn't invent a new narrative for Rawdon, and—in fact—all of his scenes are very faithfully reproduced from book to film. But he is more glamorous, more sexy, and he is more in love with her, and that was really the sort of [writing] burden of the time. I went back to London and started to write, and gradually then, you go into the process where you send the draft and they scribble on it and that goes on and on."

By the end of 2002, a shooting script was ready to go, and pre-production was beginning in earnest, but there was an unexpected delay when it looked like star Witherspoon would need more time to recuperate following her latest film project. Accordingly, shooting was postponed, and a disappointed Nair returned to her home in Kampala, Uganda, and her beloved garden there. Fortunes were soon reversed, however, and Nair was the recipient of a phone call from Witherspoon asking for film to commence at once.[40] Why? Reese Witherspoon was pregnant. If she were to star as Becky Sharp in *Vanity Fair*, it was now or never.

ALL IS VANITY

Suddenly, what had been imagined as a rather leisurely pre-production schedule was ratcheted up to warp speed, and the time to prepare the twenty-three million dollar film was trimmed down considerably. Perhaps the talent most affected by this change of plans was Maria Djurkovic,

Vanity Fair's veteran production designer. A brilliant designer of such award-winning films as *The Hours* (2002), *Billy Elliot* (2000), and most recently, *Sylvia* (2004), Djurkovic actually came to the project under odd circumstances to begin with.

"It was very, very quick," she recalls. "Basically, somebody else was going to be the initial production designer, and for reasons that I was never entirely clear about, that didn't happen. So Mira was looking for somebody else, and initially I knew her through a very, very weird coincidence. I have friends in Kampala who have nothing do with the [film] industry who are friends with Mira, who lives in Uganda as well, and they would always say [to her], 'You should meet our friend Maria who's a designer.'"

By happenstance, Nair viewed *The Hours* and reported that she wanted the designer of that film to do her next project. Djurkovic's friends in Kampala told her, "Yes, yes, that's our friend!" And from there, Nair's people placed a telephone call to Djurkovic.

"It was one of those weird situations where I was offered the film, but we never actually met, which is rather unusual. I think it was all rather accelerated," Djurkovic explains. "I originally had a six week gap before the start of the film, and I had a phone conversation with Mira…and I was to fly out to Kampala to meet her there and discuss the film. I was to get my inoculations for Kampala, but then I got another phone call. And they said, 'Reese is pregnant and we need to start on Monday.' I was at a commercial studio, and said, 'I'm actually starting a commercial on Monday,' and they said, 'Tuesday?'"

What had happened was that Djurkovic's anticipated sixteen week preparation time as originally envisioned was cut down to eight. Worse, the epic film was budgeted at a relatively low twenty-three million dollars, which meant recreating nineteenth century England was going to pose an even greater challenge. In fact, for a time it even looked as though the *Vanity Fair* team would not be able to shoot in London at all.

Ireland was considered as a substitute, but such a move would require a downsizing of scope and that was a compromise Mira Nair reportedly loathed. But then a hero rose, so to speak, when Reese Witherspoon reportedly donated some of her salary to the production. Suddenly, London was affordable again for a fifty-five day shoot.

But the crew wasn't out of the woods. Djurkovic recalls some of the anxiety about working fast and cheap. "The thing is this: if you have no money, but time, you can scramble through it. But we had no time *and* no money, so it was tough. Really tough. When you've got no money, you're going forwards and backwards and doing acrobatics the whole time. You're doing a design and you get it priced, and you realize that there's no way you can achieve it, and you have to pare it down. That's very frustrating."

Despite such hardships, Djurkovic found Mira Nair a supportive collaborator. She also found that the director had a distinctive vision for the film. And to her delight, it was one of color, passion and flamboyance.

"In a way, Beatrix [Pasztor], the costume designer, and I were given *carte blanche* to go for it, not to have to be completely rigid to the period," Djurkovic explains. "One of the major themes that Mira was keen on conveying was this whole colonial side of the country; that Britain had its tentacles all over the world, and that this had a huge impact on food, decor, design, clothes, fashions, etc. So that was a major influence.

"I spent a lot of time looking at paintings, and I submerged myself in research, and then I cast aside what I didn't want to use, but again, that was something that I had to do in a very short amount of time," she reiterates. "But we tried to include a little bit of everything to show the colonial influence. We had Japanese, Chinese, Indian, and North African. There's a little bit of everything in there."

Beatrix Aruna Pasztor was also encouraged to go for the bold. "There were a lot of white dresses and pastels in that period. Colors—like oranges, turquoise, and intense purples—were used for accenting," she told *Entertainment Weekly*. "We flipped that around."[41]

And Nair's response to the production and costume design? "I think we shared very similar ideas," says Djurkovic. "There was an embracing of the visual flamboyance. I love Beatrix's costumes, and again, she took quite a few liberties with the period; as I did as well. And with Mira, it was sort of 'Go with it girls! Go with what will give this a visual impact!' So I think that's the spirit that we embraced, and we were able to run with it.

"And run with it is—believe me—what we did," Djurkovic stresses. "As you can imagine, my feet never really touched the ground. I'm always flabbergasted by production designers who manage to be on set, because I never manage to be on set. I'm always getting the next one ready. I always see the sets in the morning, and then I'm off.

"The ridiculous thing is that I spent extraordinarily little time with Mira, and Beatrix as well. I think the costumes and the sets work very well together, but Beatrix and I barely spoke. We had one big meeting at the beginning where we discussed color and color palettes. And then every day, you'd see the results and say 'Wow, that worked!' and you'd be slightly surprised. Ridiculously, we'd go 'Hi' in the morning, and then we were ships passing in the night."

Allyson C. Johnson, Mira Nair's editor on *Monsoon Wedding*, was also swept away by the fast pace of creating *Vanity Fair*. "I had read the script, and I actually didn't even know until I got to London who the actors were going to be!" she says. "Which was interesting, because the dailies would arrive and I would say, 'Oh great—Bob Hoskins!' It was always a pleasant surprise."

There were a number of such pleasant surprises, as *Vanity Fair* boasted an eclectic and accomplished cast. Witherspoon found able support not just from Hoskins, but *Moulin Rouge's* (2001) Jim Broadbent as Mr. Osborne, *Velvet Goldmine's* (1998) Brian Slade, Jonathan Rhys-Meyers as the prickly George, and Rhys Ifans—late of *Notting Hill* (1999) and *Danny Deckchair* (1999)—as the lovestruck Dobbin. Others in the cast included Gabriel Byrne, villain of *End of Days* (1999) and *Assault on Precinct 13* (2005), as Steyne, a Byronic character he imagined as a "dark, tormented seducer,"[42] and the charismatic James Purefoy (*Resident Evil* [2000]) as Becky's beloved—but ultimately weak—gambler husband, Rawdon Crawley.

Also in the cast: the Shakespearean actress Geraldine McEwan (*Love's Labour's Lost*, 2000), the wonderful Eileen Atkins (*Cold Mountain*, 2002), and the lovely Romola Garai (*Nicolas Nickleby*, 2002) as the deluded emotionally out-of-touch object of Dobbin's affection, Amelia Sedley.

It was a big cast and a big production crew, sharing a daunting challenge: ninety locations on two continents. The film shot in Somerset and Kent in England, and at the Chatham Docks, the latter filling in for the loft of Becky's father, a painter. The first day of principal photography occurred in Gloucester, where Stanway House doubled as the mansion of Sir Pitt Crawley, Queen's Crawley.

Nair moved things along quickly by scouting many of these locations before shooting. "For instance, she'd been to Bath," Djurkovic remembers, but that preparation didn't mean it was easy getting to the locations once it was time to shoot. The *Vanity Fair* crew was often snarled in traffic.

"Traffic was just unbelievable," Johnson confirms. "Although I was in London with Mira, when you shoot there it still takes hours to get wherever you're going. We would pretty much work together on weekends because she would spend so much traveling during the week."

Sometimes, in fact, Mira Nair had her production crew moving at such a pace it actually created problems. Production designer Djurkovic had only a day to dress the aftermath of the Battle of Waterloo (at Hyde Park) and the Sedley cottage—interior and exterior, when she received a phone call from the set that the crew had moved ahead of schedule and would need Rawdon's Brussels lodgings ready for the next day.

"I was very angry," she remembers with good humor. "I wasn't happy at all, actually."

Another challenge involved creating Becky's London metropolis for the camera, a city "full of pigs, garbage and muck,"[43] that Nair hoped would resemble a period version of *Salaam Bombay!*[44]—chaotic, dirty, alive, and always in motion.

Djurkovic came up with an interesting gambit to bring the world of Old London to life, redressing Bath as Regency London. As it turns out, converting Great Pulteney Street into England's capital—a feat which involved, among other things, much scenery removal—was the high point of the film for the designer.

"That was very satisfying, very ambitious," she says. "We totally re-routed traffic. It was mad, but it was very ambitious…you could never do that in London."

The low point was, naturally, the budget restraints. For instance, Nair was denied the money she needed to shoot the Battle of Waterloo which the director likened to having *Gone with the Wind* "without Atlanta burning."[45]

"One of my big regrets and it was purely financial, is that we had to reduce Vauxhall Gardens considerably," Djurkovic laments, referring to the colorful outdoor festival where Becky expects a proposal from Jos. "I wanted to build a half-a-dozen pavilions. One Chinese, one built entirely out of seashells—really go for it. I think that Vauxhall Garden is a metaphor for the whole of *Vanity Fair*, but sadly that was a casualty of not having enough money."

Reese Witherspoon's condition was a constant source of speculation in the press, but by all accounts, she was a trooper. "She had so much energy for someone who was pregnant," Johnson says. "She still gave it her all, running across streets and everything."

And, steps were taken to hide her pregnancy. "Certain scenes were shot outside, and when the wind blew, you could tell a bit. Other times they just covered her up with baskets and things of that sort. I didn't feel the need to panic too much about that, but I know everybody was on pins and needles, really worried," Johnson remembers. "You never know. If one person starts picking up on it, then everybody is just going to be focusing on that rather than performance, and you definitely don't want that."

For Witherspoon, the pregnancy only seemed to lend authenticity to her performance, especially since Becky is with child herself for a good portion of the film's running time. Witherspoon reported that being with child only made the emotional scenes come easier to her because she felt "really hormonal."[46] The star also commented on a DVD feature about the making of the film, "The Women Behind *Vanity Fair*," that when "you're in a situation…only women can understand, it's nice to be around a female director…and female producers,"[47] a comment, no doubt, on the family atmosphere engendered on many a Mira Nair production.

While Witherspoon, Nair, Djurkovic and the rest of the *Vanity Fair* team continued shooting, Allyson Johnson worked concurrently on a first cut of the movie, so that the director and producers had a sense of what they already had in the can, and how that footage was telling the story.

"This film was so big, so much bigger than its budget, that we were constantly trying to figure out, 'Are there scenes we can cut out, so we have more [time] to do other things?'" Johnson explains. "So it was really important for me to keep up with them, and to make sure we were getting everything, and keeping the story straight.

"I think on this film, it was important to really give Mira a full view of what was shot," Johnson reflects, "and in my first cut, everything was really long. I don't usually do that, but I felt it was important for her to see everything she had. I didn't feel as comfortable cutting things out that I didn't think we'd use later."

Why? "In a film like that, you can never tell. You may not use it where you thought you were going to use it, but you might need it somewhere completely different."

After the first cut was screened, the long process of trimming the film was engaged. "A lot of the pruning came basically because we couldn't have such a long film, and again, Mira wanted that kind of quick-paced film," Johnson explains. "She didn't want to go the traditional way with this movie, so therefore there was no reason to keep the normal pace of what we know in period pieces. She has this love for fast-paced things, also this love for a film rich with many characters...and this film *definitely* had many characters.

"The one thing we were worried about was: are people going to be able to keep track of each of the characters? But it was so important to have the parallel love stories going on," Johnson explains. "A lot of the cutting really had to go back and forth and show cause and effect, so that we didn't forget why something was happening. And also, going to different countries? That was confusing. How do you get them back? Why are they coming back?"

"We were getting on pretty well, I think," suggests Julian Fellowes. "The difficulty of the process didn't—for me—come until the studio started to panic about the length of the film. They started to insist on cuts, some of which I think the film suffered from, to be perfectly honest."

In particularly, the scribe was dismayed that so much of the subplot was removed. "I think that the Amelia and Dobbin story was terribly truncated in the end, and it was very difficult to follow the beats of it," he says. "Why George agreed to marry her. Why Dobbin went on being faithful to her. How she came to think of him differently. It wasn't so much that whole scenes were taken out—which they were—but the ones that were left in were shortened. So it all became very abbreviated. But the Becky story, I think, survived. You're talking to the writer, so there are always scenes and lines that you wish you had gotten in, but I think that Mira managed with Reese to be pretty true to that.

"Sometimes, you put in a scene to make it clear when characters do another scene. And when it's taken out, your assumption as a writer is 'Oh My God it's damaged the scene that remains!' But it ain't necessarily so," says

Fellowes, when I noted to him that I found the Dobbin/Amelia sequences to be very touching. "Sometimes, when you go back to a work that's been edited or cut and you haven't looked at it for six months or a year or something, [and] when you look at it again, half the things you were worried about at the time…you can't see what your were making such a fuss about!"

By January 2004, Nair was working on sound and music for *Vanity Fair*. Again, she turned to her frequent collaborator, Mychael Danna to compose the film's score.

"Ironically, we were more on my turf for that film," Danna considers. "Certainly, it's a time period I'm very comfortable with, the early 1800s. That's the kind of music I grew up from the womb hearing, and again it's a case where Mira has such a gift for telling female stories and so, yeah, it seems in some ways to be a stretch for her, but it's a story in a culture she does understand very well.

"We used a standard, big orchestra, which we recorded in London," he describes. "The goal was to find a theme that was very memorable and very much summed up the character of Becky Sharp, and a theme that would always be there, through all the trials and tribulations and long road of ups and downs she takes through life. It's simple, energetic, almost girlish.

"I think it was fun for me to bring Mira into my world, as it were," reflects Danna. "Certainly I've worked in all kinds of music, but definitely nineteenth century orchestra music is where I came from. So it was fun to take her to London and do a score like that. I think she adored the experience, and it was really kind of fun for her to see something so—for her, in some ways—exotic.

"I love this about Mira's work, and my own career too, working on film in general," the musician says. "It's just so rewarding to be able to go from one world to another. Certainly you see in her work, there are some very significant themes that are important to her that she keeps returning to. There's definitely a thematic link between all these films, even though they're seemingly very different in very different time periods and different places. There are still some things that they've all been concerned with, and that's what's been fun about working with Mira. Whether we're working with the Philharmonia or Vilayat Khan, there are things in common and there are themes in common."

While overseeing the sound and music on *Vanity Fair*, Mira Nair was also readying herself for what would turn out to be the last leg of shooting: a trip to Jodhpar, India, in February to shoot the film's (revised) finale. The cast and crew undertook a whirlwind excursion—less than a week—to lense footage of Becky's new beginning (with Joseph Sedley) in India, shooting footage with dozens of local extras at the Mehrangarh Fort.

The film's original ending had seen a noticeably aged Becky returning to Queen's Crawley for the funeral of Pitt, and a moment when she tries to reconnect with her grown son, but is promptly rejected when he notes that it is too late to "play" at being his mother. After a brief rapprochement during a eulogy in which it is stated that "love is vanity's conqueror," the film would have faded out.

By contrast, the new ending shot in India was a more upbeat and colorful one, indicating that Becky's adventures were continuing. It included footage of Becky's luggage—her trunk emblazoned with the initials "R.S."—which tied the film back to its opening scenes and instead of suggesting a particular moral point about the journey, indicates only that life is an ongoing odyssey.

A HERO RISES AND FALLS

Vanity Fair opened September 1, 2004, with ad lines trumpeting "All's fair in love & war," and the much more dramatic, "On September 1, a heroine will rise." But Mira Nair's biggest budgeted cinematic effort to date did not meet with wide audience popularity, nor the overwhelming critical support of *Monsoon Wedding*. Once more, reviewers seemed to be of two minds about the film.

On the positive side, Roger Ebert awarded the film four stars, and many critics praised Reese Witherspoon's stand-out performance. "She does for the British Becky Sharp what English actress Vivien Leigh once did for that appealing Southern belle, Scarlett O'Hara," considered Bruce Newman in the *San Jose Mercury News*, "she makes it impossible to imagine anyone else in the role."[48]

Others including the *Sarasota Herald Tribune* noted the film was "lush," "entertaining," and "nothing to be ashamed of,"[49] but for some, the tone seemed to be one of displeasure at the perceived liberties taken with Thackeray's novel.

Variety's Todd McCarthy complained of "generally lackluster direction"[50] under Nair's guidance, and writing for *USA Today*, Claudia Puig considered that much of the "nuance, subtlety and intricacy of the classic novel" was lost while trying to make the film fit within a two hour running time.[51]

Perhaps the most frequent criticism directed at *Vanity Fair* was that the Becky Sharp of Thackeray's imagination had somehow become defanged in an effort to make her acceptable to twenty-first century mores. Although noting that some of what the author intended had shone through in "a literate well-cast, handsomely shot epic," David Ansen at *Newsweek* also remarked that Nair and Witherspoon had pulled back from the "ferocity" of Thackeray's Becky, fearful that audiences wouldn't find her "likable enough."[52]

"We all wished that it had a bigger reception," laments Allyson C. Johnson. "I think that was a little bit disappointing and frustrating, because everybody worked so hard, and it really was a beautiful film. I think I'm learning that you can just never tell what's going to happen with a movie. You just can't finish it and say, 'Oh my God, this is a fantastic film and everyone's gonna love it,' because there are so many opinions out there. Just depending on how much press you get, and what kind of press, can really affect whether the movie makes it or not. We all wish it had made a bigger impact, but it was also a very daring film. It was not going to be a mainstream film, ever."

"The first time I saw it, I was scanning the screen for anything wrong on my side of things," says Djurkovic. "The second time I was able to watch the film and I really enjoyed it. There's that thing where you come out of a movie feeling [either] a little bit flat or feeling good, and I came out feeling good."

In its first weekend, *Vanity Fair* grossed a little over six million dollars and after a brief two month spell in theatres, by November 2004, the picture had earned only slightly over sixteen million. This was considered a disappointment when measured against the performance of other recent Reese Witherspoon vehicles, and its own budget.

Perhaps more genuinely disappointing, the film was only sparsely recognized for industry honors. Nair was nominated for the Golden Lion at the Venice Film Festival, and Maria Djurkovic and Tatiana Lund were nominated for a Golden Satellite Award for best production design/art direction, but neither won. Though Beatrix Pasztor went home with a Golden Satellite for Best Costume Design, that was small consolation considering that *Vanity Fair* didn't pick up a single Academy Award nomination in any category whatsoever.

When released on DVD in early February of 2005, *Vanity Fair* racked up an additional eight million dollars in its first two weeks of general release, a sign, perhaps, that audiences were discovering the film on the secondary market.

FROM THE PAGE TO THE SCREEN

It seems there's always somebody with an opinion when filmmakers adapt a classic work of literature to celluloid. There's never a shortage of critics to claim that the movie version is unfaithful to the source material (i.e., 1995's *The Scarlet Letter* starring Demi Moore), or even that the film has misinterpreted the point of the original (i.e., Jack Clayton's 1974 adaptation of *The Great Gatsby*). This popular parlor game of second-guessing filmmakers very much represents the situation that Mira Nair's *Vanity Fair* found itself mired in upon release in the fall of 2004. Writer Julian Fellowes, for one, was fully aware of the pitfalls of the job.

"One of the things that was difficult, and this was for Mira as well as for me, is that the easiest thing to adapt is a book that nobody knows. Whatever you do—on the whole—nobody cares. The next easiest is the book that everybody knows extremely well, because you are serving something that is present in all your minds. However, the most difficult task is when you're adapting a book that everyone *thinks* they know, but they haven't read for thirty years. That was the category that *Vanity Fair* came into, and so people were making these statements in reviews that were quite simply not true.

"For instance," Fellowes continues, "I read several times that we had made Becky totally sympathetic, and that in the book she is a villainess. And of course, she isn't at all, if you read the book. In fact, Thackeray was *criticized* at the time for being so sympathetic to a woman who did not represent Victorian values.

"In a sense, Thackeray only criticizes Becky [in the book] when she finally loses touch with herself, becomes corrupted by Steyne, and drawn into his web. That's exactly the same in the film. The one moment where our Becky is represented as having gone off peak is when she thinks she can control Steyne, and she can't. The scene when he says, 'you're taking favors from a tiger.' She thinks she can manage him as she's managed everyone else, but she doesn't realize that Steyne is a much tougher nut."

Still, film scholars found plenty of ammunition in regards to Becky's "heroism" since the film's chosen ad line noted that on September 1, a "hero would rise," and the original book's subtitle contradicted that notion by terming *Vanity Fair* a novel "without a hero." Fellowes, who made a study of Thackeray while at university, has a few thoughts about this notion as well.

"The only reason Thackeray called it a novel without a hero was because he had to pretend that Becky Sharp wasn't the heroine. His publisher attacked him for writing a book about someone who was offensive to public morality, and that's why he put a section in the book where she strikes the child. And afterwards, he regretted it. He couldn't say, 'A Novel with a Heroine You Won't Approve Of,' but that probably would have been a more accurate subtitle."

In fact, as Fellowes is quick to point out, to many readers at the time of the book's publication, Becky was indeed the hero. "They adored her!" he declares. "That was what was so shocking! It was one of those books that terrified people. It's not because [the ruling class] thinks the public will reject [the work], it's because they think the audience will accept it."

Still, gazing back upon *Vanity Fair*'s reviews, it's amazing to see how picayune many complaints are. "I remember one chap—one of the journalists in Venice—said to me: 'In the book, when Becky is leaving to go to Queen's Crawley, Amelia gives her a present, but in the film, Becky gives Amelia a present!' And I said to him, 'If that's our main problem, I think we're in pretty good shape.' It makes you realize that there is a real resistance to understanding that this [film] is a different form."

The lion's share of the criticism directed at *Vanity Fair* fell into three distinct categories. The first was that Becky was not manipulative enough, or more accurately, as scheming as she appeared in the novel. The second most-oft heard complaint was that Nair's film took far too many liberties with the book, including a new ending and the inclusion of a seductive Indian dance scene at Lord Steyne's party. And finally, some reviewers didn't care for the depiction of English society, complaining that it was too ugly and mean-spirited. This last criticism pointed out that instead of a film that "glamorized the estates, the clothes, the diction" of England, this *Vanity Fair* actually invited audiences to, "Look at all those messed-up white people!" The film's approach was termed, by critic Armond White of *New York Press*, "reactionary classicism."[53]

All these points are certainly debatable, but what so many mainstream reviewers seemed to miss was the idea that this is Mira Nair's *interpretation* of *Vanity Fair*, which means that she has selected what elements from the book to weigh more heavily, and which to reduce in importance. Is this the same *Vanity Fair* that Thackeray wrote? Yes, to the extent that it can be, adapted in a different medium—almost a hundred and fifty years after its first publication—and in the hands of an artist with her own sensibilities.

Let's analyze and consider each of the aforementioned criticisms, starting with Becky's nature. In the book, there is no doubt that she is not quite so noble as she appears in the film. The Sedleys notice how taken she is with money, for instance, and that her "attraction" to their son, Joseph, is based on this fascination. In the movie, Becky is still materialistic, but Mira Nair has recast her with a modern sensibility, crafting the character as a female role model (in the tradition of Nair heroines like Mina, Maya and even Dorita).

"The beauty of Mira Nair's direction," suggests Reese Witherspoon, "is that this is not a judgment of Becky or any of the characters. There is no good and bad."[54] That may or may not be so, for Becky is certainly not judged negatively in the film, but instead lauded as a fighter. She is—to use that loaded term—the film's hero, which immediately equates with the judgment of "good."

But it is interesting *how* Becky is "good" in this adaptation. Consider a scene early in the film when Becky Sharp must leave the Sedley estate and take an exterior seat on a carriage, even though it is raining. In the book, she says she "prefers the open air," trying to put on the impression that the seating is her choice. In the film, the way the line is delivered, it's as though she is martyring herself. Life has handed her lemons, so she's going to make lemonade.

One also sees that this Becky succeeds not by trampling over others, but by actually protecting the feelings of others. She is downright obsequious at times in her efforts to make other people feel good about themselves, and that's a new twist. She validates them, whether it be about their cooking, their writing, or even their appearance. In true twenty-first century fashion, this Becky Sharp is a self-esteem builder, and that's how she rises through the ranks of insecure high society. It's not the overt scheming and duplicity of the book, it's a kind of aggressive campaign of validating others.

This approach is seen throughout the film. Early in the movie, Becky presents Amelia with a gift, a small painting by her late father. This indicates Becky has dignity, value, courtesy and something to share with others. She may be poor, but she understands and observes decorum. She has intrinsic worth as a person. She has a generous heart. In the book, as Fellowes had pointed out, the painting is already hanging on the wall when Becky arrives. That's a difference from the original text, but one that also feeds logically into the movie's modern lens. We learn more about Becky by having her give the picture to Amelia, than vice versa.

Becky is a character who, like Maya in *Kama Sutra*, is trying to break down social barriers. We cheer plucky Becky, a go-getter out to better her situation, and she never really does anything to betray our trust. She seems to love her husband and son in the movie, whereas in the book she hates her baby and cheats on her husband with Lord Steyne. This is the same character but seen with a quality we are familiar with from Mira Nair's other works. *Mercy*.

"She [Becky] never hurts these people, and that's what I think is important," Fellowes considers. "Within the book, she makes the Crawley household better…she makes it happier. She organizes Sir Pitt's stuff. She makes Mrs. Crawley happier—she amuses her. But at the forefront the whole time is her own life and self, and I don't think we betrayed that in the film. We kept that. However much she was fun or great to have around, she was always thinking of herself.

"Becky's a very liberated woman," says Fellowes. "It is a fiction that women's lib invented the liberated woman [in the 1960s]. The liberated woman has been going for hundreds of years, but nevertheless, if women's freedom and women's equality means anything, it is about taking responsibility for their own lives, and not spending their whole lives serving some kind of male originated design of what they're supposed to be like.

"Becky's like that," Fellowes stresses. "She's like the second generation of the liberated woman. The first generation was the sort of bra-burning, angry one. But the second generation wasn't that. It was the kind of Virginia Slim advert: be as feminine as you like, but make it work for you. *Use it.* Use everything you've got to get what you want. And that is how she is, and that seems to me to be a very modern archetype, and I think that's why she really chimes with a modern audience."

Regarding other liberties taken with the book, it is clear that some characters have been omitted from the film, some altered, and some stories curtailed. In good conscience, critics shouldn't complain too strongly about that. There is no choice in film, unless one wants to remain seated in the cinema for nine hours. A nine hundred page book with all of its complexity simply cannot be transferred in toto to film, an entirely different medium.

"The one thing we did alter—and this was a completely joint decision—is that we made the match with Rawdon much more of a love match than it is in the book," admits Fellowes. "Partly that's because every big, epic movie needs a love story, but particularly when it goes wrong for her with Steyne, one has to have a sense that she has lost everything; that she has lost what is of value to her through her misjudgment. Through the fact that she thought she could handle *Vanity Fair*, but in the end she was overturned by her own vanity, which is really the story.

"Thackeray has a hundred pages to talk about her loss of this and her loss of that and so on," Fellowes points out, "but we don't have a hundred pages. We have a few minutes in a film, and felt that if the marriage is really valuable to her, then the moment when Rawdon leaves—all of which is taken straight from the book, as you probably know—if she really loved him, then she would have really lost something that she wanted to keep.

"But for the rest of it, I feel that we were pretty true to Thackeray's intention, which is that she is making her life in the world, and at times, she forgets. In the book and the film she is a negligent mother. She allows Steyne to push her mothering to one side and to essentially take over her child. She thinks she's keeping her values. She thinks she's in control, but she isn't. And when she rises and rises in the world, that stuff becomes undermined and she loses control over it."

And what of the other critique, that *Vanity Fair*'s ending is made up from whole cloth, and untrue to the spirit of the book?

"We had some different endings," Fellowes acknowledges. "We had that ending which goes back to Queen's Crawley, and then Jane gives that speech at the end…which I rather liked. But the ending we got, far from being a made-up ending—which I read in the papers—is essentially the ending from the book. Except in the book they go round Germany together instead of going back to India. But he [Jos] arrives from India in the book, so to me that didn't seem like a very big departure.

"I do like the extravagance of the ending," Fellowes weighs. "There is the sense that this great adventuress is onto the next adventure. The other ending didn't have that. Really what we were choosing was either a journey in which she had learned something and had reassociated herself with her son and got back what she had lost. But that was the calmer, contemplative ending. Or, we had the sense Becky Sharp is Becky Sharp still, and that she's off to the next mountain range. And no doubt after Jos drops dead, she'll marry a maharajah. In a way, that was truer to the character, really."

As for the inclusion of Indian (and Eastern touches) throughout the film, this element also has a place. Mira Nair sees the world in terms of complexities, in terms of cause and effect, in terms of past and present. She is of Indian origin and that fact cannot be separated from this film. She is acutely aware that colonialism is the means by which the rich upper crust of Becky's time achieved its excessive wealth. That wealth was built on the backs of countries like India, Nair's home. So, it is not a betrayal of Thackeray's text to include these elements as important visuals.

In fact, for the story to make sense at all, some of this is absolutely necessary. Without understanding the wealth of the time, what is one to make of the able-bodied Rawdon's inability to find work? He is amongst the idle rich, decadent, irresponsible and—without his money—useless. He can be a soldier or get a diplomatic posting to a colony, but those are really his only options.

And Mira Nair is correct when she notes that this material is extant in Thackeray's text. Joseph Sedley is depicted in the book as having an

Indian man servant, eating Indian candies, and adorning an Indian-style frock. These are his "fascinations" and part of his life, and they are described in detail. In fact, the book actually featured other foreign countries too.

"Thackeray was born in Calcutta, and grew up rather obsessed with India. In the book, actually, there's not only India but the Far East and the Middle East," Fellowes reminds us. "We decided against that. In a two hour film that would break up the potency of it, and it was better to stick with the central image of India, because if there is one country that stands for Empire when you're dealing with Britain, it's surely India.

"In the book, Thackeray uses Empire for two or three different reasons. One, he has the luxury of writing in the 1840s about the 1810s, so he has the luxury of hindsight. And, in a way he's saying that the British are biting off a mouthful that is much bigger than they can chew. But he also uses India to suggest that there are worlds out there where it doesn't matter whether Lady Steyne has you to dinner, or if Lord So-and-So comes to your parties. There are different worlds with different values, so that one shouldn't get too bogged down in the values of one's own culture. That seems to be to be a very modern statement. When all of us are being driven by the pressures of our own civilization, we need reminding that there are places on Earth where these values mean nothing. We are—to a large degree—enslaved by them, because we choose to be. And that is true of Becky. She chooses to be captured by these values, and in a sense, snubbed by them, rather than telling everyone to piss off."

What irked the critics most, however, about *Vanity Fair* was that dance. The Indian dance featuring Becky and lorded over by Steyne. To many, it seemed out of place in Victorian England. Too different; too risqué.

"I always say, 'What do you imagine that image was in the book?'" says Fellowes. "And they say, 'I don't know,' and they haven't read the book for thousands of years. And I remind them that in the book, it's a charade where Steyne is a Turkish *pashir* and Becky is a slave girl who kneels at his feet in a slave girl, harem outfit. Well, of course, that's incredibly shocking! Just as shocking as anything Mira put on the screen. It's criticized because they've forgotten what Thackeray was trying to say. There is a very stark reminder that there are—in a sense—almost more honest values [outside

English society]. They don't masquerade and hide the sex and ambition that is driving London society as it was driving everything else."

Becky's beautifully choreographed and erotic dance works splendidly in the film, replacing one kind of performance art for another, and it also augments the visualization of Steyne's real motives, which quite obviously stem from sexual desire. Since this Becky does not make love to Steyne, it is easy to imagine her agreeing to participate in this "show," in part because she realizes that her way to reach the strata of the upper classes is through her own god-given talents: singing and performance.

In the documentaries on the DVD about the making of the film, producers even compare her to the singer Madonna, and oddly enough that's a pretty apt analogy. Some people would consider the Material Girl vulgar, her need for attention desperate, her choices questionable. But she's exactly where she wants to be: rich and powerful and iconic. So for Becky to dance (after we have heard her sing), is not that far a leap indeed.

Regarding colonialism and its impact on Europeans, Nair's version makes another unique point. At sporadic points throughout the film, her camera and characters travel to India. Frankly, the open and vivid atmosphere there seems to do wonders for the stuffy Dobbin. And look at the open, loving faces of those Indian parents and children in the scenes set there. Contrast that blissful nirvana with how the children are gloomily unhappy in England. Little George? A little bastard. Becky and Rawdon's son? Sent off to school against his will, desperate and pathetic. Is there any joy to be found in England, or only sacrifice and duty? The very air in India makes children and mums happy, and even grows Dobbin a backbone so Amelia can love him.

As for the "look-at-all-the-messed-up-white-people" argument offered by some, well, quite simply, that's how Thackeray wrote the book. *Vanity Fair* is a satire that skewers the class system and its hypocrisies. One can't make the claim that this critique was not in the novel. By revealing grotesque old lords and ladies throughout the film, Nair has merely found a visual representation of the disgusting, corrupt system. They are rotten on the outside, as well as morally.

This is empirically true to the spirit of the book, and Thackeray has even been criticized for this presentation of the characters. Scholar James Oliphant has noted that "the contemptible figures in his [Thackeray's] portrait are so preponderant that the whole effect is an utter travesty of human life."[55]

As Graham Fuller writes, "Nair visually depicts an England corrupted by imperial wealth. The movie begins with Becky's eventual sponsor and would-be seducer, the marquess of Steyne (Gabriel Byrne) decadently attired in a shimmering blue coat, being driven in a coach through crowds of impoverished Londoners, including several Chinese men whose presence indicates the burgeoning multi-culturalism."[56]

Besides, could any accurate reading of *Vanity Fair* conclude that it was Thackeray's intent to glamorize the houses and the fashions? If broached, such an approach would succeed only in validating the corrupt system Becky is trying to crack. And that wouldn't fit in with Thackeray's concept of a story without a hero, would it? One point of both the movie and the book is that materialism and social climbing is a sort of empty gesture. The upper class will never accept the lower class. And who, to paraphrase Thackeray, having achieved their goals of wealth, is truly happy and satisfied with that outcome? This is an especially timely message, "particularly in America," where people "reach for something bigger or better, or higher, whether it's money or jobs or degrees,"[57] as Reese Witherspoon says. One has the feeling that Becky sees the climbing as a good thing, a way of trying to better oneself, but in fact, it's just a symptom of rampant materialism and wanting what you can never possess.

In both the film and the book, Becky's social climbing gets her nowhere. She loses her husband, her son, and her reputation because of her efforts to reach the apex of society. She ends up working in a casino, and in Nair's version reconnects with Sedley, a man she might have married *some twenty years earlier* had she not been bent on pursuing the course she chose. So what were those twenty years for, Becky? Was it worth it?

If this entire review has seemed a rebuttal to the points made by mainstream critics who reviewed *Vanity Fair*, that's too bad. This reviewer remains shocked at the hostility the film generated. Critics were faced with a bold reinterpretation of a classic story, one taking colonialism into account and boasting a modern, feminist bent, and yet for the most part were unwilling to deal with it on those terms.

Some of these same critics applauded a film by Baz Luhrmann called *William Shakespeare's Romeo and Juliet* (1996). It was set in Verona Beach,

California, in the modern day and the adaptation included handguns and cars. It wasn't blasphemy to reparse the material that way. On the contrary, it was damn inventive, and Mira Nair's interpretation of *Vanity Fair* follows suit. This may be her *Vanity Fair* as much as Thackeray's, but it is also faithful to the spirit of the written material. And since in this medium of film, the director has primacy, there's nothing wrong with that.

A close and careful viewing of *Vanity Fair* reveals it is one of the best films released in 2004, and a timely updating of a classic. It looks like it cost a hundred million dollars, it speaks directly to a current issue in America (people living on credit well beyond their means), is beautifully photographed, and most importantly, it bring attention back to a classic work of art, and does so with new colors, a fast pace, and dynamism to spare.

6

Sneak Peek: *The Namesake* (2006)

While en route to India to shoot the climax of *Vanity Fair*, Mira Nair's selection of airplane reading led unexpectedly to the development of her next feature film. Already on her plate was a feature film adaptation of Pulitzer Prize-winning author Tony (*Angels in America*) Kushner's play *Homebody/Kabul*. Written before September 11, 2001, Kushner's piece concerned a British housewife's sojourn to an Afghanistan that didn't tally with her imagination of it.

But by the time Nair disembarked from the plane, she had traded one Pulitzer Prize winner for another. In fact, she was already deeply enmeshed in purchasing the movie rights to Jhumpa Lahiri's first novel, the *New York Times* bestseller entitled *The Namesake*. To put it in her words, Nair had a "completely visceral" response to this book.[1]

It isn't difficult to discern why the book spoke so powerfully to Nair. Lahiri's novel, a follow-up to her Pulitzer Prize-winning collection of short stories *Interpreter of Maladies*, in many ways echoes the life experience and film ethos of Nair. It concerns, among other things, the Indian experience outside of India.

Semi-autobiographical in its nature, Lahiri's novel traces the life of the Ganguli family from 1967 to the year 2000. It opens on the story of Ashima and Ashoke Ganguli, an Indian couple transplanted to Cambridge, Massachussetts, as Ashima deals with the difficult separation from their homeland, their families, and most importantly, their traditions. When Ashima gives birth to their first child, a son, this problem comes to the forefront of their lives. Bengali ascribes two names for each individual, a so-called good name and also a pet name, and though Ashima waits patiently for her grandmother to send a letter naming their son, it never arrives.

As a consequence, the boy's pet name—Gogol—becomes, to the dismay of everyone in his family, his official name in the United States.

Unfortunately, Gogol grows up hating both his name and his namesake, the Russian author of such stories as "The Overcoat." Though this name holds a meaning to his father, a professor of engineering, because of a train accident in India many years in the past, Ashoke has not shared this incident—nor this meaning—with his dissatisfied son. Gogol comes to feel oppressed by his name—which is neither Indian nor American—and as he grows, legally changes it to Nikolai.

Yet this is not all Gogol struggles with. His relationships with women, both American and Indian, help him understand that he is really of neither culture, but a hybrid of both, and at home in neither.

Like so many of Nair's films, what *The Namesake* really concerns is the concept of identity, and how we, as individuals, forge it. "The question of identity is always a difficult one," Lahiri has acknowledged, "but especially so for those who are culturally displaced, as immigrants are, or those who grow up in two worlds simultaneously, as is the case for their children."[2]

Again, this is a condition that global citizen Nair—of India, Uganda, and the United States—is quite familiar with. It's material that seems tailor-made for her touch. "Like *Monsoon Wedding* was my world in India, *Namesake* is almost exactly the world I've traveled since then, which is like when I left Calcutta for Cambridge, Massachusetts, and New York City," she said. "It's about that journey."[3]

That journey is part and parcel of *The Namesake*. Born Nilanjana Sueshna Lahiri (Jhumpa is her pet name), Lahiri was born in England in 1967, but her family moved to Rhode Island, where she was raised. Both of her parents are in education, her mother a teacher and her father the head of the cataloging department at the University of Rhode Island library.[4] Lahiri graduated from Barnard and then earned a Ph.d. in renaissance studies at Boston University before seeing stories published in the *New Yorker* and garnering such acclaim as an O'Henry Award. When published in 2003, her first novel won rave reviews.

"I've never written for anyone other than myself,"[5] Lahiri told Teresa Wiltz at the *Washington Post*, but that fact didn't stop the critics from finding her work both valuable and accessible. For instance, *Library Journal* wrote that *The Namesake* "cobbles together everyday events with mesmerizing inner dialogue and glimpses of Bengali culture,"[6] and the *Houston Chronicle* raved that the book was a "shrewdly observed excavation of family life," and termed it "dazzling and fully realized."[7]

Mira Nair bought the rights to *The Namesake* and set out to co-produce the film, budgeted at a little over nine-and-a-half million dollars with India's UTV (India United Television), Fox Searchlight and Japanese Entertainment Firm. Sooni Taraporevala, Nair's collaborator on *Salaam Bombay!*, *Mississippi Masala* and *My Own Country*, adapted the novel to screen form, and Nair reported her intention to stay "fairly close"[8] to the book, though she has made some changes.

In particular, the character of Ashima, a housewife in the book, is now a singer (to accommodate Nair's love of Bollywood music) and the Cambridge setting has been changed to New York. There have also been some reports that the role of Ashima has been made more central, particularly her struggle as a foreigner in America, and the feeling of being away from home, and in the words of Lahiri, feeling a sort of "lifelong pregnancy," a "perpetual wait, a constant burden, a continuous feeling out of sorts."[9]

"It was a very difficult book to adapt," Taraporevala suggests, while noting that she has made a specialty of just such adaptations.

"I've done a lot of adaptations. Nowadays, I think I do more adaptations than original stories. I've adapted *Such a Long Journey* (1998), which is a very dense novel. I've adapted several [novels] that have been commissioned, but have not made it to screen. I've adapted *Homebody/Kabul*, so what I'm trying to say is that *The Namesake* has been, you know, one in a series. What I loved in *The Namesake* is the inter-generational span of time. You really get a feeling of life from Ashima's journey. So that's something that interested me, and what I was interested in preserving, that kind of time span."

As for further details on the script, Sooni is cagey. "You just have to watch the movie!" she teases.

In the closing months of 2004, Mira Nair also reported that her latest film would also serve as an homage to Kolkata (Calcutta), a town where she had summered as a youth (and participated in street protest theatre). More to the point, she also saw *The Namesake*—artistically—as a tribute to the film canon of Ritwik Ghatak (1925–1976), an Indian playwright/actor /director who had made, after a fashion, the same trip from documentary film into fictional narratives Nair did, only years earlier.

One of Nair's favorite filmmakers, whose films she says she watches "virtually every night,"[10] Ghatak was a politically-active and humanist director and playwright, who, in a strange coincidence concerning *The Namesake*, once even adapted the works of Gogol. But Ghatak's work in cinema was exclusively in black and white, and so this format was actively considered for the film by Nair and her pre-production team.

"The funny thing is that this film—I always felt—should be in black and white, especially the Indian parts," says Stephanie Carroll, *The Namesake*'s production designer. "We talked about that, Mira and I, and [director of photography] Fred [Elmes] may do a bleach bypass on some scenes." A bleach bypass will take out the saturated colors, and leave more black and silver in the print.

As for the look of the film's remainder, Nair has stated she desires to capture the gothic qualities of Bengal and contrast it with the urban cool look and "desi" power of the Big Apple.[11]

But if deciding on the visual palette of *The Namesake* was a clear-cut choice, finding the right cast proved far more difficult. It was initially reported that Rani Mukherjee, an up-and-coming star of Indian films such as *Yuva* (2004), was slated to play Ashima, but soon rumors swirled that she had turned down the film because of a nude scene, or because her salary wasn't what she desired.

Later, these stories were debunked, and Mukherjee's departure from the project was revealed simply as a matter of scheduling, as the actress herself reported. She was slated to appear in director Karan Johar's next film and felt that since he gave her a break in film (in 1998's *Kuch Kuch Hota Hai*), she couldn't disappoint him.[12] Konkona Sen Sharma was to be the designated replacement Ashima,[13] but that didn't happen either. Instead, the role went to Tabu, an Indian model and actress who had appeared in such efforts as *Filhaal* (2002) and *Hawa* (2003).

For the lead role of Gogol, Mira Nair had approached another hot young Indian actor, twenty-eight-year old Abhishek Bachchan, and after meeting with him decided that he was the "right choice."[14] Unfortunately, he was soon out of the project too because of unspecified "date hassles."[15] His loss, however turned out to be Nair's gain, for she soon found a young actor with a high profile in America. She cast Kal Penn as Gogol, and he is known to a generation of teenagers for his role in the 2004 comedy *Harold and Kumar Go to White Castle*. Even more fans will come around to his work after he appears in another major 2006 release, *Superman Returns*, in which he will portray a friend of Clark Kent.

Another actress cast in the film, as Gogol's unfaithful but gorgeous wife, Moushimi, was Zuleikha Robinson, late the object of desire on television's *The Lone Gunmen* (2001). Kate Hudson had reportedly been approached for a part too, that of Gogol's WASP girlfriend, Maxine Ratliff, but that casting ultimately didn't happen. Instead, the rest of the supporting cast came to include some interesting Nair alumni, including *My Own Country*'s Glenne Headly and a young man who had gotten his start in *Salaam Bombay!*, rising star Irfan Khan.

The Namesake crew, which includes director of photography Frederick Elmes, whose films include *The Ice Storm* (1997) and *Kinsey* (2004), was originally slated to film in Calcutta during mid-to-late January of 2005 and to return to the States for filming in New York as spring sprung, in April and May. However, because of scheduling conflicts with cast members, things did not go as planned, and by late February reports in the press indicated the schedule had been re-jiggered. The shooting in New York was moved to March, and the Calcutta shooting would come afterwards, in May. Production on the film finally commenced on March 29, 2005.

"We were supposed to start shooting this January, but because of casting it was switched around," Carroll notes. "So in order to get Kal, we had to start in America first. He's doing *Superman* next."

And as for working with a new cinematographer, Carroll has been very pleased. "He's a master, and he's great to work with," she describes Elmes. "A very talented and humble man. He's working closely with Mira, and it couldn't be better." Work on *The Namesake* also takes Mr. Elmes on his first trip to India.

When interviewed for this book, Ms. Carroll had just finished shooting the big scene with Kal Penn where Gogol returns to his home and discovers the book left behind for him by his father before his untimely death.

"We just finished shooting in the very large Ganguli home," Carroll says. "We did the Ganguli's first home in Yonkers, the one from the 1970s when they first came from India. And for two weeks we've been shooting their big [second] home, the one they then move to, establishing their family in the suburbs."

This second house was harder to find, because Nair wanted to capture some of the sameness of the suburban developments, and those are harder to find in New York than elsewhere. "Mira really wanted that cookie-cutter look, which is more prevalent in California, where every house looks identical. For example, an *Edward Scissorhands* feel where every house in the development is the same. But for that movie, they built all those. This is not a huge movie, so we couldn't build a whole development," said Carroll.

The chosen house was finally discovered in East Chester, on a kind of cul-de-sac of homes that were built in the 1960s and had the right kind of "clean feel," according to Carroll, who says the production crew took over the house, redid everything (including the windows) and ultimately felt very happy with the choice of locations.

Shooting on *The Namesake* also took place at Oyster Bay, where a house doubled as the Ratliff summer cottage. "The really interesting thing about that is that for the Ratliff townhouse in Manhattan, we used the same family's beach home. We try to have that follow-through where life imitates art, so that both houses felt like they belonged together. So we went to Oyster Bay, and there's a house that's been in the family for generations, and its right on the water."

While arranging time to speak, Carroll was also hard at work preparing the second leg of shooting on *The Namesake*, namely the parts taking place in India. One of the film's major sequences would involve the train crash that changes Gogol's father forever.

"It's going to be a big thing," Carroll explains. "It'll be a bit stylized but we are recreating the crash itself. We're filming inside the car, so you won't see the cars crash. But then you'll see the aftermath and it'll be very stylized—with smoke—and I almost see it as a 9/11 in the sense of huge twisted steel reaching into the sky and girders, although in this case it'll be trains.

"Since we started production, I've researched two train tragedies in India," Carroll notes. "I have an Indian art director over there studying with his crew, finding visual references so we can plan out the budgeting. It's a lot cheaper to do it [the crash] there rather than here. So that's exciting; I've never done anything like that before."

Also, some New York scenes will be shot in India for budgetary reasons. "I have to recreate Moushimi's New York apartment and the New York disco and bridal suite for budget reasons," Carroll reveals. "I'm shipping some objects that are particularly American that I can't get over there."

In an article published in *Business Wire*, Mira Nair described her current project as her most deeply personal, noting that *The Namesake* "encompasses in a deep humane way the tale of millions of us who have known what it means to combine the old ways with a new world who have left the shadow of our parents to find ourselves for the first time."[16]

Mira Nair's adaptation of *The Namesake* is scheduled for release in 2006.

LIFE IS SUCH A COMEDY

A Conclusion to *Mercy in Her Eyes*

Director Mira Nair has stressed on many occasions that her Indian upbringing has given her "tremendous strength,"[1] and that upbringing also informs her cinematic work, granting it a unique atmosphere and texture. In her many films, Professor Nair has taken rapt audiences to the crowded streets of Bombay, asked viewers to examine the Indian diaspora in the American South and Uganda, invited us to a Punjabi wedding, and even challenged audiences to reconsider beloved literary works like *Vanity Fair* through the lens of a subject that interests her: colonialism.

Whether Nair's films are straight-faced meditations about sex such as the lush *Kama Sutra*, a comedy in which "life is a circus" as in *Monsoon Wedding*, or a personal account of a person on a quest to understand identity—personal, national or ethnic—one facet remains certain: her images always tantalize. In a world where film—to its detriment—is becoming more and more like television, ever more dependent on the crutch of close-up shots, to witness a frame bursting with life and individuality feels like a relief. The films of Mira Nair boast a tactile feeling, a tangibility that almost seems within the audience's grasp.

"All her movies are about the five senses, I think," considers Nair's frequent production designer, Stephanie Carroll. "And that's what's great about working on them. They're about life, but you can hopefully almost smell the movie. Hopefully, they appeal to people who are curious about life and emotions and other people, and maybe that's what I like about working with Mira."

In her post as a teacher at Columbia, Professor Nair has imparted her dedication and passions (including photography and gardening in addition to filmmaking) to a new generation of students, and these days, she's also exporting those personal qualities around the globe, just like her films.

On August 1, 2005, she unveiled Maisha, a screenwriting and directing workshop based on Sundance, and designed for aspiring filmmakers from Sri Lanka, East Africa, India and Pakistan.[2] Open to twelve students in its first year, and then twenty-four the following, the program is advised not just by Nair, but filmmaker friends including Spike Lee and Sofia Coppola. The program's goal is to—within five years—introduce the world to a "locally told story" produced in Uganda or Tanzania, but one that is of the "highest international standards."[3]

In other words, the next *Salaam Bombay!*

"The Maisha Advisory Committee is made up of people that are committed to helping the film culture in East Africa develop," Mira Nair told reporter Angelo Izama in early 2005. "Now that we [Spike Lee and Nair] have both seen our careers unfold into what they are today, we want to use the power of recognition to assist East African filmmakers who are struggling as well."4

In helping a new local talent find a place on the global stage, Mira Nair continues the journey she began nearly twenty years ago, and for which film aficionados of all stripes can appreciate. In addition to mercy, the director also boasts the quality of bravery.

"I don't know if there is a single theme to her work—or a single style, because what I think is great about Mira is that she tries different things," suggests longtime friend Sooni Taraporevala. "She doesn't repeat herself. She goes from *Vanity Fair* to *The Namesake*. Or she'll go from *Kama Sutra* to *My Own Country*. Maybe you can see some [common] themes in her work, but as you say, that's what critics do. What I see in her work is a complete courage to embark on different things each time."

"Most directors I've worked with have won the battle at the casting phase," Ranjit Chowdhry considers. "Then all they need to do is say: louder, softer, slower and faster. Miss Nair is different. It's best just to learn one's lines and get to the set. The rest happens slowly, across many, many takes. She is very big on nuance. I have spent many takes trying to bring some eight to fifteen different colors to a single paragraph of dialogue. I am not sure the audience picks up all these hues at a single viewing.

"I think Miss Nair is an immensely talented director who has initiated her own projects and acted as a hired hand on others. I think all the work is outstanding," the actor considers. "If one has a [Mira Nair] retrospective, then I suppose one can see dramatic threads through the work. I think she is drawn to survivors: The kids in *Salaam*. Dottie in *Perez*. Mina in *Mississippi*. And most recently Miss Witherspoon in *Vanity*. Mira herself is quite adept at surviving in this insanely difficult business. Anyone who has gone around with a begging bowl asking for money to make a film knows all too well."

Naveen Andrews sees Mira Nair in very human terms, saying the one word that encapsulates everything about the film artist is, simply, "passionate."

"I still love Mira for this," he declares. "My favorite family member in India is an aunt who is my mom's sister. This woman is very powerful in the same way that Mira is. They plant their two feet down in the ground and they have a real presence, as well as great charm. She's beautiful and all the rest of that, but Mira also has a real strength.

"At the same time, for the background she's come from, she's had to fight to get where she is today, so I've always had a lot of respect for that. As a woman from India, what she's set out to achieve and what she's achieved is really admirable, and I like her personal charm as well," Andrews muses. "I find that irresistible."

A storyteller and a survivor in the age of globalization, one ponders the imagery Mira Nair's cinema has yet to reveal. In her continuing quest for nuance, complexity, and most of all—as the spiritual heir to Satyajit Ray—mercy, this local director has made a coterie of films that appeal to international viewers with open hearts and minds.

"You called it globalization, but just the fact that we grew up in places other than India, you know, the West, forces us to confront humanity from both sides of the fence," suggests Andrews.

And maybe that's the best place to observe a rapidly changing world, and to seek to understand it better.

APPENDIX

You Know You're in a Mira Nair Film When You See...

Certain images seem almost universal in the Mira Nair canon, and these visual symbols and representations grant her work an admirable consistency from project to project. Below are four important concepts and images that recur in Nair's cinema.

1. DANCING

Mira Nair has often said she is intoxicated with life, and filled with passion for it. There is perhaps no greater way to express those feelings of *joie de vivre* than in the ecstatic discipline of dance, and importantly, dance figures in all of Nair's films. It shows up as a glimpse of happiness (*Salaam Bombay!*), cathartic balm (*Mississippi Masala*), and even an intimate expression of loneliness (*My Own Country*) and utter desperation (*Hysterical Blindness*). Dance appears in the following Nair efforts, in these particular situations:

A. *Salaam Bombay!*
   ✞ Krishna and Manju in Rekha's apartment as it rains outside.

B. *Mississippi Masala*
   ✞ Mina and Demetrius at a local club;
   ✞ In Kampala's streets during the climax.

C. *The Perez Family*
   ✞ Dorita dances on the boat to Miami, raising the spirits of her fellow exiles.
   ✞ Two couples visit a Miami disco: Carmela and Pirelli, and Dottie and her "John Wayne" security guard.

D. *Kama Sutra*
   ✞ Tara and Maya dance together as girls.
   ✞ Maya learns to dance (from Rekha) while studying to become a courtesan.

E. *My Own Country*
   ✞ Dr. Verghese's wife dances alone in an empty house.

F. *Monsoon Wedding*

⚇ Ayesha prepares and then performs a celebratory dance for Aditi's wedding.

G. *Hysterical Blindness*

⚇ In a drunken stupor, Deb dances in a feverish solitary circle at Ollie's.

H. *Vanity Fair*

⚇ In her coming out to society at Lord Steyne's mansion, Becky performs a seductive and wicked dance.

2. THEMATIC COUNTERPOINT

So many of Mira Nair's feature films set up an interesting dichotomy, examples of conflicts that balance and mirror one another in interesting fashion, as though she is arguing two sides of a debate, and synthesizing her own, new answers. Appropriate, perhaps, since Mira Nair functions in a local/global world and is both Indian and international. Complexity and paradox are represented in her quest to include counterpoint.

A. Reality vs. illusion in *Salaam Bombay!*, life on the streets vs. life as portrayed in Bollywood movies.

B. Young vs. old: The generations battle over racism, Jay vs. Mina, in *Mississippi Masala*.

C. Fear vs. passion and freedom, Carmela vs. Dottie, in *The Perez Family*.

D. Royalty vs. servitude, Tara vs. Maya, in *Kama Sutra*.

E. Modernity vs. tradition in India, in *Monsoon Wedding*.

F. Young vs. old; generations as counterpoint in *Hysterical Blindness*.

G. Upper class vs. lower class, the colonizers vs. the colonized in *Vanity Fair*.

3. AN EXTENDED MOMENT

Mira Nair loves to engage audience emotion in her films, and she often does so by lengthening or extending a moment. This can be to tease (*Monsoon Wedding*), excite (*Salaam Bombay!*), or even sadden (*My Own Country*). What's fascinating here is the way that Nair deploys her arsenal of film techniques to lengthen that moment. It might be slow-motion photography, strategic use of stock footage, or even jump cuts, but they all work to the same purpose.

A. Krishna runs through traffic, and we see his unending sprint disconnected by repetitive jump cuts in *Salaam Bombay!*

B. Dottie arrives at the shores of America, and in slightly slowed-motion, her dress balloons like a flower petal blossoming in *The Perez Family.*

C. A hazy view of trees, seen from the vantage point of a sick traveler, trying to reach home. Depicted in grainy, super 8 "stock" from Phillip Barker in *My Own Country.* Slowed down and aged so as to seem a misty memory.

D. A kiss in *Monsoon Wedding* (told in jump cuts); marigold moments (in-camera slow-motion). Finally, in the last few moments Ria is free of her secret, and jumps exuberantly out into the rain (slow-motion photography, achieved post-production in editing).

4. EXILES

Characters in Mira Nair films are often cast away from their homes, and long to return. Sometimes the banishment is caused by political turmoil (*Mississippi Masala, The Perez Family*), sometimes because of perceived personal misdeeds (*Salaam Bombay!, Kama Sutra*), and sometimes it is a class issue (*Vanity Fair*).

A. Krishna is banished from home by his mother, at least until he can raise five hundred rupees, in *Salaam Bombay!*

B. Jay and his family are exiled from their home in Kampala, Uganda, by Idi Amin in *Mississippi Masala* because Africa is for "black" Africans.

C. Juan Raul Perez, Dottie Perez and the other members of their ad-hoc family are exiles from Castro's Cuba, contending with a life of freedom in Florida, but still one disconnected from their homeland, in *The Perez Family*.

D. Maya is banished from Tara's palace after sleeping with the king in *Kama Sutra*.

E. Young George Osborne is disowned by his social-climbing father because of his marriage to Amelia in *Vanity Fair*. Similarly, Becky is disowned by the Crawleys for her unsanctioned marriage to Rawdon.

NOTES

A LOCAL STORYTELLER AT THE GLOBAL CINEMA

An Introduction to *Mercy in Her Eyes: The Films of Mira Nair*

1. Mira Nair, "Create the World You Know, Nair Tells Filmmakers," *Variety*, September 30, 2002, 14–15.
2. Mira Nair, "Eat, Memory," *New York Times Magazine*, November 14, 2004, 125.
3. Samuel G. Freedman, "One People in Two Worlds," *New York Times*, February 2, 1992, H13.
4. Mukesh Kholsa, "She Gives the 'Nowhere People' a Voice," *The Tribune*, September 27, 2001, 5.
5. Aaron Gell, "Indian Style: The Forecast Is Sunny for Mira Nair's Award-Winning Punjabi Romantic Comedy Film, *Monsoon Wedding*," *W*, March 2002, 193.
6. Ameena Meer, "Street Lessons," *The South*, February 1990, 72.
7. Bonnie Johnson, "Moviemaker Mira Nair Takes to the Streets of Bombay to Say *Salaam!* to Real Children with No Childhood," *People*, December 5, 1988, 115–116.
8. Michael Wilmington, "Movie Review, *Monsoon Wedding*," *Chicago Tribune/Metromix*, February 28, 2002. http://metromix.chicagotribune.com/movies/mmx-15649_legacy.story
9. "The Concept behind the Movie *Vanity Fair*," *Female First*, January 7, 2005. http://www.femalefirst.co.uk/entertainment/21762004.htm
10. "Jewel in the Crown. Mira Nair Interview," *Tiscali*, 2002, 1. http://www.tiscali.co.uk
11. Christopher Kelly, "*Monsoon Wedding* Director's String of Hits Blows Away Skeptics," *Knight Ridder/Tribune News Service*, March 2, 2002, K632.
12. Kalungi Kabuye, "Mira Nair Celebrates Life through Cinema," *Africa News Service*, August 19, 2002, 1008228U5489.
13. "Familiarity Breeds Content: Many Filmmakers Use Same below-the-Line Creatives for Every Set," *Daily Variety*, August 24, 2004, A1.
14. Utpal Borpujari, "Mira Nair Rejected *Harry Potter* Offer," *DH News Service* [Panaji], December 12, 2004. http://www.deccanhearld.com/deccanherald/dec12004/n7.asp

15. "*Monsoon Wedding* Director Honored," *Zap2It.com*, October 11, 2004.

16. Paul Garwood, "Indian-Born Filmmaker Wins 'Maverick Award' at Woodstock Festival," *America's Intelligence Wire*, October 9, 2004.

17. Alpana Sharma, "Body Matters: The Politics of Provocation in Mira Nair's Films," *Quarterly Review of Film & Video*, 2001, 91–103.

18. Ethirajan Anbarasan and Amy Otchet, "Mira Nair: An Eye for Paradox," *Unesco*, November 1998, 3. http://www.unesco.org/courier/1998-11/uk/dires/textl.htm

19. Rebecca Ascher-Walsh, "Mira Nair and Alfonso Cuaron," *Entertainment Weekly*, December 20, 2002, 38.

20. Richard Corliss, "A Cultural Grand *Salaam*," *Time Canada*, May 3, 2004, 46.

21. Michael Hastings, "A World of Its Own," *Newsweek*, March 8, 2004, 6.

22. Sam Wardle, "The Bollywood Invasion," *A World Connected*, February 10, 2005. http://www.aworldconnected.org

23. Lakshmi B. Ghosh, "Street Inspires Her," *The Hindu*, June 12, 2004, 2. http://www.thehindu.com/thehindu/1f/2004/12/06/stories/20041206009102

CHAPTER ONE

Mahurat: The Auspicious Beginning

1. J. Hoberman, *Village Voice*, April 11, 1995, 51.

2. Andy Pawelczak, *Films in Review*, July–August 1995, 59.

3. Darius Cooper, *The Cinema of Satyajit Ray: Between Tradition and Modernity* (Cambridge: Cambridge University Press, 2000), 3.

4. "Awards Are Temporary Hype; Mira Nair's Exclusive Interview," *Bengal on the Net*, November 30, 2001. http://www.bengalonthenet.com/php/displayfile.php?article_id...

5. Stephen Lowenstein, *My First Movie: 20 Celebrated Directors Talk about Their First Film* (New York: Penguin Books, 2002), 245.

6. Ayesha Hasan, "Professor Mira Nair Reflects on Her Film Career during Zora Neale Hurston Lecture," *Columbia News*, August 1, 2002. http://www.columbia.edu/cu/news/02/08/miraNair.html

7. Alex Luu, "Mira Nair: Celluloid Diplomat of Humanity," *Yolk*, 2002. http://www.yolk.com/v091/nair1.html

8. Caryn James, "Mira Nair Combines Cultures to Create a Film," *New York Times*, October 17, 1988, C17.

9. "Mira Nair: A Director Par Excellence," *Kerala Online*, 1998. http://www.keralaonline.com/defalutsm.asp?cap=miranair

10. Scott Tobias, "Reel Freedom: From Veteran Filmmakers to Emerging Talents, Female Directors Are Thriving in Independent Circles, Where Their Singular Vision Goes Uncompromised," *Back Stage*, December 22, 2004. http://www.backstage.com/backstage/features/article_display.jsp?vnu_content_id= 1000741248

11. John Lahr, "Whirlwind," *New Yorker*, December 9, 2002, 100.

12. Zarine Nandon, *Indo-Asian News Service*, October 17, 2002.

13. Alex Perry, "A Force of Nature," *Time Asia*, September 13, 2004, 3. http://www.time.com/time/asia/magazine/

14. "Mira Nair—*Monsoon Wedding*," *In Movies*, November 2001. http://www.in-movies.co.uk/news/interviews/interviews_66.shtml

15. Wendy Mitchell, "Period Piece as 'Complete Romp.' Mira Nair Brings Her Own Vibrancy to *Vanity Fair*," *Indiewire*, August 31, 2004.
http://www.indiewire.com/people/people_040831nair.html

16. Richard Corliss, "A Cultural Grand *Salaam*," *Time Canada*, May 3, 2004, 46.

17. John Lahr, "Whirlwind," *New Yorker*, December 9, 2002, 100.

18. Scarlet Cheng, "Mira Nair: Intoxicated with Life," *World and I*, June 2003, 98.

19. Bonnie Greer, "Mira Nair." *The Guardian/NFT Interview*, June 12, 2002, 1.
http://film.guardian.co.uk/

20. Judith Graham, *Current Biography Yearbook*, 54th vol. (Bronx: H. W. Wilson Company, 1993), 424.

21. Jeff Otto, "Interview: Mira Nair. *IGN* Talks to the Director behind Reese's Epic, *Vanity Fair*," *Film Force*, August 30, 2004, 1.
http://filmforce.ign.com/articles/543/543139p/html

22. Ethirajan Anbarasan and Amy Otcher, "Mira Nair: An Eye for Paradox," *Unesco*, 1998, 5.
http://www.unesco.org/courier/1998/11/uk/dires/text1.htm

23. Ethirajan Anbarasan and Amy Otcher, "Mira Nair: An Eye for Paradox," *Unesco*, 1998, 5.
http://www.unesco.org/courier/1998/11/uk/dires/text1.htm

24. Mitch Epstein, "Meghraj Cabaret," *Mitchepstein.net*.
http://www.micthepstein.net/work/projects/cabaret

25. John Lahr, "Whirlwind," *New Yorker*, December 9, 2002, 5.

26. Karin Luisa Badt, "I Want My Films to Explode with Life: An Interview with Mira Nair," *Cineaste*, Winter 2004, 12.

27. Cynthia Felando, *Women Filmmakers & Their Films* (Farmington Hills: Thomson Gale, 1998), 296.

28. Jennifer McNulty, "Documentary Film and Video Festival Starts September 25," *University of California Santa Cruz Currents Online*, September 17, 2001, 2.
http://www.ucsc.edu/currents/01-02/19-17.documentary.html

29. Scott Galupo, "*Vanity Fair* Shows Mira Nair's Flair for Novelty and 'Outsiderism,'" *World and I*, January 2005.

30. Shekhar Gupta, "On the Record: Mira Nair, Filmmaker: 'It's Not about Being What They (Hollywood) Are It's about Them Opening Their Eyes to Us,'" *Indian Express*, January 11, 2005.
http://www.indianexpress.com/full_story.php?content_id=62447&spf=true

31. Stephen Lowenstein, *My First Movie: 20 Celebrated Directors Talk about Their First Film* (New York: Penguin Books, 2002), 249.

32. Caryn James, "Mira Nair Combines Cultures to Create a Film," *New York Times*, October 17, 1988, C17.

CHAPTER TWO

Salaam Bombay! (1988)

1. Lakshmi B. Ghosh, "Street Inspires Her," *The Hindu*, June 12, 2004, 3.
http://www.thehindu.com/thehindu/1f/2004/12/06/stories/20041206009102

2. Barbara Osborn, "India Inside," *Film Comment*, September–October 1988, 6.

3. Mira Nair and Sooni Taraporevala, *Salaam Bombay!* (New York: Penguin Books, 1988), 7.

4. Ashish Rajadhyaksha and Paul Willemen, *Encyclopaedia of Indian Cinema—New Revised Edition* (Oxford: Oxford University Press, 2002), 212.

5. Vincent Canby, "Streets of Sao Paulo," *New York Times*, September 11, 1981, C6.

6. Mira Nair, "Eat, Memory," *New York Times Magazine*, November 14, 2004, 125.

7. Bonnie Johnson, "Moviemaker Mira Nair Takes to the Streets of Bombay to Say *Salaam!* to Real Children with No Childhood," *People*, December 5, 1988, 115–116.

8. David Sterritt, *Christian Science Monitor*, November 3, 1988, 20.

9. Jami Bernard, *New York Post*, October 7, 1988, 27.

10. Sheila Benson, *Los Angeles Times*, October 19, 1988, 1.

11. Peter Travers, "*Salaam Bombay!*," *People*, November 7, 1988, 18.

12. Barbara Osborn, "India Inside," *Film Comment*, September–October 1988, 6.

13. Vibhuti Patel, "Making a Woman's *Kama Sutra*," *Ms. Magazine*, May–June 1997, 79.

14. John Pym, *Monthly Film Bulletin*, February 1989, 42.

15. Ameena Meer, "Street Lessons," *The South*, February 1990, 72.

16. Rita Kempley, "*Salaam Bombay!*," *Washington Post*, November 4, 1988, 1. http://www.washingtonpost.com/wpsrv/style/longterm/movies/videos/salaambombay.htm

17. Richard Corliss, "*Salaam Bombay!*," *Time*, October 24, 1988, 103.

18. Leslie Camhi, "The Kids Are Alright. *Salaam Bombay!*," *Village Voice Online.* http://www.villagevoice.com

19. Shahid Khan, "*Salaam Bombay!*," *Planet Bollywood.* http://www.planetbollywood.com/Film/SalaamBombay!/

CHAPTER THREE

Mississippi Masala (1991) and *The Perez Family* (1995)

1. Peggy Orenstein, "*Salaam* America!," *Mother Jones*, January–February 1992, 60.

2. Mukesh Khosla, "She Gives the 'Nowhere People,' a Voice," *The Tribune*, September 27, 2001, 5. http://www.tribuneindia.com/2001/200110927/main8.htm

3. Charles Onyango-Obbo, "*Salaam Mississippi*," *The South*, February 1991, 74–75.

4. Samuel G. Freedman, "One People in Two Worlds," *New York Times*, February 2, 1992, H13.

5. Mukesh Khosla, "She Gives the 'Nowhere People,' a Voice," *The Tribune*, September 27, 2001, 5. http://www.tribuneindia.com/2001/200110927/main8.htm

6. Marpessa Outlaw, "The Mira Stage," *Village Voice*, February 18, 1992, 64.

7. Janice C. Simpson, "Focusing on the Margins." *Time*, March 2, 1992, 67.

8. Charles Onyango-Obbo, "*Salaam Mississippi*," *The South*, February 1991, 74–75.

9. Kate Meyers, "Sarita Choudhury," *Entertainment Weekly*, February 2, 1992, 12.

10. "Mira Nair: A Director Par Excellence." *Kerala Online*, 1998. http://www.keralaonline.com/defaultsm.asp?cap=miranair

11. Kelli Pryor, "Adding Spice to Real Life, Director Mira Nair," *Entertainment Weekly*, February 21, 1992, 34.

12. Owen Gleiberman, "*Mississippi Masala*," *Entertainment Weekly*, February 14, 1992, 36.

13. Leah Rozen, *People*, February 17, 1992, 17.

14. Stuart Klawans, *The Nation*, February 24, 1992, 246.

15. P. T. Atkins, *Rolling Stone*, February 20, 1992, 50.

16. R. A. Blake, "Love and Forgiveness," *America*, March 4, 1992, 274.

17. Cecilie S. Berry, *Cineaste*, November 1992, 66.

18. Cecilie S. Berry, *Cineaste*, November 1992, 66.

19. Peter Rainer, *Los Angeles Times*, February 14, 1992, 8.

20. Erika Surat Anderson, *Film Quarterly*, Summer 1993, 23.

21. *Library Journal*, July 1, 1990, 126.

22. Rosellen Brown, "The Year in Fiction: 1990," *Massachusetts Review*, Spring 1991, 127.

23. Kim Cunningham, "Are You Ready to Rumba?," *People*, June 12, 1995, 138.

24. Tom Austin, "Swelter," *Miami New Times*, April 6, 1994, 1H.
http://www.miaminewtimes.com/issues/1994_04_06/news/columns2.html

25. Anne Thompson, "For Mira Nair, *Vanity* Project Called Her Name," *Washington Post*, August 29, 2004, N01.

26. Tim Appelo, "*The Perez Family*," *Entertainment Weekly*, August 26, 1994, 75.

27. Stanley Kauffmann, "*The Perez Family*," *New Republic*, June 5, 1995, 33.

28. Barbara Shulgasser, "Good Actors Set Adrift in All Wet *Perez Family*," *San Francisco Examiner*, May 12, 1995, C1.

29. *New Internationalist*, November 1996, 33.

30. Lisa Schwarzbaum, "*The Perez Family*," *Entertainment Weekly*, May 19, 1995, 44–45.

31. Robert Macias, "The Best and Worst of 1995," *Hispanic*, December 1995, 16.

32. *Rolling Stone*, June 1, 1995, 70.

33. Tom Gliatto, *People*, May 15, 1995, 19.

34. Marc Stengel, "Translating Stories," *Weekly Wire/Nashville Scene*, December 22, 1997, 1.
http://weeklywire.com/22/12-22-97/nash_8-books.html

35. Daniel Baig, "Interview: Mira Nair," *Counting Down*, May 1, 2002.
http://www.countingdown.com/features?feauture_id=716479&print=1

36. Richard Schickel, "Fresh off the Boatlift," *Time*, May 29, 1995, 66.

37. Mike LaSalle, "*Perez Family* Falls Apart after a While," *San Francisco Chronicle*, May 13, 1995, E1.

38. Peter Rainer, *Los Angeles Times*, May 12, 1995, 2.

39. John Anderson, *Newsday*, Part II, May 12, 1995, 85.

40. David Denby, *New York*, May 22, 1995, 78.

41. David Sterritt, *Christian Science Monitor*, May 12, 1995, 13.

42. Nisid Hajari, "In an Awkward Position," *Entertainment Weekly*, March 21, 1997, 55.

43. Christine Bell, *The Perez Family* (New York: Harper Perennial, 1990), 152.

44. Peter Matthews, *Sight and Sound*, September 1996, 50.

45. Michael Medved, *New York Post*, May 12, 1995, 43.

46. Zachary Woodruff, "*The Perez Family*," *Tucson Weekly*, May 18, 1995, 1–3.
http://www.filmvault.com/filmvault/tw/p/perezfamilythe_f.html

CHAPTER FOUR

Kama Sutra: A Tale of Love (1997), *My Own Country* (1998), *The Laughing Club of India* (1999)

1. "Nair to Helm Fugard's *Tsotsi*," *Variety*, November 10, 1992. http:/www.variety.com

2. Yves Jaques, "*Kama Sutra*; An Interview with Mira Nair," *Online Daily of the University of Washington*, March 13, 1997, 1.
http://archives.thedaily.washington.edu/1997/031397/kama031397.html

3. Cynthia Felando, *Women Filmmakers and Their Films* (Farmington Hills: Thomson Gale, 1998).

4. Stanley Kauffmann, "*Kama Sutra*," *New Republic*, March 10, 1997, 30–31.

5. Ashish Rajadhyaksha and Paul Willemen, *Encyclopaedia of Indian Cinema—New Revised Edition* (Oxford: Oxford University Press, 1999), 200.

6. Nisid Hajari, "In an Awkward Position," *Entertainment Weekly*, March 21, 1997, 55.

7. Jenny Yabroff, "All about Eros," *Salon*, March 7, 1997, 1.
http://www.salon.com/march97/nair970307.html

8. Scarlet Cheng, "Mira Nair: Intoxicated with Life," *World and I*, June 2003, 98.

9. Tim McGirk, "Naked Ambitions," *Time Australia*, January 13, 1997, 31.

10. Kevin Thomas, *Los Angeles Times*, February 28, 1997, 12.

11. Owen Gleiberman, "*Kama Sutra: A Tale of Love,*" *Entertainment Weekly*, March 21, 1997, 55.

12. Kevin Thomas, *Los Angeles Times*, February 28, 1997, 12.

13. Jonathan Coe, *New Statesman*, June 20, 1997, 42.

14. Michael Medved, *New York Post*, February 28, 1997, 45.

15. Bill Kelley, *Sarasota Herald Tribune*, May 30, 1997, 16.

16. Brian D. Johnson, *Maclean's*, February 24, 1997, 62.

17. *Salon*, March 7, 1997.
    http://www.salon.com/March97/kamasutra970307.html?CP=SAL&D=110

18. "10 Questions: Mira Nair. The Director of *Monsoon Wedding* Shares Her Answers," *Film Force*, February 22, 2002. http://filmforce.ign.com/articles/354/354320p1.html

19. Karen Wilson, "*Vanity Fair*—Now with More Elephants!," *Gothamist*, August 20, 2004.
    http://gothamist.com/archives/2004/08/20/vanityfair_now_with_more_elephants.php

20. Joe Holley, "The Doctor Is In," *Texas Monthly*, June 1997, 48.

21. Michelle Ingrassia, "On the Front Lines of AIDS," *Newsweek*, May 9, 1994, 62.

22. Rajini Srikanth, "Ethnic Outsider as the Ultimate Insider: The Paradox of Verghese's *My Own Country*," *MELUS*, Fall–Winter 2004, 436.

23. Joe Holley, "The Doctor Is In," *Texas Monthly*, June 1997, 48.

24. Tom De Haven, "Dose of Reality," *Entertainment Weekly*, May 13, 1994, 53.

25. Kenan Pollack, "Book Watch," *U.S. News and World Report*, September 12, 1994, 94.

26. Abraham Verghese, "Last Acts," *New Yorker*, September 22, 1997, 78.

27. Edward Guthmann, "Doctor or Saint?," *The Advocate*, June 21, 1998, 67–68.

28. Terry Kelleher, "Picks and Pans," *People*, July 13, 1998.

29. M. S. Mason, "'Laughter' Shows Power of Expressing Joy," *Christian Science Monitor*, August 24, 2001, 19.

30. Alex Perry, "Learning the Yoga Way of Laughter," *Time*, January 17, 2005, A26.

CHAPTER FIVE

Monsoon Wedding (2001), *Hysterical Blindness* (2002), *11'09'01* (2002), *Vanity Fair* (2004)

1. Pat Regnier, "Local Is the New Global: In Her Hit Film *Monsoon Wedding*, Mira Nair Goes Home to New Delhi, Where Cell Phones Blend In Seamlessly with Saris," *Time International*, March 4, 2002, 65.

2. Kristin Sterling, "Professor-Student Duo Portray Co-Existence of Tradition and Modernity in India in *Monsoon Wedding*," *Columbia News*, February 25, 2005.
   http://www.columbia.edu/ae/news/02/02/monsoon_wedding.html

3. Jason Anderson, "Bridal Shower—Mira Nair's Indian Comedy Storms the Festival Circuit," *The Eye*, February 28, 2002, 2.
   http://www.eye.net/eye/issue/issue_02.28.02/film/monsoonwedding.html

4. Ashinin Bwhat, "Naseerab Recommended Me for *Monsoon Wedding*," *Rediff*, December 18, 2001. http://www.rediff.com/entertai/2001/dec/18raaz.html

5. Maria Garcia, "Invitation to the *Wedding*: Mira Nair's Award Winner Celebrates Indian Culture," *Film Journal International*, March 2002, 20–22.

6. David Edelstein, "Under the Rainbow," *Slate*, February 22, 2002.
   http://www.slate.msn.com/id/2062346

7. Duane Dudek, "*Monsoon Wedding* Moves Indian Film into Complex Aspects of Family," *Knight Ridder/Tribune News Service*, March 31, 2002, 3687.

8. Nick Vivarelli, "*Monsoon* Hits Venice Nods," *Hollywood Reporter*, September 11, 2001, 41.

9. "*Monsoon Wedding* Runs to Packed Houses in U.K.," *Times of India*, April 2, 2002.

10. David Ansen, "Runaway Bridal Party: Marriage, Punjabi Style," *Newsweek*, March 4, 2002, 60.

11. Deborah Young, "*Monsoon Wedding*," *Variety*, September 10, 2001, 63.

12. Joseph Cunneen, "Games of Love; Film Tours to Enjoy of India, Texas, Mexico," *National Catholic Reporter*, April 19, 2002, 16–17.

13. Michael Fleming, "B'way *Monsoon* Ahead," *Daily Variety*, December 16, 2002, 1–2.

14. Cynthia Karena, "*Monsoon Wedding*: Raining on Tradition—Film as Text." *Australian Screen Education*, Winter 2003, 1–4.

15. Adina Hoffman, "The Big Bash Theory: Mira Nair's Latest Movie Revels and Reels," *American Prospect*, March 25, 2002, 28–29.

16. Moira McDonald, "*Monsoon Wedding*," *Knight Ridder/Tribune News Service*, March 20, 2002, K3152.

17. Kyle Boltin, "*Monsoon Wedding*: A Discussion of Mira Nair's New Film," *Metro*, Summer 2002, 1–4.

18. Uri Klein, "*Monsoon Wedding*," *Hollywood Reporter*, May 28, 2002, 50.

19. Tom Aitken, "Resilient Loves," *Christian Century*, March 27, 2002, 34.

20. Anthony Lane, "Making Arrangements: A Wedding in Delhi and a Wake on the English Coast," *New Yorker*, February 1, 2002, 199–202.

21. Joanne Laurier, "The View from the Oasis: *Monsoon Wedding*, Directed by Mira Nair," *World Socialist Web Site*, March 30, 2002. http://wswg.org/articles/2002/mar2002/mons_M3_prn.shtml

22. Chris Hewitt, "*Monsoon Wedding*," *St. Paul Pioneer Press*, March 6, 2002.

23. Donna Freydkin, "Uma's a Mom First, Then a Jersey Girl," *USA Today*, August 22, 2002, 03D.

24. "Against the Grain: With the Studios Focused on Special Effects-Laden Blockbusters HBO Is Moving in the Opposite Direction, toward Well-Written Films with a Point of View," *Broadcasting & Cable*, November 4, 2002, 10A–11A.

25. Ruth Joao-Pierre, "Lights! Camera! Terminal!," *Business News*, January 17, 2002, 6.

26. Mira Nair, "Eat, Memory," *New York Times Magazine*, November 14, 2004, 12.

27. Ian Mohr, "*Hysterical* Sighting," *Hollywood Reporter*, August 27, 2002, 16.

28. John Dempsey, "Auds Turn Off *RFK*, but Get *Hysterical*," *Daily Variety*, August 28, 2002, 2.

29. "*Hysterical Blindness*," *Variety*, August 25, 2003, A48.

30. Terry Kelleher, "Tube," *People*, August 26, 2002, 23.

31. Stuart Klawans, "The Age of Innocence," *The Nation*, August 2003.

32. Richard Schickel, "An Omnibus of Short Films on September 11 from 11 Directors Skeptical of American Power," *Time International*, August 4, 2003, 61.

33. Malcolm Lewis, "*11'09'01*—September 11," *New Internationalist*, January–February 2003, 38–39.

34. "Mira Nair Fulfills a Dream with *Vanity Fair*. Director Fell in Love with Thackeray's Novel When She Was 16," *Associated Press*, September 7, 2004. http://www.msnbc.com/id/5868865

35. Renee Montagne, "Inside *Vanity Fair* with Director Mira Nair," *NPR: Morning Edition*, September 6, 2004. http://www.npr.org/templates/story/story.php?storyId=3890209

36. Moira Mcdonald, "Director Infuses English Story with Scents of India," *Knight Ridder/Tribune News Service*, August 31, 2004, K5308.

37. Leslie Bennetts, "Regally Blonde: While *Legally Blonde* Earned Reese Witherspoon Her $15-Million-a-Movie Price Tag and Countless Adoring Fans; Her Dramatic Test Will Be as a Hard-to-Love Redhead: The Scheming Becky Sharp in Mira Nair's Adaptation of the Thackeray Masterpiece *Vanity Fair* Opening This Month." *Vanity Fair*, September 2004, 376.

38. Mira Nair, Matthew Faulk, Mark Skeet, and Julian Fellowes, *Vanity Fair: Bringing Thackeray's Timeless Novel to the Screen* (New York: Newmarket Pictorial Moviebooks, 2004), 9.

39. Richard Porton, "Visualizing *Vanity Fair*: Nair Directs Witherspoon in 19th-Century Classic," *Film Journal International*, September 2004, 16–17.

40. Mira Nair, Matthew Faulk, Mark Skeet, and Julian Fellowes, *Vanity Fair: Bringing Thackeray's Timeless Novel to the Screen* (New York: Newmarket Pictorial Moviebooks, 2004), 22.

41. Clarissa Cruz, "Sharp Dresser: *Vanity*'s Costume Designer Uses the Color of Money for 19th Century Social Climber," *Entertainment Weekly*, September 3, 2004, 26.

42. Samantha Ross, "Feature: Gabriel Byrne Interview: A Conversation with a Most Unusual (*Vanity* Free) Suspect," *Moda Magazine*, 2004. http://www.modamag.com/gabrielbyrneinterview.htm

43. Sandesh Prabhudesai, "Mira Nair Rejects *Harry Potter* Film," *Rediff.com*. December 3, 2004. http://www.rediff.com/movies/2004/dec/03mira.htm

44. Wendy Mitchell, "Period Piece as 'Complete Romp.' Mira Nair Brings Her Own Vibrancy to *Vanity Fair*," *Indiewire*, August 31, 2004. http://www.indiewire.com/people/people_040831nair.html

45. Sheila Benson, "Interview: *Vanity Fair* Director, Mira Nair," *Seattle Weekly*, September 1–7, 2004. http://www.seattleweekly.com

46. Donna Freydkin, "Playing a *Vanity* Role, Then Walking Country Line," *USA Today*, August 18, 2004, 10B.

47. Erin Richter, "*Vanity Fair*," *Entertainment Weekly*, February 4, 2005, 118.

48. Bruce Newman, "*Vanity Fair*," *San Jose Mercury News*, August 31, 2004.

49. "All's Not Fair in Love and Movie Remakes," *Sarasota Herald Tribune*, September 1, 2004, E3.

50. Todd McCarthy, "*Vanity Fair*," *Daily Variety*, August 27, 2004, 6–7.

51. Claudia Puig, "*Vanity Fair* Serves Up Strawberry Thackery," *USA Today*, September 1, 2004, 05D.

52. David Ansen, "You Go, Girl; Reese Witherspoon Stars in a Lavish *Vanity Fair*," *Newsweek*, September 6, 2004, 66.

53. Armond White, *New York Press*, August 31, 2004. http://www.nypress.com

54. Lisa Schwarzbaum, "Upper Crusty: Reese Witherspoon Tries to Climb into High Society in the Half-Baked *Vanity Fair*," *Entertainment Weekly*, September 10, 2004, 143.

55. James Oliphant, "Criticisms and Interpretation," in *Harvard Classics Shelf of Fiction: Vanity Fair* (Bartleby.com, 2000). http://www.bartleby.com

56. Graham Fuller, "Shots in the Dark," *Interview*, September 2004, 132.

57. Thomas Chau, "Interview: Reese Witherspoon on *Vanity Fair*," *Cinema Confidential*, August 31, 2004. http://www.cinecon.com/news.php?id=0408311

CHAPTER SIX

Sneak Peek: *The Namesake* (2006)

1. Brad Balfour, "G21 Interviews Mira Nair," *New York* (*State of Mind*), 2004. http://www.g21.net/nystate22.html
2. Subhamor Das, "Jhumpa Lahiri on Her Debut Novel: An Interview with the Author," *About.com*, 2003.
3. Pam Grady, "Nair Follows Pulitzer's Trail," *Film Stew*, August 31, 2004. http://wwwfilmstew.com/Content
4. Craig Balenger, "Jhumpa Lahiri, Background and Early Life," in *Contemporary Authors New Revision Series*, vol. 134 (Farmington Hills: Thomas Gale, 2005), 1.
5. Teresa Wiltz, "The Writer Who Began with a Hyphen. Jhumpa Lahiri, between Two Cultures," *Washington Post*, October 8, 2003, C01.
6. *Library Journal*, May 1, 2005, 155.
7. Harvey Grossinger, "What's in a Name? Theme of Alienation Given Novel Approach," *Houston Chronicle*, December 26, 2003. http://www.chron.com/cs/CDA/ae/books/reviews/2319391
8. Ronjia Kulkarni, "*Namesake* Is Very Uncannily My Story!," *Rediff.com*, February 7, 2005. http://in.rediff.com/cms/l/movies/2005/feb/07mira.htm
9. Jhumpa Lahiri, *The Namesake* (New York: Mariner Books, 2003), 49.
10. Saibal Chatterjee, "Mira Nair to Shoot Next Film in Calcutta," *BBC News*, October–November 2004, 1. http://newsvote.bbc.co.uk.mpapps/pagetools/print/news.bbc.co.uk/2/hi/south_asia407 14...
11. Priyanka Dasgupta, "Tabu Takes Over from Konkona!," *Asia Africa Intelligence Wire*, February 2, 2005.
12 Subhash K. Jha, "Rani Says 'No' to Mira Nair," *Sify*, November 24, 2004. http://sify.com
13. "Mira Pottering about Aby Baby," *Asia Africa Intelligence Wire*, October 16, 2004.
14. "Abhishek in Mira's New Film," *Asia Africa Intelligence Wire*, November 12, 204.
15. "No Abhisek Bachchan for Mira Nair!," *Bollyvista.com*, 2004. http://www.bollywvista.com/article/a/32/3781
16. "Principal Photography Begins on Mira Nair's *The Namesake*; Kal Penn and Cast Shooting in Calcutta and New York," *Business Wire*, March 29, 2005.

LIFE IS SUCH A COMEDY

A Conclusion to *Mercy in Her Eyes*

1. Nona Walia, "I'm Sick of Working with Goras: Mira," *Times of India*, August 31, 2004.
2. "Mira Nair to Make Movie to Promote Indo-Pak Friendly Ties," *Press Trust of India Ltd.*, January 5, 2005.
3. Debra Kamin, "Nair Unspools Film Lab for Africans, Asians," *Daily Variety*, July 8, 2004, 8.
4. Angelo Izama, "Mira Nair on African Film Industry," *Africa News Service*, March 7, 2005.

SELECTED BIBLIOGRAPHY

BOOKS AND PLAYS

Barnouw, Erick, and S. Krishaswamy. *Indian Film*. New York: Columbia University Press, 1963.

Bell, Christine. *The Perez Family*. New York: Harper Perennial, 1990.

Cahill, Laura. *Hysterical Blindness*. New York: Dramatists Play Service Inc., 1999.

Cole, Janis, and Holly Dale. *Calling the Shots: Profiles of Women Filmmakers*. Dallas: Quarry Press, 1993.

Cooper, Darius. *The Cinema of Satyajit Ray: Between Tradition and Modernity*. Cambridge: Cambridge University Press, 2000.

Gianetti, Louis. *Understanding Movies*, 5th ed. Upper Saddle River: Prentice Hall, 1990.

Graham, Judith. *Current Biography Yearbook*, 54th vol. Bronx: H. W. Wilson Company, 1993.

Lahiri, Jhumpa. *The Namesake*. New York: Mariner Books, 2003.

Lowenstein, Stephen. *My First Movie: 20 Celebrated Directors Talk about Their First Film*. New York: Penguin Books, 2002.

Nair, Mira, and Sooni Taraporevala. *Salaam Bombay!*. New York: Penguin Books, 1989.

Nair, Mira, Matthew Faulk, Mark Skeet, and Juilian Fellowes. *Vanity Fair: Bringing Thackeray's Timeless Novel to the Screen*, New York: Newmarket Pictorial Moviebooks, 2004.

Pierson, John. *Spike, Mike, Slackers & Dykes: A Guided Tour across a Decade of American Independent Cinema*. New York: Hyperion Books, 1995.

Rajadhyaksha, Ashish, and Paul Willemen. *Encyclopaedia of Indian Cinema—New Revised Edition*. Oxford: Oxford University Press, 2002.

Thackeray, William Makepeace. *Vanity Fair: A Novel without a Hero*. New York: Modern Library Classics, 2001.

Verghese, Abraham. *My Own Country: A Doctor's Story*. New York: Vintage Books, 1994.

PERIODICALS

Aitken, Tom. "Resilient Loves." *Christian Century*, March 27, 2002, 34.

Akins, P. T. "*Mississippi Masala*." *Rolling Stone*, February 20, 1992, 50.

Anbarasan, Ethirajan. "Mira Nair: An Eye for Paradox." *Unesco Courier*, November 1998, 46–49.

Ansen, David. "Runaway Bridal Party: Marriage, Punjabi Style." *Newsweek*, March 4, 2002, 60.

Ansen, David. "You Go, Girl; Reese Witherspoon Stars in a Lavish *Vanity Fair*." *Newsweek*, September 6, 2004, 66.

Appelbaum, Alec. "60 Seconds with Mira Nair (Q and A)." *Fast Company*, October 2004, 40.

Appelo, Tim. "*The Perez Family*." *Entertainment Weekly*, August 26, 1994, 75.

Ascher-Walsh, Rebecca. "Mira Nair and Alfonso Cuaron." *Entertainment Weekly*, December 20, 2002, 38.

Badt, Karin Luisa. "I Want My Films to Explode with Life. An Interview with Mira Nair." *Cineaste*, Winter 2004, 10–15.

Bennetts, Leslie. "Regally Blonde; While *Legally Blonde* Earned Reese Witherspoon Her $15-Million-a-Movie Price Tag and Countless Adoring Fans; Her Dramatic Test Will Be as a Hard-to-Love Redhead: The Scheming Becky Sharp in Mira Nair's Adaptation of the Thackeray Masterpiece *Vanity Fair*, Opening This Month." *Vanity Fair*, September 2004, 376.

Beresford, David. "Mira Nair Wanted to Introduce India to the Joys of Sex. Her Country's Rulers Had Other Ideas." *The Guardian*, June 13, 1997, T8–9.

Blake, R. A. "Love and Forgiveness." *America*, April 4, 1992, 274.

Boedecker, Hal. "Reviews of HBO's *Hysterical Blindness* and FX's *RFK*." *Orlando Sentinel*, August 21, 2002.

Boltin, Kylie. "*Monsoon Wedding*: A Discussion of Mira Nair's New Film." *Metro*, Summer 2002, 1–4.

Bowman, James. "Porn Again." *American Spectator*, May 1997, 68–69.

Bradshaw, Peter. "As They Like It: What Critics around the World Are Saying (*Monsoon Wedding*)." *Hollywood Reporter*, March 19, 2002, 56.

Brunner, Jeryl. "On the Phone with Juliette Lewis: We Lent the *Hysterical Blindness* Star Our Mobile and Rang Her at Random for a Week." *In Style*, October 1, 2002, 300.

Brown, Rosellen. "The Year in Fiction: 1990." *Massachusetts Review*, Spring 1991, 123–146.

Butalia, Pankaj. "*Monsoon Wedding*." *New Internationalist*, March 2002, 32–34.

Cheng, Scarlet. "Mira Nair: Intoxicated with Life." *World and I*, June 2003, 98.

Clark, Mike. "Tradition, Laughter Reign in *Monsoon*." *USA Today*, March 8, 2002, 16D.

Corliss, Richard. "*Salaam Bombay!*." *Time*, October 24, 1988, 103.

Corliss, Richard. "A Cultural Grand *Salaam*." *Time Canada*, May 3, 2004, 46.

Corliss, Richard. "An Omnibus of Short Films on September 11 from 11 Directors Skeptical of American Power." *Time*, August 4, 2004, 60.

Cruz, Anne Marie. "No Go on Yoga." *People*, September 6, 2004, 160.

Cruz, Clarissa. "Sharp Dresser: *Vanity*'s Costume Designer Uses the Color of Money for 19th Century Social Climber." *Entertainment Weekly*, September 3, 2004, 26.

Cunneen, James. "Games of Love; Film Tours to Enjoy India, Texas, Mexico." *National Catholic Reporter*, April 19, 2002, 16–17.

Cunningham, Kim. "Are You Ready to Rumba?" *People*, June 12, 1995, 138.

Dasgupta, Priyanka. "Mira Plans Kolkata Shoot for *Namesake* with Rani." *Asia Africa Intelligence Wire*, September 16, 2004.

Dasgupta, Priyanka. "Tabu Takes Over from Konkona!." *Asia African Intelligence Wire*, February 2, 2005.

De Haven, Tom. "Dose of Reality." *Entertainment Weekly*, May 13, 1994, 53.

Dempsey, John. "Auds Turn Off *RFK*, but Get *Hysterical.*" *Daily Variety*, August 28, 2002, 2.

Dudek, Duane. "*Monsoon Wedding* Moves Indian Film into Complex Aspects of Family." *Knight Ridder/Tribune News Service*, March 31, 2002, K3687.

Freedmann, Samuel G. "One People in Two Worlds." *New York Times*, February 2, 1992, H13–H14.

Freydkin, Donna. "Uma's a Mom First, Then a Jersey Girl." *USA Today*, August 22, 2002, 03D.

Freydkin, Donna. "Playing a *Vanity* Role, Then Walking Country Line." *USA Today*, August 18, 2004, 10B.

Fuller, Graham. "Shots in the Dark: More Than a Century and a Half after Her Creation, the Character of Becky Sharp Still Reverberates. A New Film Shows How Social Politics and Social Hunger Have—and Have Not—Changed." *Interview*, September 2004, 132.

Garcia, Maria. "Invitation to the *Wedding*: Mira Nair's Award Winner Celebrates Indian Culture." *Film Journal International*, March 2002, 20–21.

Garwood, Paul. "Indian-Born Filmmaker Mira Nair Wins 'Maverick Award' at Woodstock Festival." *America's Intelligence Wire*, October 9, 2004.

Gell, Aaron. "Indian Style: The Forecast Is Sunny for Mira Nair's Award-Winning Punjabi Romantic Comedy, *Monsoon Wedding.*" *W*, March 2002, 193.

Geller, Conrad. "*Monsoon Wedding.*" *Cineaste*, Fall 2002, 43–45.

Germain, David. "Director Nair Rides *Monsoon* to Thackeray's *Vanity Fair.*" *America's Intelligence Wire*, September 3, 2004.

Ghosh, Lakshmi B. "Street Inspires Her." *The Hindu*, June 12, 2004, 1–3. http://www.thehindu.com/thehindu/lf/2004/12/06/stories/

Gleiberman, Owen. "*Mississippi Masala.*" *Entertainment Weekly*, February 14, 1992, 36.

Gleiberman, Owen. "*Kama Sutra: A Tale of Love.*" *Entertainment Weekly*, March 21, 1997, 55.

Gliatto, Tom. "*The Perez Family.*" *People*, May 15, 1995, 19–20.

Guthrmann, Edward. "Doctor or Saint?" *The Advocate*, July 21, 1998, 67.

Hajari, Nisid. "*Mississippi Masala.*" *Entertainment Weekly*, September 11, 1992, 94.

Hajari, Nisid. "In an Awkward Position." *Entertainment Weekly*, March 21, 1997, 55.

Hastings, Michael. "A World of Its Own." *Newsweek*, March 8, 2004, 6.

Hewitt, Chris. "*Monsoon Wedding.*" *Knight Ridder/Tribune News Service*, March 6, 2002, K5429.

Hoberman, J. *Village Voice*. April 11, 1995, 51.

Hoffman, Adina. "The Big Bash Theory: Mira Nair's Latest Movie Revels and Reels." *American Prospect*, March 25, 2002, 28–30.

Holley, Joe. "The Doctor Is In." *Texas Monthly*, June 1997, 48.

Honeycutt, Kirk. "*Hysterical Blindness.*" *Hollywood Reporter*, January 18, 2002, 67.

Honeycutt, Kirk. "*Vanity Fair.*" *Hollywood Reporter*, August 27, 2004, 9–10.

Hulse, Ed. "*Monsoon Wedding.*" *Video Business*, September 16, 2002, 15.

Ingrassia, Michele. "On the Front Lines of AIDS." *Newsweek*, May 9, 1994, 62.

Izama, Angelo. "Mira Nair on African Film Industry." *Africa News Service*, March 7, 2005.

James, Caryn. "Mira Nair Combines Cultures to Create a Film." *New York Times*, October 17, 1988, C17.

Jao-Pierre, Ruth S. "Lights! Camera! Terminal!." *Business News*, January 7, 2002, 6.

Jaques, Yves. "*Kama Sutra*; An Interview with Mira Nair." *Online Daily of the University of Washington*, March 13, 1997, 1. http://archives.thedaily.washington.edu/1997/031397/kama031397.html

Jayaraman, Raja. "Personal Identity in a Globalized World: Cultural Roots of Hindu Personal Names and Surnames." *Journal of Popular Culture*, 2005.

Johnson, Bonnie. "Moviemaker Mira Nair Takes to the Streets of Bombay to Say *Salaam!* to Real Children with No Childhood." *People*, December 5, 1988, 115–116.

Johnson, Brian D. "Possible Worlds: Movies from India and France Take Us Places Where Hollywood Never Goes." *Maclean's*, March 1, 2002, 48.

Kalungi, Kabuye. "Mira Nair Celebrates Life through Cinema." *Africa News Service*, August 19, 2002, 1008228U5489.

Kamin, Debra. "Nair Unspools Film Lab for Africans, Asians." *Daily Variety*, July 8, 2004, 8.

Karena, Cynthia. "*Monsoon Wedding*: Raining on Tradition—Film as Text." *Australian Screen Education*, Winter 2003, 1–4.

Kauffmann, Stanley. "*The Perez Family*." *New Republic*, June 5, 1995, 33.

Kauffmann, Stanley. "On a Bright Morning." *New Republic*, August 11, 2003, 22–32.

Kelleher, Terry. "Tube." *People*, August 26, 2002, 23.

Kelly, Christopher. "*Monsoon Wedding*'s Director's String of Hits Blows Away Skeptics." *Knight Ridder/Tribune News Service*, March 28, 2002, K6328.

Kempley, Rita. "*Salaam Bombay!*." *Washington Post*, November 4, 1988, 3. http://www.washingtonpost.com/wp-srv/style/longterm/movies/videos/salaambombay.htm

Klawans, Stuart. "*Mississippi Masala*." *The Nation*, February 24, 1992, 246.

Klawans, Stuart. "*Monsoon* Season." *The Nation*, March 18, 2002, 35.

Klawans, Stuart. "The Age of Innocence." *The Nation*, August 18, 2004.

Klein, Uri. "*Monsoon Wedding*. (As They Like It)." *Hollywood Reporter*, May 28, 2002, 50.

Kovacs, Elaine. "*Vanity Fair* Is Engaging Period Piece." *America Intelligence Wire*, September 2, 2004.

Lahr, John. "Whirlwind Mira Nair and Her Chelsea Production Company Mirabai Films." *New Yorker*, December 9, 2002, 100.

Lane, Anthony. "Making Arrangements: A Wedding in Delhi and a Wake on the English Coast." *New Yorker*, February 1, 2002, 199–201.

LaSalle, Mike. "*Perez Family* Falls Apart after a While." *San Francisco Chronicle*, May 13, 1995, E1.

Lewis, Malcolm. "*11'09'01*—September 11." *New Internationalist*, January–February 2003, 38–39.

Macias, Robert. "The Best and Worst of 1995." *Hispanic*, December 1995, 16.

Mason, M. S. "'Laughter' Shows Power of Expressing Joy." *Christian Science Monitor*, August 24, 2001, 19.

McCarthy, Todd. "*Vanity Fair*." *Daily Variety*, August 27, 2004, 6–7.

Mcdonald, Moira. "*Monsoon Wedding*." *Knight Ridder/Tribune News Service*, March 20, 2002, K3152.

Mcdonald, Moira. "Director Infuses English Story with Scents of India." *Knight Ridder/Tribune News Service*, August 31, 2004, 5308.

McGirk, Tim. "Naked Ambitions." *Time Australia*, January 13, 1997, 31.

Meer, Ameena. "Street Lessons." *The South*, February 1990, 72.

Meyer, Carla. "A Repulsive Beauty in '80s Jersey, Thurman's Histrionics Fit *Hysterical Blindness* Well." *San Francisco Chronicle*, August 23, 2002, D1.

Meyer, George. "All's Not Fair in Love and Movie Remakes." *Sarasota Herald Tribune*, September 1, 2004, E3.

Meyers, Kate. "Sarita Choudhury." *Entertainment Weekly*, February 28, 1992, 12.

Mitchell, Elvis. "Clashing Ingredients in a Marital *Masala*." *New York Times*, February 22, 2002.

Mohr, Ian. "*Hysterical* Sighting." *Hollywood Reporter*, August 27, 2002, 16.

Nair, Mira. "Create the World You Know, Nair Tells Filmmakers." *Variety*, September 30, 2002, 14–15.

Nair, Mira. "Eat, Memory." *New York Times Magazine*, November 14, 2004, 125–126.

Newman, Bruce. "*Vanity Fair*." *Knight Ridder/Tribune News Service*, September 1, 2004, K6104.

Onyango-Obbo, Charles. "*Salaam Mississippi*." *The South*, February 1991, 74–75.

Orenstein, Peggy. "*Salaam* America!." *Mother Jones*, January–February 1992, 60.

Osborn, Barbara. "India Inside." *Film Comment*, September–October 1988, 6.

Outlaw, Marpessa. "The Mira Stage." *Village Voice*, February 18, 1992, 64.

Pawelczak, Andy. *Films in Review*. July–August 1995, 59.

Perry, Alex. "A Force of Nature." *Time Asia*, September 13, 2004, 4. http://www.time.com

Perry, Alex. "Learning the Yoga Way of Laughter." *Time*, January 17, 2005, A26.

Pollack, Kenan. "Book Watch." *U.S. News and World Report*, September 12, 1994, 94.

Poniewozik, James. "*Hysterical Blindness*: HBO, August 25, 9:30 p.m. E.T." *Time*, August 26, 2002, 74.

Porton, Richard. "Visualizing *Vanity Fair*: Nair Directs Witherspoon in 19th-Century Classic." *Film Journal International*, September 2004, 16–17.

Puig, Claudia. "*Vanity Fair* Serves Up a Strawberry Thackeray." *USA Today*, September 1, 2004, 05D.

Pryor, Kelli. "Adding Spice to Real Life." *Entertainment Weekly*, February 21, 1992, 34.

Regnier, Pat. "Local is the New Global: In Her Hit Film *Monsoon Wedding*, Mira Nair Goes Home to New Delhi Where Cell Phones Blend In Seamlessly with Saris." *Time International*, March 4, 2002, 65.

Richter, Erin. "*Vanity Fair*." *Entertainment Weekly*, February 4, 2005, 118.

Rickey, Carrie. "Indian-Born Director Felt at Home in 1800s London." *Knight Ridder/Tribune News Service*, August 31, 2004, K5380.

Rooney, David. "*Hysterical Blindness*." *Variety*, January 28, 2002, 36.

Rozen, Leah. "*Mississippi Masala*." *People*, February 17, 1992, 17–19.

Rozen, Leah. "*Vanity Fair*." *People*, September 13, 2004, 33.

Schickel, Richard. "*The Perez Family*." *Time*, May 29, 1995, 69.

Schickel, Richard. "Rules of Engagement: Finding Modern Love in Some Surprising Places." *Time*, March 25, 2002, 70A.

Schwarzbaum, Lisa. "*The Perez Family*." *Entertainment Weekly*, May 19, 1995, 44–45.

Schwarzbaum, Lisa. "Upper Crusty: Reese Witherspoon Tries to Climb into High Society in the Half-Baked *Vanity Fair*." *Entertainment Weekly*, September 10, 2004, 143.

Sharma, Alpana. "Body Matters: The Politics of Provocation in Mira Nair's Films." *Quarterly Review of Film and Video*, 2001, 91–103.

Shedde, Meenakshi. "*Monsoon Wedding* Star Aims to Engage, Not Just Entertain." *Asia-Africa Intelligence Wire*, June 16, 2003.

Shulgasser, Barbara. "Good Actors Set Adrift in All-Wet *Perez Family*." *San Francisco Examiner*, May 12, 1995, C1.

Simpson, Janice C. "Focusing on the Margins." *Time*, March 2, 1992, 67.

Srikanth, Rajini. "Ethnic Outsider as the Ultimate Insider: The Paradox of Verghese's *My Own Country*." *MELUS*, Fall–Winter 2004.

Thompson, Anne. "For Mira Nair, *Vanity* Project Called Her Name." *Washington Post*, August 29, 2004, N01.

Travers, Peter. "*Salaam Bombay!*." *People*, November 7, 1988, 18.

Verghese, Abraham. "Last Acts." *New Yorker*, September 22, 1997, 77–79.

Vivarelli, Nick. "*Monsoon* Hits Venice Nods." *Hollywood Reporter*, September 11, 2001, 41.

Young, Deborah. "*Monsoon Wedding*." *Variety*, September 10, 2001, 63.

Walia, Nona. "I'm Sick of Working with Goras: Mira." *Times of India*, August 31, 2004.

White, Armond. "*Vanity Fair*." *New York Press*, August 31, 2004, 1–3.
http://www.nypress.com

"Abhishek in Mira's New Film." *Asia Africa Intelligence Wire*, November 12, 2004.

"Against the Grain: With the Studios Focused on Special Effects-Laden Blockbusters, HBO Is Moving in the Opposite Direction, toward Well-Written Films with a Point of View." *Broadcasting & Cable*, November 4, 2002, 10A–11A.

"Chazz Palminteri Set for the Samuel Goldwyn Co.'s *The Perez Family*; Celia Cruz Also Joins the Cast." *PR Newswire*, March 25, 1994, 0325LA009.

"Cries and Whispers." *Hollywood Reporter—International Edition*, December 7, 2004, 22.

"Early Starters." *Rolling Stone*, June 1, 1995, 70.

"Familiarity Breeds Content: Many Filmmakers Use Same below-the-Line Creatives for Every Shoot." *Daily Variety*, August 24, 2004, A1–A3.

"*Kama Sutra: A Tale of Love*." *Entertainment Weekly*, September 5, 1997, 80.

"*Kama Sutra: A Tale of Love*." *People*, March 17, 1997, 21.

"Mira Nair Fulfils a Dream with *Vanity Fair*. Director Fell in Love with Thackeray's Novel When She Was 16." *Associated Press*, September 7, 2004, 1.
http://www.msnbc.com

"Mira Nair to Make Movie to Promote Indo-Pak Friendly Ties." *Press Trust of India Ltd.*, January 5, 2005.

"Mira Pottering about Aby Baby." *Asia Africa Intelligence Wire*, October 16, 2004.

"*Monsoon Wedding*." *Africa News Service*, January 15, 2002, P1008015U9304.

"*Monsoon Wedding* Could've Done Better Than Lagaan." *Times of India*, March 30, 2002.

"*Monsoon Wedding* Runs to Packed Houses in U.K." *Times of India*, April 2, 2002.

"Nair's 'Bhenji Brigade' to Promote Asian *Masala*." *Asia Africa Intelligence Wire*, April 8, 2004.

"Nair's *Monsoon Wedding* Opens at Rainbow." *Africa News Service*, September 4, 2002, 1008247U5286.

"*The Namesake*." *Library Journal*. May 1, 2004, 155.

"*The Perez Family*." *Library Journal*, July 1, 1990, 126.

"*The Perez Family*." *New Internationalist*, November 1996, 33.

"Westwood *Monsoon*." *Hollywood Reporter*, February 21, 2002, 3.

INTERNET

Anderson, Jason. "Bridal Shower: Mira Nair's Indian Comedy Storms the Festival Circuit." *Eye.net*, February 28, 2004, 1–4.
http://www.eye.net/eye/issue/print.asp?issue_02.28.02/film/monsooonwedding.html

Applebaum, Stephen. "Mira Nair, *Monsoon Wedding*." *BBC News*, December 21, 2002.
http://www.bbc.co.uk/films/2001/12/21/mira_nair_monsoon_wedding_interview.shtml

Baig, Daniel. "Interview: Mira Nair." *Counting Down*, May 1, 2002.
http://www.countingdown.com/features?feature_id=716479&print=1

Benson, Sheila. "Interview: *Vanity Fair* Director Mira Nair." *Seattle Weekly*, September 1–7, 2004. http://www.seattleweekly.com

Borpujari, Utpal. "Mira Nair Rejected *Harry Potter* Offer." *DH News Service* [Panaji], December 12, 2004. http://www.deccanherald.com/deccanherald/dec012004/n7.asp

Camhi, Leslie. "The Kids Are Alright: *Salaam Bombay!*." *Village Voice Online*. http://www.villagevoice.com

Chatterjee, Ashok. "No Retakes for Mira Nair." *Times of India Online*, January 7, 2004. http://timesofindia.indiatimes.com/articleshow/msid-408999,prtpage-1.cms

Chatterjee, Saibal. "Mira Nair to Shoot Next Film in Calcutta." *BBC News*, 2004, 3. http://www.newsvote.bbc.co.uk/mpapps/pagetools/print/news.bbc.co.uk/2/hi/south_asia/40714...

Chau, Thomas. "Interview: Reese Witherspoon on *Vanity Fair*." *Cinema Confidential*, August 31, 2004. http://www.cinecon.com/news.php?id=0408311

Edelstein, David. "Under the Rainbow—*Dragonfly* Keeps You Guessing for a Good 20 Minutes; *Monsoon Wedding* Has a Sparkling Chaos; *Big Bad Love* Indulges Your Dissolute-Writer Fantasy." *Slate.com*, February 22, 2002, 1–5. http://slate.msn.com/toolbox.aspx?action=print&id=2062346

Geffner, David. "Mira Nair and *Hysterical Blindness*." *DGA Magazine*, September 20, 2002, 3. http://www.dga.org/v27_3/feat_mira_nair.php3

Grady, Pam. "Nair Follows Pulitzer's Trail." *Film Stew*, August–September 2004, 1–2. http://www.filmstew.com/Content/DetailsPrinter.asp?ContentID-9552.

Hasan, Ayesha. "Professor Mira Nair Reflects on Her Film Career during Zora Neale Hurston Lecture." *Columbia News*, August 1, 2002, 3. http://www.columbia.edu/cu/news/02/0/miraNair.html

Jha, Subhash K. "Rani Says 'No' to Mira Nair." *Sify.com*, November 24, 2004, 2. http://www.sify.com

Khan, Shahid. "*Salaam Bombay!*." *Planet Bollywood*. http://www.planetbollywood.com/Film/SalaamBombay!/

Khosla, Mukesh. "She Gives the 'Nowhere People' a Voice." *The Tribune*, September 27, 2001, 5. http://www.tribuneindia.com/2001/20010927/main8.htm

Kulkarni, Ronjita. "*Namesake* Is Very Uncannily My Story!." *Rediff*, February 7, 2005. http://www.rediff.com/

Laurier, Joanne. "The View from the Oasis—*Monsoon Wedding*, Directed by Mira Nair." *World Socialist Web Site*, March 30, 2002, 1–5. http://www.wsws.org/articles/2002/mar2002/mons-m30_prn.shtml

Luu, Alex. "Mira Nair: Celluloid Diplomat of Humanity." *Yolk*. http:/www.yolk.com/v091/nair1.html

McAlister, Linda Lopez. "*Salaam Bombay!*." *The Women's Show*, WMNF-FM, November 14, 1992, 2. http://www.mith2.umd.edu/WomensStudies/FilmReviews/salaam-bombay-mcalister

McNulty, Jennifer. "Documentary Film and Video Festival Starts September 25." *University of California Santa Cruz Currents Online*, September 17, 2001, 1–7. http://www.ucsc.edu/currents/01-02/09-17/documentary.html

Mitchell, Wendy. "Period Piece as 'Complete Romp.' Mira Nair Brings Her Own Vibrancy to *Vanity Fair*." *Indiewire*, August 31, 2004. http://www.indiewire.com/people/people_040831nair.html

Montagne, Renee. "Interviews: Inside *Vanity Fair* with Director Mira Nair." *NPR*, September 6, 2004, 2. http://www.npr.org/templates/story/story.php?storyID=3890209

Prabhudesai, Sandesh. "Mira Nair Rejects *Harry Potter* Film." *Rediff.com*, December 3, 2004, 2. http://www.rediff.com/movies/2004/dec/03mira.htm

Ross, Samantha. "Feature: Gabriel Byrne Interview: A Conversation with a Most Unusual (*Vanity* Free) Suspect." *Moda Magazine*, 2004.
http://www.modamag.com/gabrielbyrneinterview.htm

Stengel, Marc. "Translating Stories." *Weekly Wire/Nashville Scene*, December 22, 1997, 1–7.
http://weeklywire.com/ww/12-22/97/nash_8-books.html

Tobias, Scott. "Real Freedom: From Veteran Filmmakers to Emerging Talents, Female Directors Are Thriving in Independent Circles, Where Their Singular Vision Goes Uncompromised." *Backstage*, December 22, 2004.
http://www.backstage.com/backstage/features/article_display.jsp?vnu_content_id=100 0741248

Wilmington, Michael. "Movie Review, *Monsoon Wedding*." *Chicago Tribune/Metromix.com*, February 28, 2002, 1–4.
http://metromix.chicagotribune.com/movies/mmx-15649_lgy,0143199print.story

Wilson, Karen. "*Vanity Fair*—Now with More Elephants!." *Gothamist*, August 20, 2004.
http://www.gohamist.com/archives/2004/08/20/vanity_fair_now_with_more_elephants.php

Yabroff, Jennie. "All about Eros: *Kama Sutra* Director Mira Nair Talks about Sex in 16th Century India, and What It Means to Us Today." *Salon.com*, March 1997, 3.
http://www.salon.com/march97/970307.html

"10 Questions, Mira Nair. The Director of *Monsoon Wedding* Shares Her Answers." *Film Force*, February 22, 2002.
http://filmforce.ign.com/articles/354/354320p1.html

"Awards Are Temporary Hype; Mira Nair's Exclusive Interview." *Bengal on the Net*, November 11, 2001.
http://www.bengalonthenet.com

"Concept behind the Movie *Vanity Fair*." *Female First*, January 7, 2005.
http://www.femalefirst.co.uk/entertainment/21762004.htm

"Interview with Mira Nair." *Netribution Film Network*, 2002, 3.
http://www.netribution.co.uk/features/interviews/2002/mira_nair/1.html

"The Jewel in India's Crown: Mira Nair Interview" *Tiscali*, Summer 2002, 1–3.
http://www.tiscali.co.uk/misc/

"Jolly Good Fellowes." *Guardian Unlimited Film*, November 28, 2004.
http://filmgaurdian.co.uk/interviewpages/0,6737,1361082,00.html

"*Kama Sutra* is Bogus History and Cheesy Storytelling but What the Hell, It's Sexy." *Salon.com*, March 7, 1997, 2.
http://www.salon.com/march97/kamasutra970307.html?CP=SAL&DN=110.

"Mira Nair: A Director Par Excellence." *Kerala Online*.
http://www.keralaonline.com/defaultsm.asp?cap=miranair

"*Monsoon Wedding* Director Honored." *Zap2It.com*, October 11, 2004.

"No Abhishek Bachchan for Mira Nair!." *Bollyvista.com*, December 4, 2004.
http://www.bollyvista.com/article/a/32/3781

"*The Perez Family*." *Tucson Weekly*, May 18, 1995, 3.
http://www.filmvault.com/filmvalut/tw/p/perezefamilythe_f.html

"Screenwriters Fume over *Vanity Fair* Credits." *WENN*, September 3, 2004.
http://www.imdb.com

INDEX

ABOUT THE AUTHOR

JOHN KENNETH MUIR is the author of 17 books, including *Singing a New Tune: The Rebirth of the Modern Film Musical from Evita to De-Lovely and Beyond, Best in Show: The Films of Christopher Guest and Company, The Unseen Force: The Films of Sam Raimi,* and *An Askew View: The Films of Kevin Smith,* all published by Applause; *Horror Films of the 1970s,* a 2002 *Booklist* Editor's Choice; *Terror Television,* a 2001 *Booklist* Editor's Choice; and *The Encyclopedia of Superheroes on Film and Television.* He writes a monthly column for the Webzine Far Sector (http://www.farsector.com) and hosts a popular entertainment and nostalgia blog, Reflections on Film/TV (http://reflectionsonfilmandtelevision.blogspot.com). He lives in the historic district of Monroe, North Carolina with his wife and three cats.